Real News about the News

What role does the media play in British politics? There is growing concern that the media environment is biased, and that online news and social media spread fake news, conspiracy theories, propaganda and foreign interference. Examining TV, radio, newspapers and the Internet, Kenneth Newton unravels the real effects of the mainstream and alternative news media. With abundant evidence, Newton demonstrates that, contrary to popular belief:

- newspapers neither win nor lose elections; nor do they set election agendas;
- most citizens have a fairly mixed news diet and do not inhabit echo chambers;
- social media influences on political attitudes are generally small and actually expand the range of news people get;
- impartial and reliable public service news still provides the bulk of the nation's news diet.

Evidence shows that the main media effects on political attitudes and behaviour are positive and inform and mobilise citizens rather than influencing their voting choice.

KENNETH NEWTON is Professor Emeritus at Southampton University. He served as Executive Director of the European Consortium for Political Research and as a member of the executive of International Political Science Association and the Political Studies Association of the United Kingdom. His research publications cover social and political trust, democratic innovations, city politics and media politics and he is the co-author of *Foundations of Comparative Politics* (4th edition, with Jan van Deth, 2021).

Real News about the News

Media and British Politics

KENNETH NEWTON
University of Southampton

CAMBRIDGE
UNIVERSITY PRESS

Shaftesbury Road, Cambridge CB2 8EA, United Kingdom

One Liberty Plaza, 20th Floor, New York, NY 10006, USA

477 Williamstown Road, Port Melbourne, VIC 3207, Australia

314–321, 3rd Floor, Plot 3, Splendor Forum, Jasola District Centre, New Delhi – 110025, India

103 Penang Road, #05-06/07, Visioncrest Commercial, Singapore 238467

Cambridge University Press is part of Cambridge University Press & Assessment, a department of the University of Cambridge.

We share the University's mission to contribute to society through the pursuit of education, learning and research at the highest international levels of excellence.

www.cambridge.org
Information on this title: www.cambridge.org/9781009387033

DOI: 10.1017/9781009387040

© Kenneth Newton 2024

This publication is in copyright. Subject to statutory exception and to the provisions of relevant collective licensing agreements, no reproduction of any part may take place without the written permission of Cambridge University Press & Assessment.

First published 2024

A catalogue record for this publication is available from the British Library

Library of Congress Cataloging-in-Publication Data
Names: Newton, Kenneth, 1940- author.
Title: Real news about the news : media and British politics / Kenneth Newton, University of Southhampton.
Description: Cambridge ; New York : Cambridge University Press, 2023. | Includes bibliographical references and index.
Identifiers: LCCN 2023028760 (print) | LCCN 2023028761 (ebook) |
  ISBN 9781009387033 (hardback) | ISBN 9781009387071 (paperback) |
  ISBN 9781009387040 (epub)
Subjects: LCSH: Press and politics–Great Britain–History–21st century. | Mass media–Political aspects–Great Britain–History–21st century. | Great Britain–Politics and government–1945-
Classification: LCC PN5124.P6 N49 2023 (print) | LCC PN5124.P6 (ebook) | DDC 070.449320941–dc23/eng/20230905
LC record available at https://lccn.loc.gov/2023028760
LC ebook record available at https://lccn.loc.gov/2023028761A

ISBN 978-1-009-38703-3 Hardback
ISBN 978-1-009-38707-1 Paperback

Cambridge University Press & Assessment has no responsibility for the persistence or accuracy of URLs for external or third-party internet websites referred to in this publication and does not guarantee that any content on such websites is, or will remain, accurate or appropriate.

For Clare

Contents

List of Tables		*page* viii
1	Massive and Minimal Media Effects	1
2	The News Landscape	17
3	News Diets	37
4	Avoiding, Rejecting, Ignoring and Accepting	55
5	Digital Pessimism	78
6	Newspapers, Voting and Agenda-Setting	97
7	Media Malaise and the Mean World Effect	123
8	Personal Experience as a Reality Check	138
9	Pluralism and Democracy	156
10	Practical Lessons	175
Index		187

Tables

3.1 Average number of individual news sources used by platform, 2019	page 39
3.2 Total number of news platforms used by demographic groups, 2019	40
3.3 Use of main platforms for news by demographic group, 2019 (%)	41
3.4 'Which of the following platforms do you use for news nowadays?'	43
3.5 Top-twenty news sources, 2018 and 2019 (% of adults 16+)	44
3.6 Weekly reach of offline and online news	45
4.1 Percentage of British people who believe that conspiracy theories are definitely or probably true, 2021	60
4.2 Paranormal beliefs in the British population aged sixteen and over (%)	63
5.1 Websites/apps used for news nowadays (%)	80
5.2 News organisations followed on social media, top-five mentioned, 2022 (%)	83
6.1 Conservative and Labour swings, 1992–1997 elections, by daily national newspapers	106
6.2 Conservative and Labour swings, 1992–1997 elections, by selected demographic categories	107
6.3 Conservative to Labour swings election to election, by national newspapers (%)	110
6.4 Top media and popular agenda topics in the final week of the 2019 general election (%)	117

1 | *Massive and Minimal Media Effects*

It used to be said that the British press was the fourth estate of the realm, acting as the watchdog of the constitution, informing citizens and keeping politicians honest; now it is often said to be akin to a fifth column that undermines democracy from within. The general view is that the news media are not only powerful but also a malign influence that wields power without responsibility. Many complaints are made to support this view but perhaps the most common relates to a political bias designed to influence rather than inform its audience. This might not be so bad but for the conviction, often voiced or assumed, that people believe what they read in the papers. If so, it probably was 'the *Sun* wot won it' in the election of 1992 when the paper came out strongly for the Conservatives, which then took a surprising victory. And if that is true, it follows that the press has considerable ability to create public opinion and swing national elections. That, at least, is the common view.

More recently, concern about the British tabloids has been replaced by worries about social media and alternative websites. Their fake news, conspiracy theories, populist dogmas, anti-vaxxer beliefs and propaganda spread by Russian and American bots are widely assumed to mislead people, especially the impressionable young and politically uninformed adults. These fears are compounded by the idea that the algorithms used by some websites create echo chambers of public opinion among people who are fed with opinions they want to hear. These, it is said, polarise public opinion into political tribes that do not hear other opinions. Meanwhile, trust in the media to tell the truth is falling, which further contributes to the mood of confusion and uncertainty about what to believe.

Opinions about the powerful effects of the media are widespread and usually unshakeable and it is not just ordinary blokes propping up bars who elaborate their views in a forceful manner. Public intellectuals with international reputations often share many of the worst fears. Here are the statements of three writers in the public eye. The first is Alain de Botton, the author of fifteen books, some of them bestsellers. In his *The News: A User's Manual* he states that the news 'is the most significant single force setting the tone of public life and shaping our impressions of the community beyond our own walls. It is the prime creator of political and social reality.'[1] Pierre Bourdieu was a highly respected philosopher – widely admired and quoted in the highest academic circles. He was a professor and director of studies at the distinguished École Normale Supérieure in Paris, the author of a great many articles and some three dozen books, and the receiver of many awards, medals and distinctions in his career. This did not prevent him from writing, with assurance, something that is little short of silly:

Television enjoys a *de facto* monopoly on what goes into the heads of a significant part of the population and what they think ... with their permanent access to public visibility ... journalists can impose on the whole of society their vision of the world, their conception of problem, and their point of view.[2]

Jean Baudrillard was a French professor with the reputation of an expert on the media because he taught at the Institut de Recherche et d'Information Socio-Économique in Paris. But he too was given to making sweeping statements that have no empirical foundation:

[I]n the media and consumer society, people are caught up in the play of images, spectacles, and simulacra, that have less and less relationship to an outside, to an external 'reality,' to such an extent that the very concepts of the social, political, or even 'reality' no longer seem to have any meaning ... Caught up in the universe of simulations, the 'masses' are 'bathed in a media massage' without messages or meaning, a mass age where classes disappear, and politics is dead, as are the grand dreams of disalienation, liberation, and revolution.[3]

One problem with the Bourdieu and Baudrillard quotes is that they are contradictory. Bourdieu knows that people adopt the point of view imposed on them by journalists, and Baudrillard is equally certain that

---

[1] de Botton, A. 2014. *The News: A User's Manual*. London: Hamish Hamilton: 12.
[2] Bourdieu, P. 1998. *On Television and Journalism*. London: Pluto Press: 47.
[3] Kellner, D. 8 December 2019. 'Jean Baudrillard', in *The Stanford Encyclopedia of Philosophy*. https://plato.stanford.edu/entries/baudrillard/.

the masses are bathed in media massage without messages or meaning. What these three quotations have in common, however, is a lack of evidence.

In their book *Manufacturing Consent*, Edward Herman and Noam Chomsky propose a 'propaganda model' of the mass media in the USA that 'among their other functions, the media serve, and propagandize on behalf of, the powerful societal interests that control and finance them ... to inculcate and defend the economic, social, and political agenda of privileged groups that dominate the domestic society and the state'.[4] They allow that the American media do not always succeed in this function, but the odd thing about a book called *Manufacturing Consent* is that it does not show, or even try to show, that consent is manufactured in this way. It mainly presents case studies of the news media market objectives and content in the USA. It takes it for granted that the political agenda of privileged groups dominate society and the state. All one has to do is study the content of the media to know what the public believes. There would be no point in writing a book of this kind if the media did not succeed in manufacturing consent.

Massive Media Effects

By and large, though with exceptions, professional political scientists share these misgivings about the ways in which the news media, or the media in general, have a huge impact on what their audience think and do politically, and many go further to argue that the media undermine democracy in one way or another. Reviewing decades of research into agenda-setting, Maxwell McCombs likens the news media to teachers who repeat their lessons over and over again until it sinks into the heads of 'citizen pupils' who can then repeat it parrot-like, if required.[5] The result, according to agenda-setting theory, is that while the media are unable to tell the public what to think, they tell them what to think about. If the media are powerful enough to set the public agenda, then one might ask why are they not also powerful enough to tell the public what to think?

---

[4] Herman, E. and Chomsky, N. 2010. *Manufacturing Consent: The Political Economy of the Mass Media*. New York: Random House: x, 298.
[5] McCombs, M. 2014. *Setting the Agenda: Mass Media and Public Opinion*. New York: Wiley: 2.

Others have come up with a long list of ideas about why the media have great influence on what people think.[6] The modern news is said to contribute to political ignorance, incomprehension and confusion caused by its tidal waves of new news broadcast every day. Combined with superficiality, soundbites and photo opportunities, this mass of information neither explains anything nor relates it to what else is going on, or what went before. This, it is said, induces political fatigue which turns people away from bothering to keep up with the news. On top of that, public debate is also debased by covering complex issues and the variety of opinion about them in two-minute conflicts between two sides. Since conflict and drama sell the news, the media will provoke it or invent it if there is none.

A common theme is the mean world effect in which a constant harping on bad news about corruption, incompetence, disasters, crime and violence creates fear, alienation and distrust of the world. This undermines social capital and civic engagement. Other writers focus on the media's use of attack journalism, muckraking and investigative journalism that undermines politicians, creates cynicism and reduces faith in democracy and its institutions. The bad news and mean world effects are believed to result in falling party membership and election turnout. If the polls reported in the media tell us the result in advance of the election, there is no sense in bothering to vote. Constantly reporting the latest opinion polls is said to induce instability and short-termism in politics when politicians respond to public pressures and media outrage. At the same time, it is said that spin doctors and the importance attached to the presentation of policies make packaging more important than content. On the other hand, a case has been made that the media contribute to the pressures of ungovernability and political overload by reporting the demands and protests of myriad groups and interests, all competing for limited attention and resources.

Some distinguished commentators blame our current political tribulations on the media. Chomsky warns us of the dangers of the capitalist press and Habermas tells us how it has refeudalised the public sphere by using its power to manipulate opinion and create a population of unthinking consumers of material goods. Postman tells us that we can

---

[6] I have discussed these at greater length in 'Political Trust and the Mass Media', in Zmerli, S. and van der Meer, T. W. G. eds. 2017. *Handbook on Political Trust*. Cheltenham: Edward Elgar: 361–367.

learn little or nothing from the television. Watching it we are as children, fascinated by the moving, colourful images that amuse us to death. The general mood is summed up by Pippa Norris when she writes: 'During the past decades a rising tide of voices on both sides of the Atlantic has blamed the news for a growing public disengagement, ignorance of civic affairs, and mistrust of government. This idea has developed into something of an unquestioned orthodoxy in the popular literature, particularly in the United States.'[7]

Minimal Media Effects

Ever since Joseph Klapper published *The Effects of Mass Communication* in 1960 there has been an unresolved debate between those who believe in large or massive media effects and those who believed, with Klapper, that the media can usually do little more than reinforce existing beliefs. For the most part the maximalists have outnumbered minimalists by a large majority, but there have been a few heavyweight minimalists. In 1986, W. M. McGuire, a Yale professor of psychology and expert on the psychology of persuasion, advertising and mass communication, wrote: 'That myths can persist despite conflicting evidence is demonstrated by the robustness of the belief that television and other mass media have sizeable impacts on the public's thoughts, feelings and action even though most of the empirical studies indicate small to negligible effects.'[8] In 1993, Larry Bartels, a distinguished professor at Princeton at the time, opened an article in the foremost journal of political science in the USA in the following way:

The state of research on media effects is one of the most notable embarrassments of modern social science. The pervasiveness of the mass media and their virtual monopoly over the presentation of many kinds of information must suggest to reasonable observers that what these media say and how they say it has enormous social and political consequences. Nevertheless, the scholarly literature has been much better at refuting, qualifying, and circumscribing the thesis of media impact than at supporting it.[9]

---

[7] Norris, P. 2000. *A Virtuous Circle: Political Communications in Postindustrial Societies.* Cambridge: Cambridge University Press: 3.
[8] McGuire, W. 1986. 'The myth of massive media impact: Savagings and salvagings'. *Public Communication and Behavior*, 1: 173–257, 174
[9] Bartels, L. M. 1993. 'Messages received: The political impact of media exposure'. *American Political Science Review*, 87(2): 267–285.

This view is shared by Michael Schudson, who includes three essays on 'The Myths of Media' in his book *The Power of the News*. Covering a range of subjects from the Kennedy–Nixon election and media coverage of the Vietnam War to illusions about Reagan's popularity and the Watergate Affair, he concludes that

> Together these three chapters emphasize that the media are a central topic in our cultural and political life and that estimates of their power are frequently exaggerated ... The media are not nearly as important as the media, media culture, the talk show culture, and popular reflexes suggest ... What evidence is there that everything in American politics follows from the television image – in particular, that public opinion is a pawn of televisual politics? Not, when it comes down to it, very much evidence at all. The news establishment has a delusion not only about the power of the media but about the power of the public.[10]

Shortly after that, John Zaller changed his mind about media power. After writing an article in which he argued for 'massive media impacts' he then studied how the media affected public opinion about the Clinton–Lewinsky affair.[11] This came as a great surprise to American political scientists who expected the sustained, year-long attack journalism to ruin the president. Nevertheless, the president did not merely survive; his high poll ratings were maintained. Nor did the press manage to set the agenda. The public distrusted it and were suspicious of its motives for pursuing a campaign against Clinton. Zaller concludes that '[m]edia frenzies can briefly undermine a candidate's natural level of support but cannot permanently lower it'.[12] A politician's natural level of support, according to Zaller, is determined by the state of the economy, moderation in politics and peace, a conclusion supported by many voting studies.

Nevertheless, belief in media power was still going strong when we entered the new millennium. In that year Pippa Norris published *A Virtuous Circle*, a comprehensive and thorough study of media

---

[10] Schudson, M. 1995. *The Power of the News*. Cambridge, MA: Harvard University Press: 17, 138.

[11] Zaller, J. R. (1996) 'The myth of massive media impact revived: New support for a discredited idea', in Mutz, D., Sniderman, P. and Brody, R. eds., *Political Persuasion and Attitude Change*. Ann Arbor: University of Michigan Press: 17–78.

[12] Zaller J. R. 1998. 'Monica Lewinsky's contribution to political science'. *PS: Political Science & Politics*, 31(2): 182–189, 187.

effects in ten western European countries, the G8 and the USA, using time series, cross-sectional and experimental data in different years. After 300 pages of closely reasoned argument backed by huge amounts of statistical analysis she comes to the conclusion that:

> The second major conclusion from this study runs contrary to the media malaise thesis. The survey evidence from the United States and western Europe consistently fails to support the claim that attention to the news in general and television news in particular contribute to deep-rooted indicators of civil malaise and erosion of diffuse support for the political system.[13]

Sources of the Problem

Why, after at least more than six decades of research and untold millions of words, plus some empirical evidence, has the controversy over massive and minimal media effects not been resolved? This book argues that the research is prey to an array of pitfalls that are responsible for Bartels' 'notable embarrassments' and that if we are to establish media effects with some confidence we must keep these pitfalls in mind in order to avoid them. There are eight main problems, as discussed in the following subsections.

Problems of Cause and Effect

Difficulties in disentangling causes and effects are common in the social sciences, none more so than in the study of media effects. This is because individuals self-select the sources of political news they prefer and they often (not always) self-select sources that share their own political opinions and party identities. If Conservatives read Conservative papers and Labour supporters read Labour papers, how can we tell whether their political opinions are formed by their paper, or whether they select their paper according to their political opinions? Which is the chicken and which the egg? Equally, there is some evidence (produced in later chapters) that the commercial news media are faced with market constraints to produce what their consumers demand – they follow the politics of their readers rather than

---

[13] Norris, A Virtuous Circle, 314.

lead them. Once again, a question hangs over which is the cause and which the effect.

To complicate matters still more, political opinions and behaviour are often associated with a set of individual characteristics such as age, sex, education, income, ethnicity and political interest that are also associated with the kind and the amount of news media that people use. The result is a three-cornered tangle of variables involving the social, economic and political background of news audiences, the news media content, and the possible effects of the news media on political attitudes and behaviour that are associated with the social, economic and political backgrounds of news media audiences.

If it is accepted that self-selection means that the party-political press spends most of the time preaching to the converted, it is still possible that the media might have the effect of reinforcing the political opinions and behaviour of the party faithful. Reinforcement is not a powerful effect but it may still be important in shoring up the votes of party identifiers.

Good media effects research requires, among other things, comparison with a group exposed to a media message with a carefully matched control group not exposed to that message. It is, for example, easy to conclude that it was 'the *Sun* wot won it' if the only information you have is that *Sun* readers showed a large swing to the Conservative Party in an election. But if the swing among *Sun* readers was no greater than that among other Conservative newspaper readers, then it was not 'the *Sun* wot won it'. And if the swing among all newspaper readers was no greater than that of non-readers, then the swing was not a newspaper effect either. Chapter 6 shows that newspaper effects can look very different when control groups are introduced into the research design.

Lack of Evidence

Media studies often lack evidence, even among those who look for it, never mind the theoreticians who are not particularly interested in it. In the UK, the radio is an important and trusted source of news for many citizens but we know rather little about what news the 300 commercial stations provide, where they get it from and how often and how much they broadcast. Online websites, especially social media, are a bigger problem because information about their users is a valuable commercial commodity that is rarely available to academic researchers. There are in excess of 100,000 podcasts dedicated to political discussion. We know little or nothing about their content or who listens to them, and even less about their effects. For that matter, newspapers and TV news carry a lot of non-political news and some 'papers' contain little political news, but we know little about how readers divide their attention between the political and non-political. There is much concern at present about the effects of fake news and the politics of social media, but little is known about this vast and sprawling content, and even less about its effects. The less we know the greater the temptation to substitute plausible speculation for conclusions supported by evidence. But one person's plausible speculation is another's implausible speculation.

What Everybody Knows

One of the better research areas of media research is the growing concentration of the news media under the ownership and control of multimedia, multinational conglomerate corporations. This work is generally undertaken on the assumption, sometimes explicitly stated, that the news giant corporations produce is biased in favour of the free market economic and political interests of the business (capitalist) world. Similarly, many studies have been done on the content of the mass media to show that it is biased and full of racism, sexism, chauvinism and other unpleasant 'isms'. There is no doubt that the mass media market is increasingly concentrated in the hands of a few giant corporations, and it is clear that parts of both the mass and minority media contain biased, fake and extremist content, but the impact this has on the general public is not at all clear. The prevailing assumption, sometimes overtly stated, is that people do believe what they read in the papers and that their attitudes and behaviour are directly and strongly affected by media exposure. As an assumption it is a big leap of faith, and there is evidence to suggest that it is not true or, at least, not always true.

Blaming the Messenger

The mean world effect plays a large part in media writings. Its contention is that a concentration on bad news about violence, corruption, incompetence and disaster – if it bleeds, it leads – creates feelings of fear, alienation, hopelessness, distrust and lack of political confidence. But if the news media report the news, how do we distinguish the effects of political events being reported and the effects of how they are reported? There is a war going in Ukraine. Are the media contributing to the mean world effect by reporting the war, or is the war telling us that the world can be a brutal place? It may be that the media contribute to the mean world effect by the way it reports bad news and by the volume of these reports, but there is no avoiding the fact that wars happen and bad news of great importance should be reported. This does not solve the problem of knowing what is a real-world effect and what is a media effect, but it does teach us to be cautious about assuming that it is a media effect and that the messenger should be shot. Or, as Norris puts it: 'Claims of videomalaise are methodologically flawed so that they are at best unproven, to use the Scottish verdict, or at worse false. As a result too often we are "blaming the messenger" for more deep-rooted ills of the body politic.'[14]

A Partial View of the World

For many reasons, academic life encourages specialisation that results in knowing more and more about less and less. Within the specialised research topic of politics and the media there is now a further specialisation in certain branches of the media, especially a focus on online news and social media, rather than the media as a whole. There is something odd about this degree of specialisation which produces work on newspapers, or TV or online news, overlooking or ignoring the other media. Imagine a dietician who only studied what people eat for breakfast. Imagine an art critic who only considers the bottom three inches of the paintings they write about. Imagine a book reviewer who only reads every third or fourth chapter. No plausible conclusions can be drawn about the effects of any one medium without knowing what news people get from the others, and yet claims about the malign effects of newspapers or social media often take no account of the news that people get from other sources.

---

[14] Norris P. 2000. *Blaming the Messenger? Political Communications and Turnout in EU Elections*. Cambridge, MA: Harvard University, Shorenstein Center.

Focusing exclusively on one kind of medium, and ignoring, overlooking or knowing nothing about the others, does not result in knowing more and more about less and less; it results in knowing less and less about less and less.

The News Media Are Our Only Source of News

Almost all studies of politics and the news assume that the news media are our only source of news. Some state this in so many words. There are plausible reasons for believing this. The first is that politics are often conducted in places we cannot enter – cabinet meetings, smoke-filled rooms, private negotiations, confidential communications, caucus meetings, secret matters – or reported as off-the-record interviews. We can only learn about this news from journalists on the inside. Second, few citizens have personal contact with their political representatives, even at the local level. They have to rely on second-hand information, perhaps even third- or fourth-hand sources. Third, we all know about our household economy but for national aggregates such as gross domestic product (GDP), national productivity or balance of trade figures we have to depend on the news from economic experts who collect and disseminate this information. Besides, relatively few specialist experts and journalists know about the technical aspects of such things as global warming, the possible problems and benefits of fracking, the best way to measure GDP and the safety of Covid vaccinations. For all these things, most are dependent upon journalists' accounts of the work of experts. In short, it seems reasonable to assume that the news media are powerful because they have a monopoly of information.

The assumption may be wrong. There is some evidence (not much) that individual citizens can draw conclusions about politics, government and public policy from what they observe, experience and hear when they go about their daily lives. This is when they run up against the realities of schools, hospitals, social surveys, public transport, taxes, working conditions and the cost of living. The evidence suggests that people form their view about the state of the nation and news reports about it against the backdrop of this personal experience. The news media may not be our only source of political information, and nor does the news fall upon blank and empty minds ready to soak it up. On the contrary, citizens have other sources that serve as their own reality tests of the news they get.

The Interactions between Supply and Demand

The term 'media effects' entails two sides of a coin. That is to say the media form a system in which demand and supply interact, and in order to understand how the system works and why it works that way it is necessary to know about both sides of the system. One cannot make sense of one without the other. The commercial media must supply their readers with what they are able and willing to buy, and readers are free to decide what they want to consume. Public service news operates on a different basis but there is still an interaction between supply and demand in which audience tastes and preferences influence what the services produce. There is also a certain amount of 'back-door' commercialisation of the public services because of their need to maintain audience figures against commercial competition.

We can only understand media effects by looking at the interplay between supply (the media) and demand (their audiences). What is surprising about media research is how much of it concentrates on one and not the other. It examines the increasing ownership and control of the media and has carried out content analysis of what they produce. It has studied the practices of professional journalists and examined the economic forces that squeeze out in-depth journalism in favour of infotainment and reliance on official press briefings. On the other side of the coin, there is a fair amount of evidence about the demographics of media users and non-users and about trust in the media. These are enough for some research questions but not for media effects, which require an understanding of how supply and demand interact with each other, and especially an understanding of the ways in which people choose their news and how they react to it. Which brings us to pluralist theory.

Pluralist Theory

The lopsided view of the media is seen in pluralist theory, one of the main theories of the media in a democracy (perhaps the only one). Essentially, the theory states that the news media should be in the hands of multiple, independent sources which can present a diversity of news and opinion that allows the population to make up its own mind about political issues. The theory has nothing to say about consumers and seems to assume that citizens will be like John Stuart Mill in surveying all the evidence and the full range of opinion before making up their minds. The pluralist theory of the news media developed alongside free market economic theory in the nineteenth century and both share the assumption of perfect knowledge of the market. Pluralist theory assumes attentive citizens with a full knowledge of politics and fails to take any account of how different people with different political views process the news they get. It also assumes that the only way of guaranteeing a diversity of news is through the market competition of news suppliers, although circumstances have now been transformed, first by public service radio and television, then by the vast amount of news and comment available on the web. If pluralist theory is to have any relationship with modern circumstances it is in serious need of updating and dealing with the demand side of the equation.

Outline of the Book

With these pitfalls in mind, the book explores the effects of the media on the mass political attitudes and behaviour of the British public and its leaders. It tries to avoid speculation and assumptions as far as possible and relies on the best empirical evidence available. It points out the gaps in our knowledge and when some speculation seems sensible, given what we do know, it posts clear warning signals with the words 'might, 'may', 'could', 'suggests', indicates' and 'possibly'. It looks at the supply and demand, producer and consumer side of the equation, is aware of the fact that correlation is not causation and that causation is extremely difficult to pin down. It questions some of the most widespread assumptions about media effects and presents the evidence for doing so. And it provides evidence that suggests citizens are not entirely dependent on the media for their information and that the other ways of acquiring information may even be more important than the news.

Chapter 2 assembles information about the supply of news in the UK. So far as this is possible, given limited information, it maps out the number and the nature of TV, radio, print and online news sources as a way of sketching the main contours of the news landscape – what is available to the population of news consumers. Despite its importance for an understanding of the media system, this task has not been undertaken in the UK or in any other English-speaking country, to the best of the author's knowledge.

Since numbers alone do not tell us all we need to know, Chapter 2 also examines the content and quality of the news sources available. It compares public service with commercial TV and radio, explores the assumption that commercial news sources will usually have right-wing bias and discusses complaints about BBC bias. The concept of internal pluralism, as against market pluralism, is introduced and its crucial importance in the British news system is discussed.

Chapter 3 turns from the supply side to the demand side and examines what sorts of news people get and how much of it they get from what sources. Once again, although media effects cannot be understood without a good knowledge of media diets, they have been largely ignored by media research. Chapter 3 also considers evidence about news avoidance, echo chambers and mixed diets as well as the factors underlying the use of news from different sources.

Chapter 4 deals in general ways with the relationships between what the media say and what people believe and do. Using a common observation about evidence drawn from everyday life, it finds that apart from people who avoid the news, there are a great many who reject media messages, ignore them or accept them. Sometimes large minorities or even majorities ignore or reject media messages that have been repeated over and over again by the mass media for many years. The reasons for this are discussed in the second part of the chapter that summarises the vast amount of experimental psychology research into what is known as belief preservation or motivated reasoning. The implications of this literature for media effects is spelled out with the examples of the hostile media effect, the Lake Wobegon effect and the Dunning–Kruger effect. Decades of research on belief preservation and motivated reasoning are in direct contrast to the claims that the media have a large and direct effect on mass political attitudes and behaviour.

Chapter 5 turns to the role of online news, especially social media, and looks more closely at the evidence about echo chambers, fake news, populism, political polarisation and foreign propaganda. Once again there is a serious lack of information, but what there is does not fit well with current worries and concerns about the political content and effects of the new media and suggests a different set of conclusions.

Chapter 6 deals with national newspaper effects, especially the idea that the *Sun* has wielded considerable influence over the voting behaviour of its readers. The associations between newspaper reading and political attitudes and behaviour over the past decades is traced, together with the popular claim that the media, notably national newspapers, set the election agenda for the population.

The mass media may have an effect on mass attitudes and behaviour either directly through their news content or indirectly through their vastly larger entertainment output. Together they are said to create a mean world effect in which bad news and attack journalism create a general mood of political alienation, apathy, fear and distrust. Chapter 7 examines the evidence for media malaise induced by the news and entertainment media. The chapter presents in-depth evidence from Britain and other parts of the Western world about media use and their effects on what citizens know about polities and their disposition towards them.

The present chapter has already outlined the idea that we are all more or less dependent on the news for our political information and opinion which, if true, would explain how and why the media wield a powerful influence over society. Chapter 8 challenges this common assumption and argues that citizens absorb information about the state of the nation from the routines of their daily life at home, at work and in their localities. They use this experience to form their political attitudes, beliefs and opinions, and there is some (not much) evidence to suggest that these may be more powerful influences than the media.

Chapter 9 considers the strengths and weaknesses of pluralist theory as an account of the media's role in a democracy. It suggests that several changes and additions are necessary to make it more complete and to bring it up to date with present circumstances. The second part of the chapter uses this more complete account of pluralism to assess the role of the media in British democracy. It picks out what effects the media have and do not have and makes some suggestions about future research.

Chapter 10 argues that media effects are not simply of academic interest. It is known that British politicians since Churchill have had hostile attitudes towards the press and especially towards the BBC. They have also demonstrated their fear of media power by accommodating the wishes of newspaper owners. The chapter asks what would the government and politics of Britain look like, and how would government and democracy benefit, if leading politicians had a more realistic view of media effects on mass attitudes and behaviour?

2 | The News Landscape

If we are to understand the effects of the news media on the UK population we must, first of all, have at least a rough outline of the news available. The logic is simple. To explore the effects of any one type of news media, say newspapers, it is not enough to look only at newspapers, ignoring TV, radio and the web, which might have more powerful effects. What would we make of a metallurgist who studied the properties of an alloy by considering only one of its components, or an astronomer who studied the properties of galaxies as if they consisted solely of white dwarfs? When it comes to media effects, current fears about the impact of online fake news and conspiracy theories must be set in the context of what other news people get that might balance out, or even wipe out, any effects that online news might have. In other words, if we want to know if it really was 'the *Sun* what won it', we must test the effects of the *Sun* against other media that might have effects. Hence, we need background information about the news landscape as a whole: the size and composition of the supply side of the news.

Therefore, this chapter maps out the supply of political news and opinion in Britain. It is divided into two main parts. The first deals with the size and scope of the news media landscape, covering TV, printed material, radio and online content. The second looks more closely at the different content and effects of commercial and public service news. It considers how the public services help to create a news-rich environment that has an impact on the whole population by making news easy to access, and possibly difficult to miss. It also examines the common assumption that the commercial news media in Britain will usually be biased in favour of Conservative Party and business interests. In short, the chapter lays some of the foundations necessary to understand the overall impact of the news media system of the UK.

The News Landscape

TV

The UK produces ten dedicated TV news channels.[1] The BBC has five, Sky has two and GB News, CNBC (Europe) and Arise have one each, but another five general channels broadcast regular and extended news programmes. The BBC also has fifteen regional windows with their daily news that are required to engage with the local democratic process and facilitate civic understanding and fair and well-informed debate through coverage of local news and current affairs programmes. BBC News is a rolling 24-hour news network shared with BBC World News.

In addition to the domestic channels the MAVISE database identifies 140 24-hour news-only TV channels, not including business and parliamentary channels.[2] Of these 43 per cent are national and 57 per cent are international, and twenty-five of them are available in the UK. Wikipedia lists 275 TV channels dedicated to news and broadcasting twenty-four hours a day, seventy-four of which are in English.[3] Among the many available in the UK are Al Jazeera, Bloomberg, CCTV (China), CNBC Europe, eNCAS (Africa), Euronews, Fox News, France24, RT (Russia), NDTV (India), NHK (Japan), PBS (USA), Arise News (global) and CNN. Many other countries also have general TV channels that include regular extended news programmes. All told, some twenty-five British TV channels, plus another fourteen from abroad, are easily available in the UK, but there are untold numbers of others that provide news in their local languages.

---

[1] The vocabulary of media studies is sometimes subject to vagueness and ambiguity, starting with the word 'news'. The term covers a wide rage of subjects, most often news about sport, entertainment, health, the weather, gossip, science, nature, public figures and politics. The news programmes of most TV channels and radio stations and the content of almost all newspapers include some non-political news. In this book, unless it is otherwise specified, 'news' means political news, but unfortunately many surveys of news consumption do not define the term and it is not clear what their respondents understand by it, although at other times it is defined or one can judge its meaning from the context.

[2] European Audiovisual Observatory. 2018. *TV News Channels in Europe*. Strasbourg: European Council.

[3] https://en.wikipedia.org/wiki/List_of_news_television_channels.

Radio

The UK has few radio stations of its own that are dedicated to news, but some general stations broadcast extended news (mainly the BBC's) and there are about 380 news, or news and talk, stations.[4] More than 300 online commercial stations broadcast a weekly average of ten hours of news of all kinds, usually brief bulletins and often round the clock.[5] The length and frequency of these broadcasts increased markedly during the Covid pandemic as part of the commercial sector's contribution to spreading information and understanding of the disease. In addition, there are over 300 Ofcom-licensed community radio stations that cater for the special interests of local organisations and social groups. Ethnic, religious and language groups have some ten to twenty stations and the BBC's twenty-four-hour World Service broadcasts in twenty-seven languages.

Radio news is not as diverse as might seem at first sight because, like TV and the newspaper market, ownership and control of commercial and public stations is concentrated in a few organisations. The BBC has fifty-nine national, regional and local stations and 85 per cent of the commercial market is controlled by seven financial groups. Three companies (Bauer, Global and Independent) account for 170 stations between them and 60 per cent of the market.[6] Most of the commercial stations do not provide their own news but syndicate the same news content. While this increases the amount and availability of news, it does not necessarily add to the diversity of news content. In other words, one cannot estimate the pluralism of radio news content simply by counting the number of stations

Nevertheless, the radio news landscape in the UK is broad and varied. Ofcom notes that community radio ranges from large regional to small community stations and is run by commercial and public organisations, media trusts, local governments and individuals, with few operators working in more than one platform.[7]

---

[4] Onlineradiobox.com. Not dated. 'News radio stations' and 'News and talk radio stations'.
[5] RadioCentre.org. July 2020. 'Covid-9 Response: Commercial radio response'.
[6] Chivers, T. 16 March 2021. *Who Owns the UK Media?* London: Media Reform Coalition.
[7] Ofcom. 22 September 2009. 'Local and Regional Media in the UK'. London: Ofcom. 'Platform' has several meanings. Some use it to refer to a unique media

Newspapers and Magazines

Sales and titles of domestically produced UK newspapers have been declining for some years, a trend accelerated by the Covid pandemic. Nevertheless, there are twenty-three national dailies, thirteen national Sunday papers, ten or so national non-English-language papers, approximately 400 freebies and about 1,500 regional and local papers.[8] Scotland has 150, Wales has 50–60 Welsh-language papers and Northern Ireland has six daily and fifty local papers. There are newspapers for Catholics, the British Church, Baptists, Christian Scientists, Zoroastrians, Jews, children, seniors and students. One source lists 112 newspapers and magazines published in the UK for ethnic, language and religious groups, including Arabic, Bengali, Chinese, African, Asian, Indian, Filipino, Caribbean, Jewish, Irish, Mauritian, Muslim, Nigerian, Sikh, Greek, Gujarati, Hindi, Italian, Punjabi, Russian, Turkish and Urdu.[9] London alone has forty different language papers, and the largest language groups often have a small handful. Minority groups have little coverage in the mainstream press, so they produce their own assortment of newspapers and magazines that are notable for their small circulations and comparatively high turnover.[10]

The political magazines published in Britain cover most of the political spectrum. The list includes: *The New Left Review*, *The Salisbury Review*, *New Statesman*, *The Spectator*, *The Week*, *Private Eye*, *Tribune*, *Barn*, *Prospect*, *Socialism Today*, *Spiked*, *Chartist*, *New African*, *Politics Review*, *Total Politics*, *Scottish Left Review*, *Red Pepper*, *The Liberal*, *Monocle*, *Standpoint*, *Fortnight Magazine*, *The Internationalist*, *Lobster*, *The Irish Democrat*, *The Land*, *The*

---

outlet (e.g. a hospital radio station). Others use it to refer to a particular a form of communication – TV and radio being examples. A third meaning covers media with a similar content (e.g. social media). Still others group different devices as platforms – TV sets or mobiles. And sometimes the word refers to a computer's system of hardware and software. Sometimes the context makes the meaning clear but sometimes there is ambiguity.

[8] HoldtheFrontPage.co.uk. 13 December 2022. 'Regional Daily Newspapers in the UK'. See also wrx.zen.co.uk. Not dated. British Newspapers and News Online.

[9] Georgiou, M. Not dated. *Mapping Minorities and Their Media: The National Context – The UK*. London: London School of Economics.

[10] Firmstone, J., et al. Not dated. *Representation of Minorities in the Media: UK*. Leeds: University of Leeds.

Socialist, Solidarity, The Economist, The Critic, The Big Issue, Socialist Appeal, Liberator, Frontline, Peace News, Socialist Worker and *Weekly Worker*. Wikipedia lists another 160 foreign politics and current affairs magazines most of which are English language.

Like commercial radio, a few big players dominate the mass print media. Three companies – DMG Media, News UK and Reach – control 90 per cent of the local and regional newspaper market.[11] Two-thirds of local authority districts in the UK have no daily paper of their own, and more than half of those are the monopolies of a single publisher. Local and regional papers rely heavily on a few agencies or national news. The hyper-local news network, NUB News, has expanded, and some online-only papers have appeared, but the general trend is towards a smaller market and greater consolidation of ownership.

Like TV and radio, the print media also has a long tail of small, specialised and independent news producers.[12] The political magazine market is notable for its diverse content: those listed earlier are mostly independently owned and controlled, though most have a very small circulation. At the same time, developments in digital printing and publishing have resulted in a large number of small, local newspapers and papers for subgroups and special interest groups of many different kinds. Little is known about them.

Online News

The difficulties of collecting accurate and up-to-date information about the legacy news are magnified many times for online news. There are no centrally agreed definitions or collection of information, and some sectors are so large and scattered that a census is all but impossible. It is estimated that about 200 million websites are active, not counting the dark web that hides illegal content.

The UK has relatively few domestic online TV channels dedicated to news and most of these are the BBC's, but all the national daily and Sunday papers have online editions, as do most of the main regional papers. If local papers are added in, there are estimated to be around a

---

[11] Mediareform.org.uk. March 2019. 'Who owns the media'. Media Reform Coalition.
[12] Quinn, T. Not dated. 'News magazine: I see a whale'. Magforum.com. Magazine genres, newspapers.

thousand online newspaper in the UK.[13] Then there are some 370 news and talk internet radio stations. Overall, an approximate but conservative estimate of the number of domestic legacy sources of online news puts the figure at around 1,500, ranging from the BBC's twenty-four-hour international service down to local and community sites of mainly parochial interest.

Beyond that, access to online news from almost every nook and cranny of the globe is limited mainly by language and pay walls, but there remains a lack of information about what is available. FreeeTV.com lists 290 dedicated online news channels, to which are added uncountable hundreds or thousands of general channels with news programmes. Onlinenewspapers.com lists in excess of 8,000 online newspapers.[14] Streema.com lists 16,191 English-language news and talk radio stations. The figures vary greatly because of different definitions, ways of counting and the purpose of collecting the material.

Like all other forms of communication, the web devotes a small proportion of its space to politics defined even in the broadest way. But a small proportion of an exceedingly large number still amounts to a large number. If only 0.5 per cent of the 200 million active websites deal with political news and commentary, this amounts to around a million websites. Like the legacy media, the online market is divided between a small number of tech giants – especially Alphabet (Google), Amazon, Apple, Meta (Facebook) and Microsoft – and an incalculably huge and steadily increasing number of small, independent websites with a political content: blogs, pod casts, chat rooms, have-you-say sites, discussion forums, petitions, videos, digital native newspapers and radio stations, emails and a series of encyclopaedias, including the satirical Uncyclopedia.[15] The great majority of these are produced not

[13] wrx.zen.co.uk. Not dated. 'British Media online: UK Newspapers: national, local, daily, weekly, plus major magazines & portals'.

[14] onlinenewspapers.com. Not dated. 'Online newspaper directory for the world, England A–K, L–Z'.

[15] The media literature usually refers to TV, radio and the print media as 'legacy media' in order to distinguish them from the 'new', 'digital' or 'online' media. This terminology has its problems. British and American dictionaries define the noun 'legacy' as something bequeathed by the dead to the living, usually in a will. As an adjective the word means something received from the past or left over from previous times. However, TV, radio and print media are neither dead nor of the past. On the contrary, they are very much alive and kicking in the present. They make full use of digital technology and have a large and significant presence in online news. This book is reluctantly obliged to follow the almost

by multinational corporations but by politically involved individuals, groups and associations speaking in many different political voices for many different political interests.

The main purpose of this section of the chapter is to provide a glimpse of the uncountably vast amount of diverse news and opinion that is available from the four main forms of communication. Little is known about a large portion of the total. A simple example is provided by the Apple directory of 1,379,957 podcasts that classifies 7 per cent (96,597) of them as dedicated to news. What kind of news aimed at what kind of market to what effect is unknown.

The News System

A simple headcount of news suppliers is a useful starting point for a rough idea of the size and composition of the news market, but it is only a start because it has nothing to say about the content and the quality of the news supplied. News sources are not all of the same quality, but the problem is that quality is not a subject for measurement. Nevertheless, it would be a mistake simply to assume that counting heads is a satisfactory way to measure pluralism: the *Sun* is not the equal of the *Financial Times*; nor is *News Thump*, a satirical website, on the same footing as Channel 4 News.

Quality is subjective and difficult to pin down, but content is different and one of the most frequently voiced complaints is biased reporting, especially on the part of the commercial media which is said to favour right-wing and conservative interests. Regular publications on the growing concentration of ownership and control of the mass media in the hands of multimedia and multinational corporate giants is largely based on the assumption that these will usually, perhaps inevitably, present a distorted account of the news that favours business interests. There is, of course, evidence of this in Britain where the national press is largely owned by multimillionaires whose newspapers generally (not always) support the Conservative Party. Nevertheless, it is by no means true that the commercial media are always or inevitably biased politically.

> universal use of 'legacy' as a category covering TV, radio and the print media, but rejects the implication that they are dead or dying or of the past and have been replaced by the 'new', 'digital' or 'online' media.

The Golden Chains of the Market

The relationship between commercialism and political bias is complicated by economic forces that encourage either political bias or impartiality. These forces are not well understood or much researched, but one seems to be the nature and size of the market. Local papers with a small market cannot afford to alienate a significant part of their populations so the incentive is to avoid the news or treat it impartially. In contrast, Britain has a large national newspaper market that runs into tens of millions and it is not just financially viable but sometimes profitable for national dailies to proclaim their partisan affiliations.

A second economic pressure favouring political neutrality is that three-quarters of the British population prefers it.[16] This is not the only criterion that people use in selecting their news media, but it is an important consideration for some and may help to explain the popularity of public service TV news and the more impartial papers – the newspapers of record. It might be said that these are better described as independent papers with liberal values in the sense that they support such values as liberty, equality and fraternity, but are not necessarily or consistently party political or generally in favour of a particular ideology and do not necessary take a position on capitalism versus socialism. Commercial news sources do not always support the interests of big business.

Nor do the particular interests of commercial media necessarily coincide with the general interests of the business classes and the parties that represent them. The first priority of any business is to look after its own balance sheet, which may put pressure on it to maintain its circulation by selling what its readers want to buy. If so, the economic interests of papers may not coincide with the interests of the wider business community of which they are a part. There are examples to illustrate the point. In the 1997 general election, the Murdoch papers split their support between the Conservatives and Labour. *The Times* stayed faithful to the Conservatives but the *Sun* switched to Labour. But then *Times* readers are mainly true-blue Tories, while polls in 1997 showed that the majority of *Sun* readers

---

[16] Newman, N., Fletcher, R. and Schultz, A., et al. 16 June 2020. *Digital News Report 2020*. Oxford: Oxford University, Reuters Institute; BBC Media Centre. 15 June 2020. 'Reuters Institute study finds BBC News is America's most trusted news brand'.

were going to vote Labour. *The Sun* then switched back to the Tories for the 2010 election but only after the polls reported a large Conservative lead.[17] During the referendum on Scottish independence in 2015 the *Sun*'s English edition opposed it and the Scottish edition was in favour. In the US presidential election of 2016 Murdoch's Fox News angered Republican campaign managers because it supported unelectable right-wing Republican candidates who appealed to the channel's ageing, white viewers, rather than the party's main election hopefuls. Meanwhile the *Wall Street Journal* supplied its business readers with what they wanted and continued its tradition of not endorsing anyone.

As one writer puts it, Murdoch 'likes to support the party most likely to win *and* the one most likely to further his economic interests'.[18] Another says, '*The Sun* newspaper is a great weather vane, but it doesn't decide the direction of the wind'.[19] To understand what shapes the political policies of the Murdoch media it is often best to follow the money, that is, the bottom line of Newscorp's balance sheet, rather than the policies of the larger business community and the party it supports.

The Murdoch media are not alone in following the politics of their readers. Nor are they the first to come under pressure from their customers. The circulation of the *Financial Times* was threatened by its endorsement of Labour in the 2005 general election. In 2012 most Conservative dailies supported the government's poll tax but soon modified their tone when mass public opposition erupted. In 1956 the *Manchester Guardian* (as it was then) and its sister paper, *The Observer*, put their sales at risk when they provoked strong reader criticism regarding its opposition to the Suez invasion. In 1989 the *Sun* ran a story about the what they alleged to be the appalling behaviour of Liverpool football fans in the Hillsborough. The story turned out to be a fabrication and in spite of two full-page apologies, there is still a boycott of the paper in Liverpool.

'The first law of journalism', according to the journalist Alexander Cockburn, is '[t]o confirm existing prejudice, rather than contradict

[17] For more information see Chapter 6.
[18] Martinson, J. 1 May 2015. 'As the papers loudly declare party allegiances, it won't just be one that wins it'. *The Guardian*.
[19] Straw, W. 30 September 2009. 'Sun's circulation down 35% from mid-1990s peak'. Leftfootforward.org.

it'.[20] Commercial news organisations cater for the preferences of their audiences and in the final analysis will follow them to protect their sales. It is also a brave newspaper editor who suppresses a major scoop because it is not in the interests of the political party the paper generally supports.

Public Service and Commercial TV

The mixed British system combines public service and commercial media. There is no clear distinction between the two; they have features in common and mutually influence each other, but there are still differences. Commercial media are wholly commercial, whereas the BBC is allowed to supplement public funds with commercial income. Both are supposed to be completely independent of government and political parties, but in practice it is not unknown for British governments to put political pressure on the BBC and ITV either through strong and public criticism of their news reports, or in the case of the BBC through control over its charter and licence fee. The need to maintain its audience figures has resulted in some 'back-door commercialism' on the part of the BBC which has moved closer to the commercial model of programming and content.

As far as the news is concerned, the most important similarity is that the same public service rules apply to both public service and commercial TV and radio. They must not editorialise with political opinion, as newspapers can, and they must not broadcast political advertising except under strict fairness rules imposed on party-political and election broadcasts. And they should observe a long and elaborate professional code of conduct for journalists. When commercial TV was legalised by the Television Act of 1954 its broadcasting licence required it to produce news that was balanced, accurate and impartial. The BBC agreed to the same rules which it had been following since its foundation. The details of these duties have been modified several times since they were first laid down in the 1954 Act, and Ofcom has further elaborated the duties of due impartiality and accuracy, but the general principles remain the same.[21]

[20] Lavin, C. 19 May 1996. 'The first law of journalism: To confirm ... ' *Chicago Tribune.*
[21] Ofcom. 5 January 2021. 'The Ofcom broadcasting code. Section five: Due impartiality and due accuracy'. London: Ofcom.

Still, public service news has been attacked for its political bias. This may be inevitable, no matter how hard and successfully public services pursue the ideal of total impartiality. It is impossible to maintain perfect balance, accuracy and impartiality in a world of fast-moving events, tight deadlines and limited resources. It can also be argued that pure political impartiality is impossible anyway because the very words we use in discussion are value loaded. Nevertheless, public service and commercial TV and radio have managed to get as close or closer to balance, accuracy and impartiality as any other sources of news in the UK or elsewhere. It is also important to distinguish between accuracy and impartiality, the former being a matter of factual reliability and the latter concerning opinions. Barwise and York note that the BBC has been accused of partiality but rarely of inaccuracy.[22]

Nor is it possible for even the most balanced, accurate and impartial news organisation to escape unwarranted accusations of bias because of 'the hostile media effect'. This occurs when those with strong but different views about an issue are convinced that the same report about it is biased against their own position and in favour of the opposition view, regardless of how objective, impartial and balanced the report may be. The effect is most frequently found among those with the strongest political opinions and the minorities on the fringes of public opinion, so the effect tells us more about hostile individuals than about the media. For example, the *Daily Mail* has been described as very or fairly left wing, mainly by people who describe themselves as very right wing, and the *Guardian* has been described as very or fairly right wing, mainly by people who describe themselves as very left wing.[23]

In recent years the hostile media effect has been fuelled by deepening political divisions, culture wars and cancel culture. Distrust of the BBC increased from 11 per cent in 2018 to 27 per cent in 2022, most among poorly educated males with less interest in the news and who only used social media to access such content.[24] More than half of the distrusters were Conservative voters and two-thirds voted for Brexit. If this trend

---

[22] Barwise P. and York P. 2020. *The War Against the BBC*. London: Penguin Random House: 9–10.
[23] Smith, M. 7 March 2017. 'How left or right-wing are the UK's newspapers?' London: YouGov.
[24] Reuters Institute. 2020. *Digital News Report 2020*. Oxford: Oxford University, Reuters Institute, 17.

is general to most news media then it seems that the hostile media effect may be spreading beyond the political fringe to the general population.

Among the public services, the BBC is often the most heavily criticised for bias. A small minority on the political left in the population are given to complaining about its right-wing bias, but they are usually balanced out by a small minority on the political right which complains of its left-liberal bias.[25] More seriously, governments have attacked both the BBC and ITV for its reporting of some issues, the BBC more frequently than ITV. According to some, the BBC's independence has been compromised from the start when it came under pressure from the government over its reporting of the General Strike in 1936. Most recently, however, it has been brought to task for its attempts to maintain balance and impartiality by giving air time to small but vocal minorities that are, the critics claim, beyond the pale of acceptable politics.[26] Pure political impartiality may be theoretically impossible, and in practice even those who approximate it are coming under attack by those who believe they are entitled to their own facts as well as their own opinions.

Judgements about political bias are usually a matter of opinion, but what is not subjective is the fact that the public service regulations that govern the BBC, ITV and Channel 4 produce news that is different in content, kind and quantity from commercial TV and radio.[27] Research

---

[25] Moore, M. and Ramsay, G. 2017. 'Caught in the middle: The BBC's impossible impartiality dilemma', in Jackson, D. et al. eds., *UK Election Analysis, 2019: Media, Voters and the Campaign*. Bournemouth: University of Bournemouth: 92.

[26] For an extensive analysis of government relations with the BBC and general criticism of the BBC for bias see Barwise P. and York P. *The War Against the BBC*. London: Penguin Books.

[27] What follows is a short summary of a large body of evidence about the features and effects of public service broadcasting in northern Europe – see Curran, J., Iyengar, S., Lund, A. and Salovaara-Moring, I. 2009. 'Media system, public knowledge and democracy: A comparative study'. *European Journal of Communication*, 24(1): 5–26; Nikoltchev S. 2007. *The Public Service Broadcasting Culture*. Strasbourg: Council of Europe; Aarts, K. and Semetko, H. 2003. 'The divided electorate: Media use and political involvement'. *Journal of Politics*, 65 (2): 759–784; Vliegenthart, R., Schuck, A. and Boomgaarden, H. 2008. 'News coverage and support for European integration, 1990–2006'. *International Journal of Public Opinion Research*, 20(4): 415–439; Aalberg, T. et al. 2013. 'International TV news, foreign affairs interest and public knowledge: A comparative study of foreign news coverage and public opinion in 11 countries'. *Journalism Studies* 14(3): 387–406; Toka, G. and Popescu,

across Europe, including Britain, finds that compared with commercial news the public services broadcast more news, both domestic and foreign, and do so more frequently during the day and with a greater concentration in peak viewing and listening hours. A Council of Europe study reports that although public services make up only 14 per cent of all TV channels, they account for 30 per cent of the total output of TV news.[28] Public service news also delivers more hard information about policy and politics. The difference between hard and soft is fuzzy, but hard news is generally concerned with major and urgent issues of national and international politics and policy, while soft news is more about political personalities, appearances and human interest stories.

Public services also broadcast longer news programmes that cover more subjects and have space for in-depth and detailed discussion. Commercial channels and radio stations often have shorter news programmes, if any, and tend to place them in off-peak hours when audiences are smaller, keeping peak hours for entertainment programmes that attract larger audiences and more advertising revenue. Research also finds that public service journalism is more professional and politically neutral with higher standards of reporting.

The contrasts between public and commercial news are matters of degree rather than kind but they are found across the countries of Europe, and they have consequences for their populations. In broadcasting more and longer news programmes at peak viewing hours, public service broadcasters make it easier to access the news. People with an interest in politics will always find the time and a way to keep up with events, but the less interested are also more likely to fit news into their daily routines if it is broadcast frequently throughout

M. 2009. 'Public television, private television and citizens' political knowledge'. EUI Working Papers, RSCAS, 2009/66, San Domenico di Fiesole, European University Institute; Fraile, M. and Iyengar S. 2014. 'Not all news sources are equally informative: A cross-national analysis of political knowledge in Europe'. *The International Journal of Press/Politics* 19(3): 275–294; Kennedy, P. J. and Prat, A. 2019. 'Where do people get their news?'. *Economic Policy*, 34(97): 5–47; Dimitrova, D. and Strömbäck, J. 2013. 'Election news in Sweden and the United States: A comparative study of sources and media frames'. *Journalism*, 13(5): 604–619; De Vreese, C., Banducci, S., Semetko, H. and Boomgaarden, H. 2006. 'The news coverage of the 2004 European Parliamentary election campaign in 25 countries'. *European Union Politics* 7(4): 477–504.

[28] European Audiovisual Observatory. 2013. *Television News Channels in Europe*. Strasbourg: European Council, 7.

the day. Consequently, attention to the news is not just a product of personal characteristics but also of news systems because countries with a news-rich environment are likely to have better-informed and more understanding citizens.

Studies of media political systems in northern Europe find good evidence to support this claim. One of them finds an association in Britain between watching BBC News regularly and higher levels of political knowledge.[29] More than this, the study predicts that there will be differences between the wholly public BBC, the wholly commercial ITV and the part public-part commercial Channel 4. The prediction is confirmed by the evidence: consistent viewers of BBC News are better informed than their ITV equivalents, and Channel 4 viewers fit neatly between these two. The study concludes that 'BBC and to a lesser extent Channel 4 News viewing tend to be associated with Britons' ability to answer the full battery of current affairs knowledge questions ... ITV news consumption is negatively associated with a person's ability to correctly answer knowledge questions, all else being equal'. In this case, 'all else' covers age, education, political interest, the amount of time spent watching TV news and exposure to radio, newspaper and online news. Of these variables, the older age groups, the more politically interested and those who watch BBC TV are significantly better informed about both hard and soft news. Nevertheless, the main effect is driven more by age and political interest than differences between channels. In this case, as in many others in the following chapters, social, economic and political factors play a stronger part in determining effects than the media.

The link between public service news and the public's knowledge of politics is amply confirmed by other studies. They find that the added increment of information is not limited to those with an interest in politics who watch a lot of news and accumulate a lot of information. It extends to those who are not much interested in politics and do not seek it out, but come across it because they watch a lot of public service TV – they fall into the news rather than jumping into it. An early study of the role of television in the British general election of 1964 shows that even those with a weak interest in politics improved their knowledge of party policies if they watched party and election broadcasts on

---

[29] Soroka, S. et al. 2013. 'Auntie knows best? Public broadcasters and current affairs knowledge'. *British Journal of Political Science*, 43(4): 719–739.

The News System 31

TV. They watched these programmes because the three channels in those days were obliged by public service rules to broadcast them, and there were no other channels to watch. The study concludes that 'TV has retained its power to inform right down to the lowest motivation group in the sample'.[30] Recent studies across Europe show that the same thing still occurs, although perhaps less so now because it is possible to switch to any number of other channels.

This finding has a set of further consequences. First, those who are interested in politics and are well informed about it benefit from a virtuous circle in which the more they know and understand, the better able they are to accumulate more knowledge and understanding.[31] The result is a knowledge gap between the politically interested and well informed and the uninterested and poorly informed. The uninformed fall further behind if they are less able to navigate the news system and have fewer hooks on which to hang new information and improved understanding. However, public service research shows that there is an additional process at work in which the politically uninterested also accumulate knowledge if they fall into the news, and are more likely to do this if they live in a public service country and watch its TV channels and news. Perhaps this applies to public service radio as well, but that is not known. Note that the public interest regulation of news broadcasting applies to both public service and commercial TV and radio in the UK.

Second, public service countries have a smaller knowledge gap than countries with wholly commercial TV. The knowledge gap is reinforced in commercial systems but diminished in the information-rich and easily accessible news environment created by public services.

Third, most research on media effects on audiences focuses on the characteristics of individuals in the audience. For the most part these are the demographic variables of age, education, socio-economic status, sex and ethnicity, together with interest in politics, party identification and position on the left–right scale. Public service research shows that these are not the only factors of importance. Whatever their personal characteristics, individuals in countries with public service broadcasting are likely to be better informed than those in

---

[30] Blumler, J. G. 1972. 'The political effects of television', in Holloran, J. ed., *The Effects of Television*. London, Panther: 70–104.
[31] Norris, P. 2000. *A Virtuous Circle*. Cambridge: Cambridge University Press.

commercial-only systems; public service countries create a news-rich environment which rubs off on large parts of the population, even those with less interest in the news. The country one lives in matters.

Fourth, self-selection is one of the most difficult problems that bedevil media effects. If the politically interested and engaged spend most time with the news media, how can we tell whether it is the media or the political interest of individuals (or both) that accounts for their knowledge of politics? Which is cause and which is effect? Falling into the news avoids the self-selection problem, because those who fall usually have little interest. So if we hold constant the variables normally associated with political interest and knowledge, such as education, age and income, and still find that those who watch a lot of public service TV know more, we can conclude that it is TV that makes the difference. The evidence is that they do know more and therefore we have good reason to conclude that the public service news is at least partially responsible for closing the knowledge gap.

The nationwide effect of public service news leads to a further observation, known as the rainmaker effect, after the biblical saying that the gentle rain from heaven falls on the just and the unjust alike.[32] Hence the rainmaker effect is about the top-down influences that have effects on individuals whatever their particular individual characteristics. In the same way that we talk about a toxic culture in an organisation or institution that influences everybody in them, so the rainmaker effect can have an impact on the population living in an area – a community, region or country. There is evidence of a public service rainmaker effect in a comparative study of twenty-five European countries, including Britain, that examines the association between media use and social trust.[33] Social trust exists between the individual members of society, as against political trust between electors and politicians. The aim of the research was to examine the direct effects of different kinds of media exposure on the social trust of individuals, and the indirect effects that the media might have on the general

[32] Putnam, R., Pharr, S. and Dalton, R. 2000. 'Introduction: What's troubling the trilateral democracies?', in Pharr, S. and Putnam, R. eds., *Disaffected Democracies: What's Troubling the Trilateral Democracies?* Princeton: Princeton University Press: 3–27.

[33] Schmitt-Beck, R. and Wolsing, A. 2010. 'European TV environments and citizens' social trust: Evidence from multilevel analyses'. *Communications*, 35 (4): 461–483.

culture of a country, and from there to have an effect on its individual members. The study compares the effects of public service and commercial channels, and for extra confidence in the results the data were run for two separate years to see if they produced the same result, which they did. The research used the standard statistical technique of multilevel analysis to measure direct, individual level effects and top-down country effects. Irrespective of individual viewing habits, trust was lower in countries that watched, on average, a lot of TV. But the strength of the effect was also dependent on which channels were watched. Those living in a strong public service country were more trusting, and that includes individuals who favoured commercial channels as well as those who preferred public service TV. Hence the rainmaker effect on social trust in countries with public service TV fell on those who watched it and on those who did not.[34] The rainmaker effect has not been much researched and the mechanisms by which it might work are not well understood, so caution is needed in drawing conclusions, but it remains an intriguing research subject.

The effects of public service TV and radio are likely to vary according to the proportions of the public–commercial mix. The larger the public service sector the bigger its impact is likely to be. The more independent it is of commercial income and pressures the more it may differ from commercial media and the greater its effects might be. And the more independent it is of government and political pressure the more likely people are to trust its news, the more people will watch it and the greater is effects may be.[35] And, lastly, if both public service and commercial news channels are bound by public service rules to produce reliable and impartial news, the greater their combined effect on the population is likely to be. These are all hypotheses arising out of

---

[34] See also Jacobs, L., Hooghe, M. and de Vroome, T. 2017. 'Television and anti-immigrant sentiments: The mediating role of fear of crime and perceived ethnic diversity'. *European Societies*, 19(3): 243–267; Jacobs, L., Meeusen, C. and d'Haenens, L. 2016. 'News coverage and attitudes on immigration: Public and commercial television news compared'. *European Journal of Communication*, 31(6): 642–660; Zmerli, S., Newton, K. and Schmitt-Beck, R. 2015. 'Mass media and political trust in Europe: Testing for "rainmaker" effects', in Poguntke, T., Rossteutscher, S., Schmitt-Beck, R. and Zmerli, S. eds., *Citizenship and Democracy in an Era of Crisis: Essays in Honour of Jan W. Van Deth*. Abingdon: Routledge: 75–92.

[35] Kennedy, P. J. and Prat, A. 2019. 'Where do people get their news?' *Economic Policy*, 34(97): 5-47

the evidence and awaiting testing, but the research already published shows that public service news makes a positive difference. This is of special importance for the UK where it is a main feature of the news system.

Discussion

We know remarkably little, sometimes nothing, about large parts of the modern news media landscape of the UK, and the evidence we do have is often rough and ready. It varies from one source to another depending on definitions and the purposes for which the data were collected. But what we do know is that TV, print media, radio and the web produce a vast and uncountable amount of news from almost every part of the globe, representing almost every political opinion under the sun. In constitutes only a small proportion of the total volume of all media content, but nevertheless a small percentage of a vast total is still a very large amount.

The great majority of online news sites are small, digital natives. They number in the tens of thousands, at least, and while most are in foreign languages or behind pay walls, there are still large numbers of open-access, English-language sites. More importantly, the mainstream legacy media have reconfigured themselves to fit the digital age, and it is now possible to go online to access some 1,500 British newspapers, hundreds of radio stations and a few dozen TV stations dedicated to the news.[36] The number of newspapers is declining, along with diminishing circulations, but many are now available to the general public who can access them online.

The raw numbers of news sources show that there are more than enough to meet the demands of pluralist theory for many, varied and independent news sources, but this conclusion needs qualification. Both the digital and the legacy media are marked by divergent trends. On the one hand, the mass market is increasingly dominated by a few giant multinational multimedia conglomerate corporations, and on the other, the specialist and niche markets are populated by a large and ever-increasing number of small independents.

---

[36] The legacy media (sometimes known as the 'old' or 'traditional media') consists of radio, TV and the press, as distinct from the 'new', 'online' or 'digital' media. The labels can be misleading and lead to confusion and false assumptions, as we see in later chapters.

Raw numbers tell only half the story because they do not take account of the content and quality of the news. If one simply counts heads, then newspapers of record are the same as the tabloids and Al Jazeera TV is the equal of RT, the official Russian state channel (now removed from all broadcast platforms in the UK). Some researchers trying to measure news pluralism in British by counting heads have come to the conclusion that the system, especially the mainstream media, is not pluralist. This runs into problems.

First, it takes no account of the divergent paths of the mass market towards ever-increasing consolidation, and the niche market towards ever-increasing diversity and fragmentation. Second, it takes no account of the difference between a partisan news source with a bias and an internally pluralist source that aims to be accurate, balanced and impartial. Third, there is a problem with assuming that a single news source will have a single political view, and that many organisations will express many different points of view. This also is not the case. Ofcom distinguishes between the wholesale and retail provision of news.[37] In theory the wholesale measure (supplying news to retail outlets) should be less pluralist than the retail measure. This is because wholesale news is provided in bulk packages of news to many retail outlets, whereas many independent retail outlets produce their own news, thus contributing to the pluralist variety of political voices. The distinction is blurred when wholesalers allow their outlets a degree of independence in writing their own news, as the BBC regional and local services do. It is also blurred when different retailers buy the same news from one wholesale source, as seems to be the case with many commercial radio stations. Wholesalers add to a news-rich environment but do not contribute to a diversity of political voices; small retailers may add only a little to a news-rich environment but they help to increase the diversity of news and opinion.

There is also the point, already made, that different regional versions of the same paper, and different newspapers with the same owner, can and do express different points of view about issues such as Scottish independence and Brexit. The same has been true of weekly and Sunday editions of the same paper. The result is that a single wholesale media organisation may produce a diversity of news, while many retail

---

[37] Ofcom, 21 October 2011, 'Measuring media plurality'. London: Ofcom.

media outlets may not. Simply counting heads is not necessarily a measure of media pluralism of ownership or diversity of content.

A long-running and common assumption is that commercial media, especially those of the multimedia multinational conglomerates, will produce news biased in favour of free market, right-wing interests. This is not always or inevitably so. First, there is a market for impartial and accurate news, which is why we have newspapers of record. Second, in the final analysis the commercial press follows its own bottom line, which means giving readers what they want to read, or risk a decline in sales. If there is a conflict between the paper's own interests in maintaining its circulation, and those of the broader business class, the paper's interests will generally win.

Pluralist theory is also built on an assumption that does not stand up to the facts of the modern world. The theory was developed in the early Victorian age and its main claim is that democracy is best served by a free market system in which many different news sources with many different points of view compete with each other. There was, in those days, no public service news to produce accurate, impartial and balanced news which now plays a major role in the system. Nor, in those days, did they envisage the emergence of giant corporations that control many, if not most, of the mainstream news outlets. And nor was it possible, in those days, to predict the increasing diversity of a vast number of small digital sources of news and opinion, and the problems this has produced because of fake and unreliable information.

The Victorian era of a few newspapers and political pamphlets has been replaced by a vast array of TV channels, radio stations, newspapers and websites that deliver round-the-clock news and opinion, seven days a week, in almost every language in the world and representing the views and interests of almost every social, political, ethnic, religious and geographical group. There is more to say about pluralist theory of the news in a democracy and we return to it in Chapter 9.

Perhaps the main point to be made about this brief account of the British news media landscape and system is the central importance of public service news. It dominates mainstream TV and radio news, and plays a major online role (which is explored more thoroughly in Chapter 3). In many respects the British news system is similar to other Western countries, but it is different from most because the public services are the most significant single feature of its news landscape.

3 | News Diets

In a utopian democracy, as in a perfectly competitive economic market, every citizen would be fully informed about the news and the range of opinions about it. They would regularly check different sources to make sure that they have all the facts and have understood the complexities of the issues. We know that this does not and cannot happen in the real world. Most people are not that interested or concerned about politics, so they take short cuts, rely on gut instinct and economise on time and effort in a variety of different ways.

We know that some people are politics and news avoiders, and that at the other extreme there are news junkies who attend closely to the news. In between these two extremes there is probably a majority who get a varying amount of news in a typical day. This chapter explores how large each of these groups is, who they are and, if they access news at all, do they get a reasonably mixed diet or do they live in echo chambers of their own making? Understanding these choices is likely to involve the individual characteristics of news consumers and avoiders – including age, sex, income, education, ethnicity and news literacy – and life cycle considerations of family, work and retirement that allow more or less time for the news. It may also depend on the user-friendliness of different kinds of news – their ease of access – as well as the importance of the news at any given time.

News Avoiders, News Addicts and Others

The 'beer and skittles' theory claims that the huge growth of the entertainment industry, especially TV, has distracted people from politics and news about them. The evidence we have does not support this claim. A series of social surveys starting in 1981 finds that large minorities of a quarter to a third are not interested in politics. This was the case in Britain in 1981, when there were only a few TV channels, in 1990, when the first cable channel was launched and

15 per cent of the population owned a computer, and again in 2017, with the digital age in full swing.[1] The growth of the entertainment industry has little to do with politics and news avoidance, and nor does the media landscape of different countries. The Reuters Institute *Digital News Report 2019* finds that news avoidance can vary greatly between countries with the same level of media development, and be very different in countries with the same level of development: in the USA and Poland, 41 per cent sometimes or often actively avoid the news; in the UK and Brazil it is 35 and 34 per cent; in the Netherlands and Malaysia it is 29 per cent.

A second explanation of news avoidance attributes it to apathy, a view often voiced with a touch of self-righteousness by those who think they are better than others. This does not fit the evidence either. In 2017 the Reuters Institute at Oxford University found that 24 per cent of the British avoid the news mostly because it was depressing, they did not trust it and they felt they had no political influence. These feelings were heightened two years later when news avoidance jumped to 35 per cent, driven by anger, sadness and boredom over Brexit.[2] This is not apathy but, on the contrary, an engagement with politics and a feeling that nothing could be done about it. A growing awareness of fake news made things worse, but that all changed overnight when, in May 2020, the danger of Covid-19 sank in and it was necessary for personal safety to know about the pandemic and government measures to control it. All the main news channels, and especially the BBC, reported big jumps in the numbers tuning into the news and government briefings.[3] The BBC usually registers the largest spike in audience numbers during times of national emergency or crisis.

Part of the explanation for news avoidance is the difficulty of understanding and evaluating politics and the range of views about them.

---

[1] Harding, S., Phillips D. and Fogarty M. P. 1986. *Contrasting Values in Western Europe: Unity, Diversity and Change*. London: Macmillan: 77; Ashford S. and Timms, N. 1992.*What Europe Thinks: A Study of Western European Values*. Aldershot: Dartmouth: 89.

[2] Mayhew, F. 12 June 2019. 'Reuters Digital News Report 2019: People actively avoiding news because of Brexit'. *PressGazette*.

[3] Newman, N., Fletcher, R., Kalogeropolous, A. and Nielsen, R. 2019. 'Reuters Institute Digital News Report 2019'. Oxford: Oxford University, Reuters Institute; Tobitt, C. 17 March 2020. 'Coronavirus leads to "staggering demand" for trusted TV news'. *PressGazette*; Ofcom. 17 December 2021. 'Covid-19 news and information: Consumption and attitudes'. London: Ofcom.

News Consumers

The vast amount of ever-changing political events, the bewildering array of opinions about them and the variety of news brands reporting them makes it difficult to know which sources to trust, how to make sense of the reports and what is important and unimportant. Age is consequently one of the most important social characteristics associated with a lack of interest in the news, but that picks up considerably with the acquisition of experience and knowledge, although those with lower levels of education and income are still less engaged than the chattering classes with higher levels.[4] News avoiders are disproportionately found among the young, the poor and the poorly educated; news junkies are mainly well paid and educated.

News Consumers

Tables 3.1, 3.2 and 3.3 present an overview of the number of news sources used by social groups. The figures must be treated with a pinch of salt because they rely on self-reported responses to social surveys, and we know that these rely on the accurate recall of behaviour and are sometimes the overestimations of people who want to present themselves as good citizens who keep up with the news. Nevertheless, it is worth presenting them now and checking them against other methods of data collection quoted later. The year 2019 is selected because this

Table 3.1 *Average number of individual news sources used by platform, 2019*

All platforms	Any Internet	TV	Printed papers	Radio
6.7	3.6	2.7	2.6	2.0

Source: Ofcom, *News Consumption 2019*. London: Ofcom: table 10.1.
Note: The average of 6.7 across all platforms cannot be calculated by totalling the rest of the figures in the respective columns, because the average must take account of the population size in each cell. For example, the TV and printed paper values in the first part of the table are similar, but many more people watch TV news than read a paper.

---

[4] Ofcom. 2019. *News Consumption in the UK: 2019*. London: Ofcom: figure 2.3; Newman, N., Fletcher, R. and Karogeropolous, A. Reuters Institute. 2018. *Digital News Report 2018*. Oxford: Oxford University, Reuters Institute: 33.

Table 3.2 *Total number of news platforms used by demographic groups, 2019*

All platforms total	Female	Male	16–34	55+	ABC1	C2DE	Minority ethnic	White
6.7	6.2	7.2	7.0	6.2	7.5	5.8	8.2	6.4

Source: Ofcom, *News Consumption 2019*. London: Ofcom: table 10.2.
Note: The average of 6.7 across all platforms cannot be calculated by totalling the rest of the figures in the respective columns, because the average must take account of the population size in each cell. For example, the average of the eight demographic groups does not add up to the average total.

was the last normal year before Covid-19 caused an unusual upsurge in news attention.

The figures show that people get more sources of news when they go online than they get from TV, the press or the radio, and that men, the young, those of higher socio-economic status and minority ethnic groups access more sources than others. Differences of sex and social status fit neatly with what is known about political and social interest and activity, but the age and ethnic minority figures are surprising and in need of explanation. The young see more news sources because they find many of them when they go online. Chapter 2 noted that minority ethnic groups and political organisations produce a large number of magazines and newspapers because their interests are not sufficiently dealt with in the mainstream media. They also go online more frequently than the white population which means that, like the young, they use more news sources than the average for the country. Other than that, TV remains the main source of news for three-quarters of the population, even for half the youngest age group. Older people depend mostly on the legacy media, especially TV and to a lesser extent newspapers.

Overall, the population uses an average of 6.7 different news sources. This might seem a rather high figure for a national average, and it might well be given that it relies on accurate self-reporting of behaviour and possible overestimation. Yet it is not difficult to imagine a figure approaching the average. Individuals might take a national daily, a Sunday and a local weekly paper or a freebie. They might listen to a general radio station over breakfast and to a music station during the day. In the evening they could watch the peak-time news on TV, perhaps switching on different days between the BBC, ITV and

Table 3.3 *Use of main platforms for news by demographic group, 2019 (%)*

	Total	Female	Male	16–24	65+	ABC1	C2DE	Minority ethic	White
TV	75	75	76	51	94	76	74	65	77
Internet	66	66	67	83	40	72	61	82	64
Radio	43	42	45	26	49	47	39	32	45
Paper (printed only)	38	35	40	20	58	41	34	34	39
Newspapers (printed or websites/apps)	49	47	51	35	64	56	42	48	49

Source: Ofcom, *News Consumption* 2019. London, Ofcom: table 2.3.

Channel 4 depending on what else they were watching. Online news is not yet the largest provider of news for most people but it adds substantially to the diversity of sources, as shown in Table 3.1. News digests and aggregators have also expanded the range and variety of news and a fifth (19 per cent) of UK adults use them and 25 per cent say they use search engines.[5] The national average will also be increased by the minority who read political magazines and like political comedy.

Multisourcing

Ofcom's 2019 *News Consumption Report* presents more detailed evidence about how individuals mix the four main sources (platforms in Ofcom's use of the term) of news (Table 3.4). As expected, a minority of 10 per cent use only one source, almost wholly relying on TV, and a slightly larger minority use all four. In between the great majority use two or three, with a national average of 3.5. This figure refers to the four main forms of news, not to the various news outlets reported in Tables 3.1, 3.2 and 3.3 It is notable that TV makes up the largest part of all fifteen combinations, underlining again its importance in the news system. Radio, by and large, is the weakest link for news.

Another Ofcom table allows us to push the analysis a step further with a list of the top-twenty news sources in the country (Table 3.5). These figures reveal two simple but important points. First, BBC 1 is by far the most popular single source of news in the country, with almost two-thirds using it. If BBC 1, BBC News, BBC 2 and BBC radios 1, 2 and 4 are added, then the corporation has a blanket reach of 90 per cent or more of the country. The second point is that the legacy media fill fifteen of the top-twenty spots. Only Facebook, Google, Twitter, WhatsApp and Instagram make it into the top twenty. Moreover, the legacy media dominate the reach of online news. When the Ofcom sample is asked to name its most-used digital news source, the legacy media are mentioned three times as much as the digital natives in the top twenty.[6] The BBC takes the lion's share

---

[5] Ofcom, 27 July 2021. 'Young people turn away from TV news to keep up to date online'. London: Ofcom.

[6] 'Digital natives' has been given two meanings: people who have grown up in the digital (computer and online) era and organisations created in this era that have an exclusively online presence. The term as used here refers only to organisations, people being identified by age group or generation.

Multisourcing

Table 3.4 'Which of the following platforms do you use for news nowadays?'

			%
One only		TV	10
		Radio	1
		Printed newspapers	1
		Internet	1
	Subtotal		13
Two			
		TV and Internet	14
		TV and printed papers	6
		TV and radio	5
		Internet and printed papers	2
		Internet and radio	3
		Radio and printed papers	0
	Subtotal		30
Three			
		TV, radio and printed papers	7
		TV, printed papers and Internet	14
		TV, radio and Internet	13
		Internet, radio and printed papers	1
	Subtotal		35
Four		Internet, radio, printed papers and TV	14
None of these			3
Average			3.5

Source: Ofcom. *News Consumption 2019*. London: Ofcom: table 2.42.
Note: This table is based on those who use the four main platforms, but not other sources, so it is likely to slightly underestimate multisourcing.

of those who go online for news, with 62 per cent of the population saying they use its website or apps for news, almost twice as many as the next on the list, the Google search engine with 34 per cent.[7]

In recent years, audiences for TV news and readers of printed newspapers have declined, and although both have moved to the web

[7] JigSaw Research. 21 July 2022. *News Consumption in the UK: 2022*. London: Ofcom: figure 8.2.

Table 3.5 *Top-twenty news sources, 2018 and 2019 (% of adults 16+)*

	2018	2019
BBC One	62	58
ITV/ITV WALES/UTV/STV	41	40
Facebook	33	35
BBC website/app	23	25
BBC News channel	26	23
Sky News channel	24	23
Google (search engine)	17	19
Daily Mail/Mail on Sunday	18	18
Channel 4	18	17
Twitter	14	16
WhatsApp	10	14
Instagram	9	13
BBC radio 2	12	12
The Guardian/Observer	11	11
The Sun/Sun on Sunday	11	11
BBC 2	14	11
Channel 5	10	10
BBC Radio 4	9	9
BBC Radio 1	9	9
Metro	9	9

Source: Ofcom, *News Consumption 2019*. London: Ofcom: figure 3.2. Based on the question 'Thinking specifically about <platform>, which of the following do you use for news nowadays?'

and found many customers there, the gain has not filled the gap. Nevertheless, the legacy media continue to dominate the online market for news, as Table 3.6 shows. In 2019 the online reach of the BBC, *Mail*, *Guardian* and Sky News put them in the top four places, with the BBC head and shoulders above the rest. Twelve legacy news organisations were in the top-fifteen places for online reach, the remaining three being filled by digital natives. Moreover, many of the digital natives borrow heavily from the agenda and content of the legacy media, as do the news aggregators. Some digital native news agencies use the legacy media to curate their material. In contrast, Table 3.6 shows that five alternative and radical digital natives also make it into the top twenty for reach although they fill the bottom five places in the table. With

Table 3.6 *Weekly reach of offline and online news*

TV, radio, print	%	Online	%
BBC TV and Radio	68	BBC News Online	50
ITV News	36	Mail Online	16
Sky News	26	Guardian online	14
Daily Mail/Mail on Sunday	15	Sky News online	14
The Sun/Sun on Sunday	15	Huffington Post	11
Regional/local paper	12	Sun online	9
Daily Mirror/Sunday Mirror/Sunday People	11	Mirror online	9
Metro	11	Local paper website	9
Channel 4 News	10	MSN	8
Commercial radio news	9	BuzzFeed	8
The Times/Sunday Times	8	Telegraph online	7
Guardian/Observer	6	Times online	7
The Telegraph/Sunday Telegraph	6	Metro online	6
London Evening Standard	4	ITV news online	6
The Express/Sunday Express	4	Independent/Indy100	6
i newspaper	3	The LADBible	6
		Breitbart	2
		Westmonster	2
		The Canary	2
		Another Angry Voice	2

Source: Reuters Institute, *Digital News Report 2019*, Oxford: Oxford University, Reuters Institute: 68.

small reaches of between 2 and 6 per cent of the population they are the minnows on the online news world.

Habit and ease of access probably explain part of the continuing popularity of the legacy media, especially among older people, but there is also a close correspondence between reach and trust in news organisation.[8] The exceptions are the *Financial Times* because of its special focus, and the *Times* with a pay wall. As with the legacy media,

---

[8] Sipitt, A. June 2019. *Political Trust in the UK*. London: Full Fact.org; Ibbetson, C. 16 December 2019. 'Do people in the UK trust the media'. London: YouGov.co.uk; Edelman.com. 2019. *2019 Trust Barometer*: table 46; Jennings W. and Curtis C. 29 April 2020. 'No, trust in the media has not collapsed because of coronavirus'. London: YouGov.co.uk.

those who use a particular online source tend trust them more than the general population – they trust 'my' media.

It is not enough to distinguish between the legacy and online media and draw a clear line between them, as much of the discussion about online news and social media does, because the legacy media accounts for a large proportion of the news of the digital natives. An Ofcom survey asks 'Which, if any, of the following news sources do you follow on [social media sites]?', and 56 per cent of Facebook users said it was the BBC. Once again, TV channels and national papers fill most of the top spots for social media news – Sky News, ITV, *Mail*, *Guardian*, *Sun*, Channel 4, CNN and local newspapers. The prevalence of legacy news in social media is not limited to Facebook. The BBC is also the most commonly used news source on Twitter, Instagram and Snapchat, along with other legacy newspapers and TV channels.[9]

Nor does this exhaust the legacy media's presence in the news of the digital natives because the Huffington Post, MSM and BuzzFeed also cull, recycle and curate news from other sources, primarily the mainstream legacy media. As a result, it is wrong to assume that those who get news from social media are mainly being fed alternative or extremist accounts of it with large amounts of fake news and conspiracy theories. That sort of content certainly has a presence on the web but most of those who get online news and news from social media are getting mainstream legacy reports.

Cross-Media Diets

A YouGov survey examines how many of those who read one paper every day on the web also look at another at least once a week.[10] This study differs from the previous ones quoted in this chapter because it tracks the actual crossover traffic of people on their computers and laptops. It avoids, therefore, the possibly unreliable information culled from interviews which depend on good memories and no exaggeration of news consumption. As one might expect the two papers that have the largest web readership, the *Guardian* and *Mail*, have the largest

---

[9] Ofcom. 2018. *News Consumption in the UK: 2018*. London: Ofcom: table 7.11
[10] Smith, M. 3 January 2018. 'Which newspaper websites get the most crossover readership?'. London: YouGov.co.uk.

crossovers with other papers, but the *Independent* and *Telegraph* are not far behind. More than four out of five *Independent* readers check out the *Guardian* at least once a week and a third of *Telegraph* readers do the same with the *Guardian*. A majority of *Telegraph* readers also see the *Financial Times* and the *Express* and almost as many see the *Independent*. A third of *Express* regulars see the *Guardian* and a third see the *Independent*. As one might expect, the tabloids with the least political content, the *Star*, *Sun* and *Mirror*, have the lowest crossover rates and there is a clear tendency for tabloid readers to see other tabloids and for broadsheet readers to see other broadsheets. The *Times* is an exception, probably because of its pay wall. The general picture, however, is of a good deal of crossover reading between the national dallies, which confirms the diversity of news consumption suggested by survey research.

A second computer-tracking study was carried out by UKOM/Nielsen home and work panel use of desktop and laptop computers.[11] This research covers the six largest online newspaper sites at the time (*Mail, Guardian, Telegraph, Sun, Independent* and *Times*), plus the BBC, so it has a broader scope than the YouGov study in the previous paragraph. The total monthly number of unique visitors to these websites was thirty-two million. As expected, the BBC accounts for the largest single amount of cross-media traffic because it is easily the largest and most trusted source of online news, but there is a large amount of other crossover traffic as well. Almost half of *Guardian* readers visited the *Telegraph*'s website and vice versa. More than half of *Sun* readers watched BBC News and more than half overlapped with the *Mail*, while more than a third read the *Guardian* and the *Telegraph*. Just under two-thirds of *Telegraph* readers watched BBC News and half of them also read the *Mail, Guardian* or *Telegraph*. Once again, broadsheet readers overlap most with each other; tabloid readers overlap less and when they do, they overlap with each other.

Social Media and the Young

Half the population now gets news from the social media. This does not mean that half the population gets all its news from this source, only some of it. Television remains the most popular source of news for

---

[11] Ofcom. 2012. *News Consumption in the UK: 2012*. London: Ofcom: table 4.59.

three-quarters of the population, followed closely by online sources (66 per cent) and then by social media (49 per cent). But those who do use social media for news tend to get it in rather different ways and, as a result, get rather different news. Some prefer to go straight to their preferred source while others rely more on posts from third parties, either organisations or individuals. The young (18–24), women and lower social grades (C2DE) tend to favour posts from social media, messaging apps and news aggregators. They see a lot of trending news but also news stories and comments from friends and family. Men, older people (65+) and ABC1s generally prefer to go straight to their preferred news organisation and make less use of social media posts.[12] However, overall, a half or more of the news that social media users get is from news organisations and only a fifth of these are digital natives. The main news organisation is the BBC, but Sky News, ITV, the *Guardian* and the *Mail* are also used across the four main social sites. That said, the news that social media users get is far more mixed than from any other source and includes BuzzFeed, LADbible, CNN, Huffington Post, YouTube and national dailies.

The very young (12–15) differ again. Almost two-thirds claim to be 'quite' or 'very' interested in politics, and most rely heavily on TV for news and current affairs, with BBC 1 and 2, once again, the most important single source for almost half (45 per cent). ITV is also important (30 per cent). The next most heavily used news sources are the six main social websites, led by YouTube with a 27 per cent reach. News links posted on social media, and commented on, by friends, family and people followed are the main news they see on social media. Parents are overwhelmingly important for both learning about news and the most trusted sources of news. The BBC is the most trusted, social media the least.

The chapter has covered TV, newspapers, radio and online news, and while there are other sources of news such as party leaflets, independent news sheets, podcasts and political meetings, little is known about them. Eleven per cent read political magazines, mainly *Time*, *The Economist*, *The Week* and *Private Eye*, and 6 per cent use podcasts for news on a full range of subjects, not just politics.[13] Political

[12] Ofcom. 2018. *News Consumption in the UK: 2018*. London: Ofcom: table 16.7.
[13] Ofcom. 2022. *News Consumption in the UK: 2022*. London: Ofcom: figure 9.1; Reuters Institute. 2022. 'Digital news report 2022'. Oxford: Oxford University, Reuters Institute: 29.

magazines may be important carriers of news and opinion but they cannot rival TV, radio and newspapers for reach and mass influence.

Time Spent with the News

Ideally, we would like to know how much attention people pay to the news, setting aside non-political news about weather, sport, celebrities, health and entertainment. Do they listen to the radio with half an ear while making a meal? Do they skim the front-page headlines before turning to other sections of the paper? Do they tune in and out of TV news while checking their mobile or chatting to someone else?[14] Do they pay close attention to news reports about subjects of special interest to them: taxation, the cost of living, education if they have children, health services if they are ill or unemployment if they are jobless?

There are no answers to these questions at present, but information about how long they spend with TV news is provide by a Broadcasting Audience Research Board (BARB) report commissioned by Ofcom. The data are collected from attachments to TV sets that measure what programmes are switched on and for how long, so it avoids the possible problems of surveys.[15] Taking the eight main TV channels as a whole, the average person watches around sixteen minutes thirty seconds of TV news a day, but almost three-quarters of the 65+ age group watches close to twice that amount, and the 16–24 age group watches less than a sixth. Making allowances for the non-political news content of most TV news, a rough guess is that people watch political news on TV for around 10–12 minutes a day. The total average daily viewing time is close to 211 minutes.[16] In other words, and this point is important, TV news has a remarkably broad reach across the population but not much depth. Of course, TV is only one way of getting news; nevertheless, watching the news, the nation's favourite source, accounts for about 5–7 per cent of all viewing time.

The same is true of video viewing on the web. YouTube reported a huge increase during the pandemic in March 2020, and although there

---

[14] Ofcom studies suggest that a lot of people multi-task while watching TV. See Jigsaw Research. 24 July 2019. *New Consumption in the UK 2019*, London: Ofcom: table 2.73.
[15] Ofcom. 2019, *Communications Market Report 2019*. London: Ofcom.
[16] BARB.co.uk. 12 May 2020. 'Record TV viewing in April'. London: BARB.

was some interest in virus-related topics, news and current affairs was watched by 10 per cent of the population, placing them far below music, how to videos and jokes, pranks and challenges.

Factors Underlying News Consumption

News sources have different combinations of functions and purposes which influence how they are used at different times of the day and over a lifetime. The radio is good for multitasking at home and in the commute to and from work. It can deliver both in-depth and breaking news. Some music stations have news headlines on the hour. TV news is most popular at peak viewing hours in the early evening, sometimes in the morning, and especially at times of national crisis and emergency when large numbers turn to it for important information. Newspapers are read over breakfast, in the lunch hour and while commuting, and besides news, editorials and analysis they contain other attractions. Papers are shared in households, at work and left on the bus or train for others to pick up. Unlike radio and TV, they are not for multitasking. Sunday papers are more likely to carry discussion, analysis and longer articles. Online news is the most varied and flexible of them all and is used for extensive news reporting, time-shifting, breaking news, grazing, podcasts, videos, blogs and online editions of TV channels and newspapers, as well as digital native, news aggregators, news digests and search engines. Those who use a computer at work and are at ease with it make more use of it for news and tend to use it to graze briefly during downtime.

The young are least interested in politics, or in conventional politics at least. They make heavy use of the BBC and other national TV channels, and also of the web. Older people are more politically involved and make heaviest use of newspapers and TV. Retired people watch more television than the average and have more time for the news. Higher-income groups with computer skills developed at work use digital technology and tend to graze news on digital hardware. Those with special interests in particular issues tend to scan a range of news sources and use aggregator sites and publications to help them do this. In unusual times of elections and referendums, terrorist attacks and pandemics, attention to the news bounces and centres on the most reliable and trusted sources, particularly the BBC.

Those with higher levels of formal education and news literacy skills tend to be more interested in politics and more attentive to the news.[17] They prefer reading to watching it and access a wider array of sources, paying more attention to credibility cues and preferring newspapers of record. They place less trust in social media and search engines, but are increasingly turning to selected podcasts. The less well educated and less news literate prefer to watch or listen to the news and make more use of social media and tabloids.[18] Inequalities of income, social status and education account for much of the difference between those who pay most and least attention to news and much of the differences in the kinds of news they use. Nonetheless, TV news, especially the BBC, is the most common sources of news for most of the population.

The news is all around us and in one form or another it can be found in all the corners and waking hours of normal life. It has been described as a 'doorstep' matter, like the doorsteps that we cross when we move from one room to another without so much as a thought about them.[19] Most individuals believe it is a civic duty to keep up with it although some weigh this against their feelings of alienation, anger, sadness and lack of power over events. But even they and the active avoiders find it difficult to avoid the news. Some who do not actively seek it out believe that it will come to them anyway.[20]

---

[17] News literacy is a background understanding of politics together with a knowledge of different news sources – what to trust and where to find it. It takes time and trouble to accumulate news literacy so age and education are the most important social characteristics associated with it and with an interest or lack of interest in the news. See Ofcom. 2019. *News Consumption in the UK: 2019*. London: Ofcom: figure 2.3; Newman, N., Fletcher, R., Kalogeropolous A., Levy, D. and Nielsen, R. 2018. *Reuters Institute Digital News Report 2018*. Oxford: Oxford University, Reuters Institute.

[18] Ofcom. 2020/2021. 'Adults media use and attitudes report: 2020/2021'. London: Ofcom: 33; Reuters Institute. 2018. 'Reuters Institute Digital News report 2018'. Oxford: Oxford University, Reuters Institute.

[19] Haller, H. and Norpoth, H. 1997. 'Reality bites: News exposure and economic opinion'. *Public Opinion Quarterly*, 61(4): 555–575; Killick, A. 2017. 'Do people really lack knowledge about the economy? A reply to Facchini'. *Political Quarterly*, 88(2): 265–272.

[20] Goyanes, M., Ardèvol-Abreu, A. and Gil de Zúñiga, H. 11 October 2021. 'Antecedents of news avoidance: Competing effects of political interest, news overload, trust in news media, and "news finds me" perception'. *Digital Journalism*: 1–8.

Discussion

The evidence we have suggests three main groups of news consumers in the British population. News avoiders form 15–30 per cent of the population depending on how it is measured and defined. There is no clear division between those who actively avoid the news and those who are not interested enough to go out of their way to keep up with it. But in any case, it is difficult to avoid altogether. At the other extreme, between 20 and 33 per cent use all four of the main news platforms, often two or more from each, plus other more minor and occasional sources. The majority in between use two or three main sources each, and a few others sporadically.

This suggests two conclusions: first, Chapter 1 finds that, although there is a vast amount of it, news forms a small part of the total of volume of mass communications in society; second, this chapter finds that most people use only a small part of the news available, although they use it on a fairly regular, weekly basis. In other words, the public uses only a small proportion of the total amount of news available, and that, in turn, is only a small proportion of the total media content. There is no doubt about the hyper-pluralism of news supplies, but whether the demand for it is pluralist or not is a matter of opinion depending on how one evaluates the figures in Tables 3.1, 3.2 and 3.3 and how much importance is attached to the internal pluralism of the public service news.

It is often claimed that a new technology will transform society. History shows that it rarely transforms, but more usually results in slow change in which the new is gradually mixed and blended with the old. So it is with the news media. Digital technology has changed the ways in which the majority get their news, and the market for terrestrial television news and printed papers is in decline, but most have stuck with the tried and tested legacy media that they know and trust. Hence, legacy news continues to have the broadest reach, but many are increasingly turning to computers, smartphones and tablets to get it – old wine in new bottles, or rather news produced by the old, pre-digital media accessed via the new digital technology. At the same time, TV sets are not in decline, they just get bigger.

This exploration of the supply of news and the demand for it throws light on some common misconceptions. There is a fairly common assumption that the web is an expanding source of radical, new and

Discussion

unconventional content produced by digital natives, and it is in some ways. It is home to all sorts of fringe, extremist, unconventional and radical political content, as well as thoughtful, mainstream, original critical material. The former attract attention and concern from the mainstream media but actually few tune in to, or even come across, online material produced by believers in lizard overlords, climate denial, the deep state, vaccine misinformation, flat earth, QAnon, the perils of wind farms, millennial cults, 5G, white supremacists, holocaust deniers, devil worship... the list goes on. The general public may know about these things, and many do because the mainstream media tells us about them, but like the Loch Ness Monster, they have heard about it, though not many have actually seen it first hand.

Part of the problem is confusion caused by the language of 'old' and 'new' media that obscures the difference between the means of communication and its content. The term 'new media' is often assumed to be a package of new technology and digital natives that is separate and entirely different from the 'old media', which is a package of old technology and legacy media. When it is realised how much use the 'old' legacy news has made of the new technology, a different view of the new media emerges.

A second misconception is that the proliferation and fragmentation of online websites will help to create echo chambers of opinion. There is little evidence to support the idea but, on the contrary, evidence to suggest that most citizens have a relatively small but mixed news diet, and that cross-media traffic between websites of a different political colour is not at all uncommon. Those who come closest to living in echo chambers because they rely on one source of news are mostly dependent on public service news, which is not conducive to the creation of echo chambers.

The third misconception is that the proliferation and fragmentation of the news media is helping the fragmentation and instability of the electorate. Smartphones are used effectively by groups of activists to organise protests and pop-up demonstrations, but if one takes a step back from a focus on smartphones, Twitter, Facebook, Instagram and Snapchat to take in the content of the web as a whole, the world looks different. And if ones takes a bigger step back to view the national news media and its users as a whole, then it is apparent that the diet of most people has a large common, overlapping core provided by the mainstream legacy media. And even then, it is still to be shown that online media are responsible for fragmentation and instability rather than many other features of our disturbing times.

And lastly, this preliminary account of news diets reveals the importance of individual attributes in the selection of news sources. Age, sex, social status, education and ethnicity are closely tied to preference for online, TV, newspaper or radio news. The better educated prefer to read the news in a broadsheet, the less well educated prefer to watch it or read a tabloid. The old spend more time with the news, mainly watching it on TV and reading a paper. The young tend to access news from more sources, mainly because they go online where there is easier access to a greater variety of news. Ethnic groups and radical political minorities produce their own newspapers, magazines and radio stations, and make heavy use of online news. Men and people of fifty-five and over prefer hard news, women and younger people prefer soft. The young who use social media as their main source of news are especially likely to prefer soft news. Political interest and identity are also important influences on what news sources people trust and to turn to, and how they treat the news they receive. The demograpy of news diets is important because it complicates the problems of establishing media effects, as we will find out in later chapters.

4 | Avoiding, Rejecting, Ignoring and Accepting

For the past six decades the mainstream media has been pumping out information about the dangers of smoking and abusing alcohol. They have also produced an unbroken drum-beat of information about the need to eat and drink sensibly. They have emphasised over and over again the need to take at least moderate exercise. They have routinely advised caution about sunbathing and the dangers of sunburn. They have conducted smaller but urgent campaigns against driving too close to the vehicle in front and drink driving. For eighteen months during the Covid pandemic every TV channel, newspaper and radio station in the country was saturated with daily news about Covid as a highly contagious and deadly disease that requires masks, social distancing, the avoidance of crowds and then inoculation.

While many people, sometimes large majorities have absorbed this information and changed their beliefs and behaviour, in other case large minorities, sometimes majorities, have continued with their lives as if they had never come across the media campaigns. This chapter is about the different ways individuals respond to the news and public information campaigns, even when the same message is repeated incessantly by all the mainstream media over long periods of time and even when the information is backed by experts, scientists and professionals armed with the best evidence. The chapter identifies four main ways of responding to the news media – avoiding, rejecting, ignoring and accepting – and considers each in turn.

The second part of the chapter then turns to the mountain of experimental psychology that examines what is variously called belief preservation, motivated reasoning, heuristics or cognitive bias. This research investigates how individuals can preserve their beliefs, even against overwhelming evidence, simple logic and compelling argument that shows them to be false. Though rarely even mentioned in the media political effects literature, this research casts serious doubt on the assumption that the news industry has a large, possibly decisive, influence over mass attitudes and behaviour. However, what happens in experimental laboratories is not necessarily repeated in the outside world, so the chapter also investigates whether individuals in the real world can preserve their beliefs and behaviour against the best media efforts to change them.

News Avoiding

Estimates of news avoiders vary from single figures to around a third of the population, depending on how it is defined and measured, but it is unlikely that even the most allergic can avoid the news all together. There are regular news programmes on the main terrestrial TV channels and on radio stations. Many music radio stations broadcast news headlines on the hour. Anyone turning on a TV news broadcast for sport or weather is likely to have to suffer some political news before turning to these topics. Searching a newspaper for something else is likely to result in the sight of a news headline or two. A political comment about politics may be dropped into a group chat about other things. At times of crisis there is a bounce in attention to the news and during the early months of Covid almost the entire nation tuned into government press conferences. News is ubiquitous and hard to avoid, so perhaps the problem is not so much those who try to avoid the news in general but those who try to avoid specific messages to be found in some parts of the news. Perhaps they select the daily paper that fits their own political beliefs, or perhaps they avoid the general news by focusing on special news sources.

News Rejecting and Ignoring

In 2019, before Covid changed smoking habits and the use of face-to-face interviewing to collect information about them, 13.8 per cent of people aged eighteen years and above in the UK said they smoked cigarettes.[1] This is a small fraction of those who smoked forty or fifty years ago, and the numbers continue to fall, but nevertheless, millions are still spending money on something that can do them (and others) nothing but medical harm. The evidence is that most smokers are

---

[1] Office for National Statistics. 7 December 2021. 'Smoking prevalence in the UK and the impact of data collection changes: 2020'. London: HMSO.

aware of the dangers though some are ignorant or misinformed about some aspects of them, or claim not to know.[2] Either way, most smokers have ignored the torrent of information broadcast by the media over the past six decades as well as the warning messages on packets.

According to official government figures almost two-thirds (63 per cent) of adults were above a healthy weight in England in 2022 and, of these, half were obese.[3] In 2019–20, 10,780 hospital admissions were directly related to obesity and just over a million were obesity related, which was a 17 per cent increase on the previous year. In that year, 61 per cent of adults took at least 150 minutes of exercise a week, 11.5 per cent were fairly active (30–149 minutes), but 27 per cent (around 13.5 million individuals) were inactive (fewer than thirty minutes).[4] Physical disabilities account for a proportion of this number, but this leaves millions among the 80 per cent who fail to meet minimal government targets.[5]

Most adults drink some alcohol during the week, but almost 10 per cent (five million) self-reported drinking alcohol five or more days a week, and a quarter of them exceeded the recommended limits for men and women.[6] In 2019 there were 7,565 alcohol-specific deaths in the UK, an 11 per increase on 2001.[7] In 2018–2019 there were almost 1.3 million estimated admissions where the primary or secondary diagnosis was alcohol linked, 8 per cent higher than the previous year.

The numbers have declined steeply since 1979, but in 2019 there were 210 fatal traffic accidents involving drink driving, 1,390 serious collisions and another 3,750 slight collisions. In that year there were 41,737 convictions, which is probably the tip of the iceberg since many

---

[2] Cummings, K., Hyland, A. and Giovino, G. et al. December 2004. 'Are smokers adequately informed about the health risks of smoking and medicinal nicotine?'. London: National Institute for Health, Suppl. 3: S333–40.

[3] Office for Health Improvement and Disparities. 5 July 2022. *Obesity Profile*. London: OHID.

[4] Sport England. April 2022. *Active Lives Adult Survey November 2020-21 Report*. Loughborough: Loughborough University, Sport England.

[5] Farrell, L., Hollingsworth, B. and Propper, C. et al. 2013. 'The socioeconomic gradient in physical inactivity in England'. Bristol: University of Bristol, Centre for Market and Public, Working Paper No. 13/311.

[6] Office for National Statistics. 2018. 'Adult drinking habits in Great Britain: 2017'. London: ONS.

[7] Office for National Statistics. 2021. 'Alcohol-specific deaths in the UK: Registered in 2019'. London: ONS.

drivers are not pulled over and tested.[8] The government has issued many public safety warnings about driving too close to the car in front, placing road signs and markings on many stretches of motorway, but even in the middle of these many drivers take no notice and drive dangerously close to the vehicle in front. According to the Department for Transport Road Casualties Great Britain statistics, 'following too close' was a contributory factor in 7,271 road accidents in the UK in 2019, including 28 deaths, 600 serious accidents and 3,000 slight accidents.[9]

In 2018 (illegal) drug use in England and Wales was running at 9.4 per cent of the population in England and Wales, with some 3,200 drug-related deaths and 714,000 drug-related hospital admissions.[10]

According to Cancer Research UK, 86 per cent of melanoma skin cancer is caused by exposure to the UV of natural and artificial sun and all cases are preventable.[11] This fact, and the steps needed to guard against it, are widely known and understood by the population in general. Nevertheless, a 2017 survey by the British Dermatological Association finds that 35 per cent of British people were sunburnt while in the UK in 2017, and of these 28 per cent were sunburnt three times. Almost half (46 per cent) were sunburnt while abroad.[12] Cancer Research UK records that there are 6,744 new cases of melanoma skin cancer a year, a 140 per cent increase since the 1990s.[13] The World Health Organization anticipates more than 3,000 deaths from this form of cancer in 2025.[14]

In all the cases discussed so far it is likely that most were aware of what the media were telling them and the dangers of their own behaviour to themselves and others, but they chose to ignore the message. They could also choose to simply deny the evidence and advice in the

---

[8] Quittance.co.uk. 2022. 'UK Drink-Driving Statistics (2022)'. London: Quittance.
[9] Department of Transport. 24 November 2022. 'Road accidents and safety report'. London: Gov.UK.
[10] NHS Digital, 28 January 2021. 'Statistics on drug misuse 2020'. London: NHS Digital.
[11] Cancer Research UK. Not dated. 'Melanoma skin cancer risk'. London: Cancer Research UK.
[12] British Association for Dermatologists. 7 May 2017. 'Home and away – Brits getting sunburnt in the UK and abroad'. London: British Association for Dermatologists.
[13] Ibid.; Cancer Research UK, 'Melanoma skin cancer risk'.
[14] Melanoma UK. Not dated. 'Melanoma facts and stats'. Melanoma UK.

same way that flat-earthers deny that the world is round. Climate change is another example. Although public opinion has changed substantially and is likely to continue to change, one current survey finds that 29 per cent of the British are not at all, or not very concerned about it; another reports that 29 per cent believed that it would not harm them in their own lifetime; a third finds that 30 per cent do not see climate change as a threat; a fourth reports that 24 per cent think the threat of climate change has been 'over-exaggerated'.[15]

Covid is one of the best cases for the understanding of media influence because it involves an almost total saturation of news about the pandemic's nature and danger, and the behaviour necessary to minimise the risks of catching and spreading the disease. We also know that the vast majority of the population paid unusually close attention to media reports about Covid and that they were able to correctly answer questions about it (Chapter 5). The great majority took notice and acted upon what they had learned, but large minorities of 22 to 49 per cent believed with varying degrees of conviction in one or more of twenty-one different conspiracy theories about Covid and the vaccination programme.[16] These include the claims that the virus is a hoax, is man-made in an attempt to reduce the world population, an attempt by global companies to take control, or a way to: make money; collect DNA data; destroy the West; implement a police state; carry out mass sterilisation; and conceal the attempt to swap the real world for a simulation. The true believers convinced of these things were impervious to the influences of the mainstream media. Ignorers accept a media message but do not comply with it, but deniers take a simpler route and reject the message as false.

Large minorities subscribe to other conspiracy theories (Table 4.1). More than fifteen million people subscribe to the view that a single group of individuals definitely or probably controls world events and about ten million agree that mankind has probably made contact with

---

[15] Bell, J., Pouchter, J., Fagan, M. and Huang, C. 14 September 2021. 'In response to climate change, citizens in advanced economies are willing to alter how they live and work'. Washington, DC: Pew Research Center; Fagan, M. and Huang, C. 18 April 2019. 'A look at how people around the world view climate change'. Washington, DC: Pew Research Center.

[16] Freeman, D. et al. 2020. 'COVID-19 vaccine hesitancy in the UK: The Oxford coronavirus explanations, attitudes, and narratives survey (Oceans) II'. *Psychological Medicine*, 52(14): 3127–3141, table 5.

Table 4.1 *Percentage of British people who believe that conspiracy theories are definitely or probably true, 2021*

Single secret group controls world events	28
Most likely that humanity has made contact with aliens	20
Harmful side effects of vaccines hidden from public	19
US government knowingly helped terrorist attack in 9/11	12
Global warming and climate change a hoax	9
Likely that 1969 moon landings were fake	9
A secret group of Satan-worshipping paedophiles has taken control of parts of the US government and mainstream US media	8
AIDS virus created and spread around the world by secret group/organisations	7
The official account of the Nazi Holocaust is a lie and the number of Jews killed by the Nazis during World War II has been exaggerated on purpose	4

Source: C. Ibbetson, 18 January 2021. 'Where do people believe in conspiracy theories?'. YouGov, The Globalism Project.

aliens. The percentage figures at the bottom of the table may seem small but even the smallest of 4 per cent amounts to some two million individuals.

Rejecting Newspaper Advice About Voting

We are used to being told how many newspapers readers vote as their paper recommends and, indeed, there is normally a close correspondence between the two. There are also small to large minorities, occasionally majorities, who reject this advice. In the 2015 election, for example, the *Telegraph*, *Mail*, *Times*, *Express*, and *Sun* were Conservative papers and yet 31, 41, 45, 49 and 51 per cent of their readers respectively did not vote Conservative. One in three of Labour's *Mirror* readers did not vote for the party.[17] The corresponding figures for the five Conservative papers in the 2017 election were 21, 26, 42, 23 and 41. As before, a third of *Mirror* readers did not vote

---

[17] Kellner, P. 8 June 2015, 'General election 2015: How Britain really voted'. London: YouGov.co.uk.

Labour.[18] Large minorities ignore the advice of their paper about how to vote.

A more exacting test of the association between reading a partisan paper and voting in elections involves tracking changes over time. Do people who change their vote also change their newspaper in order to align the two or, alternatively, do they change their vote if their paper changes its party support? There is little evidence that either of these occur. The most exhaustive analysis of newspaper reading and voting switching focuses on the 1992–1997 period in which there was a good deal of vote churning and also the unusual case of a paper switching, namely the *Sun*'s conversion to Labour. The study concludes:

> The 1997 election provided a clear opportunity for the power of the press and of Britain's top-selling newspaper in particular to reveal itself. In practice on the evidence of this chapter *The Sun* did not evidently bring the Labour Party new recruits. Equally, Labour's new recruits did not prove particularly keen to switch to the *Sun* ... Like social class the partisanship of British newspapers is clearly part of the structure of British voting behaviour, but whether they can explain the flux [in voting] is very much open to doubt.[19]

Brexit as a political issue is very different from general elections insofar as the Leave and Remain votes were divided according to education, age, social grade and income, but not along normal party-political lines.[20] Political beliefs also distinguish Leavers from Remainers, with two-thirds of Leave voters being classified as authoritarian, 53 per cent on the political right and 75 per cent anti-welfare. But just as significant, minorities of readers do not follow their newspaper's party-political line in general elections in the same way that significant minorities do not agree with their paper about Brexit.[21] Of the Leave papers (*Sun, Express, Mail, Star* and *Telegraph*) 30, 30, 34, 35 and 45 per cent respectively of their readers voted Remain. Of the Remain papers (*Mirror, Times, Financial Time* and *Guardian*) 44, 30, 22, and

---

[18] Curtis, C. 13 June 2017. 'How Britain voted at the 2017 general election'. London: YouGov.co.uk.
[19] Norris, P., Curtice, J., Sanders, D., Scammell M. and Semetko, H. 1999. *On Message: Communicating the Campaign*. Sage: London: 168–169.
[20] Moore, P. 27 June 2016. 'How Britain voted at the EU referendum'. London: YouGov.co.uk.
[21] Swales, K. Not dated. *Understanding the Leave Vote*. London: National Centre for Social Research.

9 per cent voted Leave. Once again, we see large minorities ignoring what their paper says.

Three years after the referendum there were many examples of Leavers switching to Remain papers and Remainers switching to Leave papers. In 2019 a fifth of new *Telegraph* readers were Remainers, 40 per cent of new *Times* readers favoured a no-deal Leave, a third of *Mirror* readers were no-deal Leavers, a third of new *Sun* readers were Remainers and a quarter of new *Mail* readers were Remainers.[22] Although the referendum was a divisive, tribal issue, many members of the tribe ignored what their newspaper was saying and followed their own, individual opinions. As we will see in Chapter 6, it is wrong to assume that all newspaper readers choose their newspapers for their politics, just as it is wrong to assume that readers will accept the political policies and voting advice of the newspaper they read.

Believing What the Papers Do Not Say

While some parts of the population rejects or ignores what the media say, there are also many millions who believe what the media do not say. Multiple surveys over the years show that large numbers in the British public believe in paranormal phenomena. The figures vary a little from one study to another but they mainly paint the same general picture. Table 4.2 presents one set of results.

These items differ from those discussed earlier in the chapter because, unlike smoking, lack of exercise or drink driving, they do not involve personal costs or danger and can, therefore, be worn lightly. For example, 24 per cent claim to have taken advice from a fortune teller, but only 9 per cent say they believe what they were told. It is one thing to flippantly cross a fortune teller's palm with silver out of curiosity or fun, but it is another to believe what they say and quite a different thing to smoke a pack or two of cigarettes a day or eat and drink to the point of obesity. Nevertheless, the figures in Table 4.2 show how many Britons hold fast to beliefs that are only occasionally mentioned in the mainstream media and then usually with a scepticism ranging from mild surprise to outright ridicule.

---

[22] Taylor R. 12 July 2019. 'What do British newspaper readers think about Brexit?'. London: LSE.

Table 4.2 *Paranormal beliefs in the British population aged sixteen and over (%)*

Premonitions	58
Life after death	47
Telepathy	41
Guardian angels	38
Belief in ghosts	38
Seen a ghost	38
Dreams predict the future	35
Some governments conceal existence of extraterrestrial beings	31
Magpies unlucky	28
Spilling salt unlucky	22
Carry a lucky charm	16
13 an unlucky number	15
Witches and wizards	13
Certain magical words and spells	12
Some crop circles the work of extraterrestrial forces	9
Horoscopes accurately predict life events	8
Breaking a mirror unlucky	7

Source: Ipsos, 31 October 2007. Survey on Beliefs. London: Ipsos.

Although the UK falls far short of the claimed 25 per cent of Americans who are creationists, a recent YouGov poll reports that one in seven Britons (14 per cent) think it's probably or definitely the case that the universe was created by God in seven days, and evolution was just part of his creation plan. Another survey finds that 9 per cent in the UK believe that humans and other living things were created by God and have always existed in their current form. One study that is sceptical of these figures finds that

> [O]nly 3 per cent reject the idea that plants and animals have evolved from earlier life forms, while 6.8 per cent reject the idea that humans have evolved from non-human life forms. Only 4 per cent (some two million) qualify as young earth creationists, and among those who attend religious services at least once a month, 14.3 per cent reject plant evolution, 28.6 per cent reject human evolution and 10.2 per cent think the earth is young.[23]

---

[23] Farrell, J. 27 January 2015. 'New survey finds creationism in Britain has been overstated'. *Forbes*.

Another YouGov poll finds that 41 per cent believe that Princess Diana's death was not an accident and a third believe it was an assassination. Between a quarter and a seventh believe it involved MI5, the security services or the SAS.[24]

There are many other examples of invented knowledge, fake history, alternative medicine, voodoo science and cult beliefs that are collected under the general heading of 'counter-knowledge', and less politely as zombie ideas. A small library of books have been written about them.[25] The books cover, between them, such things as: the presence of alien constructions in the Andean forests and Easter Island; predictions based on the Bible or the dimension of the pyramids (themselves built by aliens); the end of the world is nigh; lost tribes, the Arc of the Covenant and the Holy Grail; a flat earth or a hollow earth; myths about 5G; satanic rituals; Masonic conspiracies; extrasensory perception; the Q link pendant; alien abduction; Nostradamus; the Protocols of the Elders of Zion; near death and pre-birth experiences; biorhythms; the Loch Ness Monster; evolutionary physics on the fourth level of understanding; crystal medicine; Mayan cosmology and the many uses of complementary and alternative treatments (e.g. aromatherapy, craniosacral therapy and cranial osteopathy, analysis of the hair, healing hands, detox therapies, super foods, wellness myths, the rainbow diet, reflexology, applied kinesiology). This list could have been longer and no doubt readers can add a few of their own.[26]

Many of these attract a tiny following, but some attract millions, and collectively they add up to many millions. Damian Thompson's book, *Counter-Knowledge*, documents how the public thirst for books of pseudohistory, fake archaeology and bogus astronomy seems to be unquenchable, with sales that run into the millions and tens of millions.[27] Books on miracle diets and nutrition, sometimes written by people with dubious qualifications or none at all, can sell like hot

---

[24] Jordan, W. 7 September 2013. '38% of Brits think Princess Diana's death 'NOT an accident'. London: YouGov.co.uk.

[25] See, for example, Fritze, R. 2009. *Invented Knowledge: False History, Fake Science and Pseudo Religions*. London: Reaktion Books; Shermer, M. 2003. 'Why smart people believe weird things'. *Skeptic*, 10(2): 62–73.

[26] For a long list of list of alternative medical practices from acupressure to zero balancing see https://en.wikipedia.org/wiki/Naturopathy.

[27] Thompson, D. 2008. *Counter-Knowledge: How We Surrendered to Conspiracy Theories, Quack Medicine, Bogus Science and Fake History*. London: Atlantic Books.

cakes. Likewise, books explaining the mystery of the universe or provide self-help advice about how to become rich, successful, famous, beautiful or happy in ten easy steps can go to the top of the bestsellers list and stay there for weeks. Counter-knowledge is big business with complementary and alternative health treatment estimated to have a world market of some 200 million people and 80–90 billion dollars a year and rising.[28] In the UK, 16 per cent of the population used complementary and alternative medical treatments in 2015 and around 10 per cent (6 million) uses homeopathic treatment. The number is rising annually. The beauty market is huge, with more than £1 million spent on anti-ageing and anti-wrinkle products that are known to have little or no physical effect. Helen Mirren, a 'Face of L'Oreal', is reported as saying 'I'm an eternal optimist – I know that when I put my moisturizer on it probably does fuck all, but it just makes me feel better'.[29] Feeling better is important, but for effects on the skin most people would be better served by taking the free advice to give up smoking, staying out of the sun and drinking less alcohol, although that advice, as we have seen, is often unwelcome.

However, mass beliefs of an unusual and eccentric nature must be treated with some caution. First, rooted beliefs and behaviour can change (e.g. smoking, climate change, drunk driving) markedly over time as evidence about them accumulates and the message gets through to the public. Some forms of counter-knowledge also come and go over time and others are not held with strong conviction or seriousness. In fact, some are little more than jokes. A group of Jedi Knights banded together to have themselves recorded as a religion in the 2001 census. Interest in the Loch Ness Monster, like Bigfoot and the Yeti, probably involves more curiosity and fun than belief.

There may also be a difference between beliefs of conviction and convenience. Possibly some believed, against all evidence to the contrary, that Brexit would release £350 million a week for the NHS, but others may have used it as a convenient excuse for their real, but publicly less acceptable, reasons for voting to leave. Few, other than

---

[28] Grandviewresearch.com. Not dated. 'Complementary and alternative medicine market size, share and trends analysis report'. Report ID: GVR-1-68038-725-4; Ernst, E. 18 January 2020. 'The-extraordinary popularity of homeopathy = an extraordinary lie'. edzardernst.com.
[29] Singh, A. 2 August 2017. 'Helen Mirren admits L'Oreal moisturiser "probably does f— all"'. *The Telegraph*.

Remainers making a point, complained when the promise dropped out of sight within hours of the referendum result being announced. Similarly, some people may have hidden their needle phobia behind all sorts of other implausible reasons for refusing inoculation against Covid.[30] In the USA, the evidence that the 2020 election was not stolen is so overwhelming (and rarely supported by any of the mainstream media) that it is difficult to believe that many really believe it to be true. The rest continue to use it as an excuse for continuing their support for Trump and his kind of politics, or as one researcher puts it, a form of partisan cheerleading.[31]

Two further points should be made. First, blogs, alternative websites, YouTube, podcasts and social media are often blamed for the creation and popularity of fake news and extreme beliefs, but most of the beliefs and behaviours mentioned in this chapter date back to early history – fake news, conspiracy theories, beliefs in the occult and paranormal, voodoo science and snake oil, false history, beauty potions, tobacco, alcohol and drug addiction, racism, sexism, ageism, gluttony, laziness, drugs, millenarianism, rejection and fear of science, eccentric religions, collective hysteria and moral panics are as old as the oldest profession.

Many of the things now said to be closely associated with, and promoted by, legacy and digital native news sources have their origins in previous centuries. Mass market consumerism was firmly rooted in the Netherlands in the seventeenth century, unaided by multimillion-pound advertising campaigns and social media influencers.[32] For that matter, modern communications technology has helped to spread and strengthen the global and borderless world, but that also existed in an early form in the seventeenth-century Netherlands.[33] There is much concern about fake news in social media, yet Ramses the Great (1279–1213 BC) used it to good effect. Racism, sexism, nationalism and most other 'isms' were commonplace for centuries before the

---

[30] Wills, E. 7 December 2020. 'Covid-19 vaccination: Needle phobia – it's the jab, not the vaccine, some fear'. BBC News.

[31] Jerit, J. and Zhao, Y. 2020. 'Political misinformation'. *Annual Review of Political Science*, 23: 77–94.

[32] Schama, S. 1988. *The Embarrassment of Riches: An Interpretation of Dutch Culture in the Golden Age.* Los Angeles: University of California Press.

[33] Brook, T. 2008. *Vermeer's Hat: The Seventeenth Century and the Dawn of the Global World.* London: Bloomsbury.

invention of the printing press and many centuries before hate radio, the xenophobic vitriol of social media and the counter-knowledge of our own age.

Second, the modern mass media are undoubtedly able to broadcast news more widely and quickly than ever before, but it is important not to exaggerate their significance. In his celebrated study of news dissemination in eighteenth-century Paris, Robert Darnton starts by pointing out that it was not by newspapers, which were not permitted. Instead, news communication went through phases, starting with insider gossip at court, which turned into public rumour and eventually into scandal books. Darnton writes:

> We tend to think of them [the eighteenth-century media in Paris] by way of contrast to the all-pervasive media of today. So we imagine the Old Regime as a simple, tranquil, media-free world-we-have-lost, a society with no telephones, no television, no e-mail, Internet, and all the rest ... It had a dense communication network made up of media and genres that have been forgotten ... In short, the communication process took place by several modes in many settings. It always involved discussion and sociability, so it was not simply a matter of messages transmitted down a line of diffusion to passive recipients but rather a process of assimilating and reworking information in groups – that is, the creation of collective consciousness or public opinion.[34]

We can trace Darnton's account of how news spread by word of mouth further back in time than eighteenth-century Paris. From the eleventh to the sixteenth century, central and northern Europe produced numerous apocalyptic, millenarian, anarchic and violent social movements, some involving several thousand followers recruited by little more than the word of mouth.[35] During this period Columbus returned from America with tobacco and potatoes and soon after, as recounted in Charles Mann's fascinating *1493: Uncovering the New World Columbus Created*, mass demand for them spread quickly across continents without the help of modern communications technology.[36]

---

[34] Darnton, R. 2000. 'An early information society: News and the media in eighteenth-century Paris'. Washington, DC: American Historical Association.
[35] Cohen, S. 2001. *States of Denial: Knowing about Atrocities and Suffering*. Cambridge: Polity Press.
[36] Mann, C. 2011. *1493: Uncovering the New World Columbus Created*. New York: Vintage Books.

Richard Brown records in detail how, in the late seventeenth and early eighteenth century in Boston, family and public news was conveyed mainly by word of mouth, but also by letters and hand-delivered messages.[37] News was mainly exchanged and discussed by a small and select elite but important public information was read out to assemblies of people summoned by drums, bells, cannons and trumpets and, if sensational, it could spread 'like a contagion'. In one case, family and the business ties of merchants also carried news from parts of Europe and the Caribbean, although this took weeks to arrive by boat and was seasonal and irregular. Newspapers and a postal service followed in the 1720s and although papers were expensive and had a limited run until the early nineteenth century, later they started to spread news beyond small, local elites, thereby undercutting their gatekeeping powers as the self-appointed guardians of knowledge and information.

The Psychology of Belief Preservation

The evidence that large numbers can stick to their own opinions whatever the media say or do not say will come as no surprise to hundreds of psychologists who have conducted research exploring the various ways in which individuals can hold on to beliefs that are contrary to all logic, evidence and argument. From experimental work in the 1950s to the research of Nobel Prize winner Daniel Kahneman in 2021, they have produced a volume of work on this subject so large that this section cannot possibly do it justice.[38] Fortunately, there is a succinct summary in Cordelia Fine's *A Mind of Its Own: How Your Brain Distorts and Deceives*. It summarises an impressive mountain of research in the following way:

> Tussling against our desire to know the truth about the world are powerful drives to protect our self-esteem, sense of security and pre-existing point of view. Set against our undeniably impressive powers of cognition is a multitude of irrationalities, biases and quirks that surreptitiously undermine the accuracy of our beliefs.[39]

[37] Brown, R. 1989. *Knowledge Is Power: The Diffusion of Information in Early America, 1700–1805*. New York and Oxford: Oxford University Press.
[38] For a recent history of irrationality see, Smith, J. 2020. *Irrationality: A History of the Dark Side of Reason*. Princeton, NJ: Princeton University Press.
[39] Fine, C. 2005. *A Mind of Its Own*. London: Icon Books: 204.

The Psychology of Belief Preservation

Our brains can do this either from the errors of thinking rooted in mental processes (cognitive bias) or from emotion and strong attachment to beliefs (belief preservation, motivated reason, heuristics). The focus here is on the second of these and on the ways in which the psychology of belief preservation helps us understand the various ways in which people respond to the news of the day.

Beliefs about the world and about ourselves form part of our core personality, part of our ego that 'fights fiercely to defend its honor'.[40] Some psychologists treat beliefs and ideologies as like the material possessions we treasure and preserve.[41] As a result, '[a]nyone who has made a decision is usually extremely reluctant to change it, even in the face of overwhelming evidence that it is wrong'.[42] They can do this in many different ways. First, they can focus, consciously or unconsciously, on sources of news and opinion that reflect their own views back to them while bypassing or skating over disagreeable ones. Many people self-select a newspaper because of its politics. They can also choose to talk politics with people who agree with them, avoiding the unpleasantness of disagreement.

Nevertheless, most will routinely come across information and opinions they don't like, but belief preservation has ways of dealing with this. One of the most common is to subject hostile opinion to more exacting tests of logic and evidence, while they accept opinions they like with less (or no) critical scrutiny. Confirmation and disconfirmation bias is used by so many people in so many circumstances that it has been described as 'a ubiquitous phenomenon in many guises'.[43] In everyday language it is known as 'the knee-jerk reaction' and in politics it is found in the hostile media effect that allows some people to dismiss information out of hand for no better reason than they dislike it. Perhaps the clearest example in Britain is the way that the BBC is criticised by minorities of both the left and right wings of politics for being biased against them and for the opposite camp. Another more

---

[40] Mlodinow, L. 2012. *Subliminal: The Revolution of the New Unconscious and What It Teaches Us About Ourselves*. London: Allen Lane: 200.
[41] Abelson, R. P. 1986. 'Beliefs are like possessions'. *Journal for the Theory of Social Behaviour*, 16(3): 223–250; Molnar, A. and Loewenstein, G. 2022. 'Ideologies are like possessions'. *Psychological Inquiry*, 33(2): 84–87.
[42] Sutherland, S. 2009. *Irrationality*. London: Pinter and Martin: 95
[43] Nickerson, R. S. 1998. 'Confirmation bias: A ubiquitous phenomenon in many guise'. *Review of General Psychology*, 2(2): 175–220.

recent form of confirmation bias is the way that real news has been defined as fake, and fake news as real, a simple and convenient way of dismissing mainstream news in a way that requires minimal thought, evidence, logic and argument. Conspiracy theories go hand in hand with fake news because they explain how groups are so powerful that they can manipulate events and still keep their existence secret. By definition there can be no evidence to bring to bear on their existence so it is necessary to explain them with made-up, fake news.

These are extreme examples of belief preservation among partisans of a true-believer kind, but there are plentiful milder versions. Sutherland writes: 'I have demonstrated that belief – and even current hypotheses that there is no reason to hold strongly – are remarkably resistant to change.'[44] He gives five main reasons for this: avoiding evidence that might disprove their beliefs; disbelieving the correct evidence; interpreting new evidence to make it support their beliefs; selectively remembering items that support their beliefs; and the desire to protect self-esteem. The belief preservation literature stresses the fact that it applies not just to extremists, partisans and true believers but to everyone. It does not claim that everyone does it all the time, because there are plenty of examples of people changing their minds, but all of us try to preserve our beliefs a lot of the time.

Once it has taken root, misinformation can be very difficult to correct even when it is harboured by open-minded moderates.[45] We often tend to remember the first facts we learn about a matter and stick with them when told they are wrong. Research also finds a 'boomerang' or 'backfire effect' in which attempts to correct misinformation about political issues result in a strengthening of false beliefs, not a re-examination of them. People are good at inventing things that explain away inconvenient facts. Some supporters of the invasion of Iraq, on the grounds that it had weapons of mass destruction, believed that they had actually been found, in spite of the frequently reported evidence that they had not. We also invent, or choose to believe,

---

[44] Sutherland, *Irrationality*, 109.
[45] Nyhan, B. and Reifler, J. 2012. *Misinformation and Fact Checking: Research Findings from Social Science*. Washington, DC: New America Foundation, Media Policy Initiative; Anderson, C., Lepper, M. and Ross, L. 1980. 'Perseverance of social theories: The role of explanation in the persistence of discredited information'. *Journal of Personality and Social Psychology*, 39 (6): 1037–1049.

excuses that help us protect our beliefs: Covid, not Brexit, is the cause of our economic problems; the papers destroyed Jeremy Corbyn and Boris Johnson; Partygate was blown up out of all proportion by Johnson's enemies and in any case doctors, nurses, teachers and Labour leaders were doing the same thing; delays to get through border controls in Dover are caused by the French. A common form of protection is to blame the papers for their bias and their readers for believing it, a convenient way to combine self-deception and ego-inflation in order to preserve belief and condemn others for their ignorance and stupidity. The social theorist and biologist, Robert Trivers, sums it up bluntly: 'We are thoroughgoing liars, even to ourselves … we deceive ourselves the better to deceive others.'[46]

Memory is also powerful. According to the neuroscientist Dean Burnett, 'much of what your brain does is dedicated to making you look and feel as good as possible … And one of the ways it can do this is by modifying your memories to make you feel better about yourself.'[47] The fading effect involves the recall of happy events rather than unpleasant ones.[48] This, in turn, is associated with the availability heuristic, which is the ease with which something comes to mind and can be recalled from the past. In political life we are more likely to recall the successes (real or not) of our favoured political leader and to forget their failures, doing the reverse for the opposition.

Trust and distrust in the media are important, and since distrust of the news media is quite widespread in Britain it helps to explain why many people reject some of the news they receive. There is also a mild and more widespread form of the hostile media effect seen in surveys showing that people tend to trust 'my media' more than the media in general.

Political beliefs, party-political support and partisanship are also associated with the trust of some news media and distrust of others. Partisanship has a strong influence on the selection of news sources and goes hand in hand with a resistance to correcting disinformation, the boomerang effect, the invention of facts and willingness to believe

---

[46] Trivers, R. 2011. *Deceit and Self-deception: Fooling Yourself the Better to Fool Others*. London: Penguin: xv, 3.
[47] Burnett, D. 2016. *The Idiot Brain*. London: Guardian Books: 59.
[48] Walker W., Skowronski, J. and Thompson, C. 2003. 'Life is pleasant – and memory helps to keep it that way!' *Review of General Psychology*, 7 (2): 203–210.

them, the distortions of memory and the availability hypothesis. Extreme cases of partisanship are linked with fake news, the hostile media effect and conspiracy theories. In short, trust and partisanship are among the most important drivers of denying, ignoring or accepting the political news.

The preservation of self-esteem is also aided and abetted by the Lake Wobegon syndrome. It is named after the Garrison Keillor radio show *A Prairie Home Companion* where, in the little town of Lake Wobegon in the USA, 'all the women are strong, all the men are good-looking, and all the children are above average'. It captures the idea that people often think of themselves as better than others. An accumulation of surveys shows we are prone to believe that we are better drivers, better judges of character and more honest and moral than others, that we are more knowledgeable and intelligent about politics, better at spotting fake news, less likely to be taken in by it, more rational in our political judgements, more objective and less self-serving in our political behaviour and attitudes, and more likely to see right and history as being on our side. And, of course, unlike others we do not believe everything we read in the papers. 'Ironically, people tend to recognize that inflated self-assessment and overconfidence can be a problem – but only in others.'[49]

The Lake Wobegon effect helps people enhance their self-esteem and it takes a peculiar turn with the Dunning–Kruger effect. The experimental psychologists David Dunning and Justin Kruger gave their subjects a set of mental tasks involving logical reasoning, grammar and social skills.[50] The subjects were then asked to assess their own performance relative to others in the experiment. Those who performed badly in the tasks did not realise it; on the contrary, they ranked themselves alongside the best. Meanwhile those who had done well underestimated their score compared with others. The poor performers did not lack self-esteem or self-confidence, but they did suffer from a dual burden in which their lack of skill in performing the tasks was compounded by their inability to recognise their lack of skill.

In a second stage of the experiment several weeks after the first, the poorest and the best performers were invited back, given the tests of

---

[49] Molodinow, *Subliminal*, 199.
[50] Kruger, J. and Dunning, D. 1999. 'Unskilled and unaware of it: How difficulties in recognizing one's own incompetence lead to inflated self-assessments'. *Journal of Personality and Social Psychology*, 77(6): 1121–1134.

five of their peers to 'grade', and asked to assess how competent each of the five had been in completing the test. Seeing how well some others had performed did not lead them to revise their estimate of their own performance. One the contrary, they tended to raise their already overinflated self-estimates, although the difference was not statistically significant. Once again, they suffered from a double problem: they were unable to do well in the tasks and they were unable recognise the ability of others. But their self-confidence remained unshaken.

Charles Darwin is reputed to have said: 'Ignorance more frequently begets confidence than does knowledge.' The role of confidence and overconfidence in politics has not been much studied, but it may be important for belief preservation when it helps individuals to reject the advice of experts and stick resolutely to misinformation that others and the mainstream media believe to be mistaken, plain wrong or ridiculous. However, when it is linked with the Dunning–Kruger effect it can be doubly dangerous, for it suggests that self-confidence can be linked in some individuals who are too ignorant to recognise their own ignorance and not intelligent enough to recognise their own lack of intelligence. The consequences are seen in American research conducted in 2014 that found that only one out of six Americans could find Ukraine on a map, and the farther their guesses were from its actual location, the more they wanted the USA to intervene with military force.[51] There is no necessary or inevitable association of ignorance with confidence, but when they are combined, it may help to explain why some minorities with ideas that confound all logic, evidence and science are loud and forceful in their beliefs.

Self-confidence is especially important for political careers. Politicians must believe that they have something important to offer and that they are better leaders than most, and in front of the TV cameras they must give the impression of being knowledgeable and on top of things at all times. Besides that, fierce criticism is a routine part of the job, so they need an uncommon amount of self-confidence to carry on regardless. The Dunning–Kruger effect may help to explain why some supremely self-confident politicians in high places are not notably intelligent or well informed.

---

[51] Dropp, K., Kertzer, J. and Zeitzoff, T. 8 May 2014. 'The less Americans know about Ukraine's location, the more they want U.S. to intervene'. *Monkey Cage*.

To complicate matters, those gifted with mental agility and creative intelligence may find it easier to justify their erroneous theories and ideas about the world. Philip Tetlock identifies a type of adviser he calls 'hedgehogs' because they know one big thing and stick to it come what may by minimising the evidence that contradicts it and maximising evidence that reinforces it. They are more likely to resist changing their minds in the face of unexpected evidence and to defend their deterministic explanation of the past. They are good at convincing themselves and others, partly because they advocate bold and simple explanations for complex things. They are more likely to dig themselves into intellectual holes, but they have all sorts of ways of rationalising their failures: I was almost right, those who got it right were lucky, I will be proved right in the future, I made the right mistakes, something out of the blue happened, my grand theory just needs a bit of tweaking.[52] There are clever fools in political life who use their intelligence to defend crackpot ideas (no names, no pack drill) just as there are average folk who are neither clever nor foolish but sensible in their judgements.

The social sciences also have their own examples of belief preservation. Exasperated by postmodern relativism in which everything, including science, is a social construction, Alan Sokal published 'Transgressing the Boundaries: Towards a Transformative Hermeneutics of Quantum Gravity' in the journal *Social Text*. The article purported to be an affirmation of the postmodern approach but was actually a deliberate farrago of meaningless, high-fallutin' phrases, silliness, confusion, obfuscation, vagueness, jokes, absurdities, clichés, jargon, parody, misattributions, misinterpretations, eloquent bunkum and calculated flattery of *Social Text*'s contributors and editors.[53] But it was written by a professor of mathematics and physics, no less, with degrees from Harvard and Princeton and professorial positions at New York University and University College, London. The editors were

---

[52] Tetlock, P. 2005. *Expert Political Judgement: How Good Is It? How Can We Know*. Princeton, NJ: Princeton University Press.

[53] Sokal, A. 1996. 'Transgressing the boundaries: Toward a transformative hermeneutics of quantum gravity'. *Social Text*, 1(46/47): 217–252. Sokal's detailed annotation of the article and another nine chapters on its broader implications are found in Sokal, A. ed. 1998. *Beyond the Hoax*. Oxford: Oxford University Press. See also Koertge, N., 1998. *A House Built on Sand: Exposing Postmodernist Myths about Science*. New York: Oxford University Press.

apparently completely unaware of its intent but, pleased to have confirmation of their central belief from a scientist, it was published. As belief preservation scholars would predict, when the hoax was revealed, the editors preserved their beliefs and denounced Sokal for his unethical deception that would demoralise students.

Discussion

If different individuals can react in different ways to the same message from the same source, and any given individual can react in different ways to the same message from different sources, what does this tell us about the persuasive power of the media involved? These things occur on a daily basis. Some trust the BBC and accept its reports; others distrust it and treat its news with scepticism. Some might trust a report because it appears in the broadsheet they read, but would distrust it if it appeared in a tabloid, a broadsheet of a different political colour or on an anonymous website. Large minorities or even majorities do not vote for the political party their newspaper supports and many do not follow their paper's line on the EU referendum. They can stick to the paper they usually read if they decide to change their vote, and they can stick to the party they usually support if their paper switches to the opposition.

These variations in behaviour direct attention away from the media to the audiences of the media, to the people who avoid, deny, ignore or accept a message and their reasons for doing so. As Chris Bail, a sociologist who has spent his career studying how social media shapes political polarisation, puts it: 'our focus upon Silicon Valley obscures a much more unsettling truth: the root source of political tribalism on social media lies deep inside ourselves'.[54]

These observations drawn for the real world have been confirmed by an army of experimental psychologists in their decades of research. They find that individuals can preserve their beliefs no matter what evidence, elementary logic or argument is presented to them and that they can do so by using one or more of a large number of mental processes to retain the belief that they are right. Moreover, the researchers insists that everyone is prey to these mental processes and

---

[54] Bail, C. 2021. *Breaking the Social Media Prism*. Princeton: Princeton University Press: 10

there is plentiful evidence to confirm the claim. This does not mean that everyone preserves their beliefs all the time, but we can all do it some of the time whether we are clever or not, well informed or not, well educated or not, sensible or not. Belief preservation seems to be a human constant.

The desire of some individuals to protect their own beliefs and behaviour, whatever the media say, suggests a modification to Abraham Lincoln's famous statement: 'You can fool some of the people all of the time, and all of the people some of the time, but you cannot fool all of the people all of the time.' Knowing what we now know about belief preservation suggests that: 'All the people want to fool themselves some of the time, some want to fool themselves all the time, but not all want to fool themselves all of the time.' This does not mean that the media have no influence, but it does suggest that we should be exceedingly cautious in drawing conclusions about their power to mould public opinion and behaviour. Even when the public has followed media advice on things such as smoking, global warming and Covid we cannot assume that this is the media at work. Public trust in the media is generally low, which makes it all the easier to reject or ignore them. Trust in scientists, professionals and experts is much higher and on the issues of global warming, Covid and smoking, the public has probably taken their advice, which has been reported in the media. We may want to congratulate the media for their persistent reporting of the experts, but the messenger cannot take much credit for changing mass attitudes and behaviour any more than Pheidippides could take credit for the Athenian victory over the Persians in the battle of Marathon. And if the media cannot take credit for the good, can they be blamed for the bad?

The issues that have involved large shifts in public opinion suggest that they are matters amenable to empirical evidence. The effects of smoking have been amply demonstrated and mass behaviour has changed accordingly, but by definition, we cannot produce evidence for the conspiracy theory that world events are controlled by a single, secret group of people. We have conclusive medical evidence about Covid, and most accept it; we do not have evidence about premonitions, life after death, telepathy or ghosts, and millions continue to believe in them.

However, hard evidence does not count for some people and some issues. Significant minorities continue to smoke, tailgate, drink-drive,

Discussion

deny evolution and believe that the world was created 6,000 years ago. Large numbers, sometimes majorities, continue to abuse alcohol, overeat and take no exercise, no matter what the experts and the media say. And large minorities continue to maintain their political beliefs and voting decisions despite reading a paper that doesn't agree with them.

People react to media messages about politics, as in other things, in different ways. Some accept the message, some ignore it and some deny it, depending on the individuals and on the source of the message. How individuals react is often dependent on their beliefs about politics and on their political attachments and these, in turn are associated with a set of standard variables that are usually closely linked to political beliefs and behaviour: age, sex, education, socio-economic status, ethnicity, religion. These are the variables that influence what news media individuals choose to trust and use, and how they react to news from those and other sources. As a result, there is often an alignment between individual characteristics, individual beliefs and behaviour and the news media attended to most closely. But it is the individual characteristics that are the drivers of both political attitudes and behaviour and the ways in which people avoid, deny, ignore or accept media messages. The medium is not the message; the message is the message and the message is what the public make of it.

5 | *Digital Pessimism*

Chapter 4 dealt in general terms with how individuals can react in different ways to the same news. This chapter takes a closer look at how different individuals use and react to online and social media news and how this can result in different effects. It does this bearing in mind the conclusion of earlier chapters that online and social media are not necessarily the only or the most important sources of news for large sections of the population. It also takes account of the fact that most online and social media news comes from legacy TV channels and newspapers.

In the early days of digital communications, many were optimistic about how the new technology would transform politics by opening up lines of communication, bypassing the old hierarchical forms of communications controlled by elites, reaching the computer-literate young who had previously been politically uninvolved, linking up groups and communities and generally contributing to free and open communication in which all could have their say. Gradually the mood changed, and over the past fifteen years or so a series of worries, fears and concerns about the new media have accumulated. Some fear that the diverse new media system would provide politically uninterested citizens with every opportunity to avoid the news in favour of entertainment. At the same time, the politically interested, it was said, might pick out the partisan news that resonated with their own politics and ignore other sources. Between them, cable news and the web could allow sections of the population to form isolated, self-selected echo chambers of news and opinion, and the result would be a fragmented and polarised political system.

Echo chamber fears were reinforced by the algorithms used by some social media and other websites to feed people with the political opinion and news their web activity suggested they wanted to receive. This concern was linked with the illegal use for political purposes of big data gleaned from online activity. There is also a concern that the rise of populism is encouraged by the political content of the web and social media. When terrorists were caught it was reported that they had accessed terrorist websites which, it was assumed, were responsible for converting them to the cause. More alarm was added when the terms fake news, alternative facts and post-truth came into common use and were linked to online conspiracy theories and social media. Then, when Covid struck, fake news and conspiracy theories took an especially dangerous turn. Algorithms cannot distinguish between real and fake news. And finally in recent times, Russian and American propaganda bots added to a pessimistic view of online politics.

There can be no doubt that digital technology has changed the world and that its effects penetrate every corner of social, political and economic life in one way or another. The technology is invaluable in many ways, but it may be politically dangerous as well. This chapter, therefore, marshals the evidence we have about the political effects of online news and social media and deals particularly with echo chambers, algorithms, political polarisation, populism, fake news and foreign bots.

Online News

The first task is to examine which online news websites are most popular in order to get a general impression of what the web contributes to the nation's diet. Table 5.1 shows the top-twenty sites in Ofcom's *News Consumption Report 2022*. It contains a disparate range of sources: legacy TV and newspapers, digital natives, aggregators, mainstream and alternative, broadsheets and tabloids, local and national papers. There is little here to suggest a concentration of sources around any particular political party, political interest or radical, alternative or mainstream social movement. On the contrary, the list of twenty contains a heavy preponderance of mainstream TV channels and daily newspapers, with a few aggregators and a single alternative website. This is more evidence of old wine in new bottles.

Echo Chambers

Also known as filter bubbles or news cocoons, echo chambers are created when news organisations supply their audiences with the news they want to hear, and also when individuals pick news outlets that supply them with a biased and incomplete version of events that confirms their own views. Echo chambers are not new, but what is

Table 5.1 *Websites/apps used for news nowadays (%)*

	2018	2022
BBC website/app	63	62
Google (search engine)	46	34
YouTube website/app	13	21
Sky News website/app	17	20
Guardian/Observer website/app	17	19
Daily Mail website/app	17	18
Google News	11	17
Yahoo News website/app	11	11
Any local newspaper website/app	11	10
Apple News app	6	10
ITV/ITN website/app	10	8
MSN News website/app	11	8
CNN website/app	7	8
BuzzFeed website/app	8	7
Huffington Post website/app	12	7
The Telegraph website/app	9	7
The Independent website/app	8	6
The Sun website/app	6	6
Channel 4 website/app	5	6
LADbible website/app	5	6
TV broadcaster websites/apps	74	74
Newspaper websites/apps	53	53
Aggregators	42	42

Source: Ofcom, *News Consumption in the UK 2022*: table 8.2.
Note: The question 'Which of the following do you use to get news?' was asked of those who used only non-social media online sources for news. The figures for 2018 and 2022 are not strictly comparable. Because of Covid, face-to-face interviewing could not be used in 2020, but that does not seem to make much difference.

new is (1) the huge number and variety of news sources that allow individuals to pick only those that reflect their own opinions back to them and (2) the algorithms that feed people with news and opinion that is consistent with their own political views.[1]

---

[1] Algorithms of this kind are prone to data-gathering problems that can result in the false targeting of messages – see Elbanna, A. and Engesmo,
J. 19 August 2020. 'A-level results: Why algorithms get things so wrong – and how we can fix them'. *The Conversation*. textplore.com.

Chapter 3 produced evidence that few in Britain confine themselves to one source of news: most mix different news platforms in a variety of different ways; there is a surprising amount of crossover online traffic involving news of different political colours; and the alternative political websites with fake news and conspiracy theories, which are assumed to be responsible for echo chambers, have a small to insignificant reach across the population. Most of the small minority that does use only one news source go to the BBC for it.

There is also good research that tackles echo chamber concerns more directly. In common with other Western countries, a large majority of British citizens (76 per cent) expressed strong support for the ideals of impartial and objective news. Two-thirds supported the idea that news outlets should give equal time to all sides. Three-quarters think that British television news channels should have to try to be politically impartial.[2] It does not necessarily follow that audiences treat the news impartially. On the contrary, they may choose to believe or reject it according to their own opinions, but the point is that they prefer impartial rather than partial and biased sources.

Nevertheless, the problem remains that social media and search engines may not supply balanced and reliable news, so users of online news may be trapped unwittingly in bubbles created by algorithms. To test this possibility, one study compares the news repertoires of those who use them and those who do not, to see if it makes any differences to the variety of news they get.[3] And, indeed, it does, but not in the expected way. Social media users go to an average of 2.92 sources of online news and non-users to 1.7. Search engine users go to an average of 3.61 online news sources, non-users to 1.97.[4]

[2] YouGov. 13 November 2020. 'Do you think British television news channels should have to try to be politically impartial, or should they be allowed to express their own political views?' London: YouGov ; Robertson, C. T. 23 June 2021. 'Impartiality unpacked: A study of four countries'. Oxford: Oxford University, Reuters Institute.
[3] Fletcher, R. 24 January 2020. 'The truth behind filter bubbles: Bursting some myths'. Oxford: Oxford University, Reuters Institute; Fletcher, R. and Nielsen, R. 12 July 2021. 'Why people that use search, social, and aggregators have more diverse news diets'. Oxford: Oxford University, Reuters Institute; Fletcher, R., Kalogeropoulos, A. and Nielsen, R. 2023. 'More diverse, more politically varied: How social media, search engines and aggregators shape news repertoires in the United Kingdom'. *New Media & Society*, 25(8): 2118–2139.
[4] Nielsen, R..K. 30 May 2017. 'Where do people get their news?'. Oxford: Oxford University, Reuters Institute.

The explanation for this surprising result is some rather unsurprising behaviour patterns. About half the population (47 per cent) avoid search engines and social media in looking for the news. They are creatures of habit who go straight to a preferred online source they trust – mostly the BBC or a national newspaper. The other half uses 'side door' entrances to the news provided by their preferred search engine, social media or news aggregator – Google, Yahoo, Bing, Google News – which cast their net more widely over an array of news providers and, therefore, present their users with more news sources. The BBC's share for this group drops to about 15–20 per cent, and the share of other news sites rises, including the *Guardian*, *Independent*, *Mail Online* and *Telegraph*. As a result, their news repertoire is broader and more diverse, and yet even though they are fed news from the more reliable broadsheet papers, they trust this news less than those who go straight to their preferred source. There is a general distrust of news on the web compared with that of TV, radio and printed papers.[5]

That social media users go to more online news sources of news is significant for their diets but it does not tell us what sorts of news they get from what sorts of sources. Ofcom's 2022 survey of news consumption shows us this with the figures in Table 5.2. It shows that the BBC is consistently the second or third site followed by five of the six main social media sites, and it ranks first in Facebook, the most popular of them.

Ofcom's conclusion that social media users come across more varied news from a larger number of sources is consistent with another study of eight western European countries, including the UK. This finds that across all countries and all age groups, only a minority of social media users say that they come across news content on these sites that is consistent with their own views. Fewer than one in five of the 18–29 age group claim that they often see news on social media that is in line with their own political views, and only 11 per cent of the 50+ group do so.[6] It is possible that some go out of their way to see news that is inconsistent with their own opinions but most are likely to come across

---

[5] Brennan, S. 17 March 2020. 'COVID–19 has intensified concerns about misinformation: Here's what our past research says about these issues'. Oxford: Oxford University, Martin School.

[6] Matsa, K., Silver, S., Shearer E. and Walker, M. 30 October 2018. 'Younger Europeans are far more likely to get news from social media'. Washington, DC: Pew Research Center.

Table 5.2 *News organisations followed on social media, top-five mentioned, 2022 (%)*

Facebook
BBC	54
Any public figure	41
Any journalist	29
Sky News	27
Daily Mail	21

Twitter
Any public figure	59
BBC	54
Any journalist	52
Sky News	26
Guardian/Observer	17

Instagram
Any public figure	60
BBC	45
Any journalist	44
Sky News	29
LADbible	14

Snapchat
Any public figure	34
Any journalist	33
BBC	28
Daily Mail	25
The LADbible	20

TikTok
Any public figure	34
Any journalist	33
BBC	28
Daily Mail	25
LadBible	20

YouTube
Any public figure	23
BBC	29
Any journalist	29
Sky News	14

Source: Ofcom, 2022, *News Consumption in the UK: 2022*, London: Ofcom: figure 7.7.

it by accident or because a website, a legacy media outlet or another individual links them up to it.

Shared news between friends, family and contacts is part of the explanation for the more mixed diet of social media and search engine users, and because social media contains a mixture of people who are related by both strong and weak ties, shared news can come from all sorts of political quarters. Hence, 'social media, search engines, and aggregators are actually more likely to show people news from outlets they wouldn't normally use, leaving them with news diets that are more balanced across multiple outlets with different editorial lines'.[7] As a Reuters Institute report concludes: 'There are numerous studies that either find weak evidence of filter bubbles or, at best, mixed evidence. There are almost no studies that find a very strong evidence of these kinds of effects.'[8]

Political Polarisation and Populism

Online and cable news media are thought by some to be a cause of political polarisation. If society is divided into different camps that get their news from self-selected partisan and biased sources they are less likely to come across alternative views and opinions. The chances for mutuality, understanding, consensus and compromise will be reduced accordingly. This is known as the Fox News effect in the USA, after the right-wing cable TV channel that is said to promote a right-wing drift in American politics. A stronger form of the theme claims that extremist websites have the power to indoctrinate people and convert them to extremist causes.

There is little evidence to support a Fox News effect in the USA, and the British evidence of a similar effect of radical news is no stronger.[9] News diets for a large majority in the UK are heavily loaded on mainstream sources, including their online websites. Radical left- and right-wing websites form a small to tiny portion of them. Few

---

[7] Fletcher, R. and Nielsen, R. 12 July 2021. 'Why people that use search, social, and aggregators have more diverse news diets'. Oxford: Oxford University, Reuters Institute.

[8] Fletcher, R. 24 January 2020. 'The truth behind filter bubbles: Bursting some myths'. Oxford: Oxford University, Reuters Institute.

[9] Prior, M. 2013. 'Media and political polarization'. *Annual Review of Political Science*. Vol. 16. Palo Alto, CA: Annual Reviews: 101–127.

individuals rely on a single main source of news, and even those who do also tune into the mainstream media, especially the BBC. This does not preclude the existence of radical, extremist, single-minded true believers using the web to communicate and organise, but in the main these form small pockets in the population.

However, populist movements have become widespread in recent years, and some claim that the media, both old and new, are behind this. Once again, the evidence does not confirm this. One study of eight European countries and the USA finds that populism in all nine countries is strongest among the older, less well-educated and poorer sections of population.[10] Populists are rather more likely to prefer TV news than non-populists and they prefer commercial channels to public service ones. In Britain they are slightly heavier users of social media compared with non-populists, especially Facebook, as well as ITV, the *Mirror*, *Express* and *Sun*. Non-populists lean towards the *Financial Times*, Channel 4, *Telegraph*, *Times*, *Guardian* and BBC.

However, the data suggest more overlap of news diets than separation. As one would expect from the evidence of previous chapters, the largest single news source for populists and non-populists alike is the BBC – populists 74 per cent, non-populists 82 per cent – followed by ITV which divides into 54 per cent populists, 34 per cent non-populists. At the other extreme the *Financial Times* is split 2:6 for populists and non-populists, and the *Express* is split 9:6. The evidence suggests that the British news media are rather weakly associated with populism and that the main variables associated with it are age, income and education, which are also the variables associated with voting for Brexit.

Just as the news diets of populists and non-populists overlap substantially in the middle, so also do the media themselves. Whether they are organised on a single left–right populist continuum or in a 4 × 4 matrix that cross-classifies populism/non-populism with left–right dimensions, the mainstream news channels and newspapers tend to overlap a lot in the middle. Alternative websites are outliers, with The Canary and LADbible on the left and Westmonster on the right. Polarisation of the media is less pronounced in Germany but much

---

[10] Fletcher, R. Not dated. 'The rise of populism and the consequences for news and media use'. Oxford: Oxford University, Reuters Institute.

stronger in the USA. There is little evidence here to suggest that online media are responsible for right-wing or populist politics in the UK.

Fake News

Of all the topics in this chapter, it is most difficult to provide a coherent account of fake news because there is so little evidence. Perhaps that is why this is the longest section of the chapter. The term is used in different and sometimes vague ways to include things that are arguably not fake news (satire?), or to exclude things that are arguably a large part of it (the fake news propagated by governments and leading politicians). Some prefer to use the terms 'false news' or 'disinformation', which can also be defined as false information deliberately spread and used to deceive. Misinformation is unintentionally mistaken information communicated in good faith. Others say the term fake news is so vague and confusing that it is best not to use it at all.[11] The problem is that whatever term is substituted in place of 'fake news' is likely to suffer the same fate of being used in different ways to refer to slightly different things. In surveys it is sometimes unclear what respondents understand by it. And yet, however it is defined, one fact stands out: much is written and much is claimed yet remarkably little is known about it. Or as one source puts it: 'with the partial exception of the United States ... we lack even the most basic information about the scale of the problem in almost every country'.[12]

Defining fake news as a form of falsehood intended to primarily deceive people by mimicking the look and feel of real news, an early overview of American studies finds that only a small fraction of the online audience is exposed to fake news, although it warns that its impact *may* be quite substantial for a small proportion of people.[13] A more recent American report using tracker devices on TVs, desktops and mobile media instruments finds that fake news comprised 1 per

---

[11] Hern, A. 7 February 2018. 'MPs warned against term "fake news" for first live committee hearing outside UK'. *The Guardian*.

[12] Fletcher, R., Cornia, A., Graves, L. and Nielsen R. February 2018. 'Measuring the reach of "fake news" and online disinformation in Europe'. Oxford: Oxford University, Reuters Institute; Ipsos, 6 September 2018. 'Fake news, filter bubbles and post-truth are other people's problems ... ' London: Ipsos.

[13] Tandoc, E. 25 July 2019. 'The facts of fake news: A research review'. *Sociology Compass*, 13(9), emphasis added.

cent of overall news consumption and that no one spent more than a minute a day with it.[14] A study of France and Italy found that none of the websites that most often contain false news reach more than 3.5 per cent of the online population and most reach less than one. Many of the visits to false news sites were fleeting and the time spent with them on Facebook was a small fraction of that spent with *La Repubblica* and *Le Monde*. Between them, these two accounted for more time than the twenty most popular false news sites in each country. The study is careful to point out that it deals only with part of the overall problem of false news and that three of the twenty false news websites in France (none in Italy) generated as much, if not more, Facebook news interaction as established new brands. Nevertheless, the study concludes that false news has more limited reach than is sometimes assumed. This is consistent with what independent evidence-based analysis has found in the United States and with a study of tweeting activity about the 2019 EU election.[15]

These studies are noteworthy and consistent, but their conclusions are not compatible with what the general public tells us in the surveys. One found that 71 per cent of Facebook users in Britain came across 'some' or a 'great deal' of fake news there, while this figure was 67 per cent for Twitter users.[16] Another report finds that 54 per cent say they very/fairly often see news stories that deliberately say things that are not true.[17] A third finds that 54 per cent encounter fake online news every day and that at its peak there were 200 million monthly encounters with it on Facebook.[18] Almost half (43 per cent) admit to sharing fake news with others, 47 per cent of those aged 18–24.

It is not possible to attach great precision to these figures because they are built on memory and impressions about a vaguely defined

---

[14] Allen, J. et al. 2020. 'Evaluating the fake news problem at the scale of the information ecosystem'. *Science Advances*, 6(14).

[15] Fletcher, R., Cornia, A., Graves, L. and Nielsen R. February 2018. 'Measuring the reach of "fake news" and online disinformation in Europe'. Oxford: Oxford University, Reuters Institute. See also Cinelli, M., Cresci, S., Galeazzi, A., Quattrociocchi, W. and Tesconi, M. 18 June 2020. 'The limited reach of fake news on Twitter during 2019 European elections'. *PLoS One*, 15(6): e0234689.

[16] Yapp, S. 2019. 'Vast majority of UK adults oppose unregulated political advertising online'. Intuit Research/Norsta.

[17] Ipsos Public Affairs. 2 September 2018. 'Fake news, filter-bubbles, post-truth and trust'. Ipsos.

[18] JournoLink. Not dated. 'Fake news statistics – how big is the problem?'. JournoLink.

matter that is also widely discussed and in the front of people's minds. Nevertheless, there is a huge gap between the majorities who claim to see it and the comparatively tiny minorities it reaches according to tracker devices. What explains this disparity?

There are many possible reasons but two stand out, namely the fake news propagated by governments and leading politicians, and the multiplier effect of the mainstream media. Examples of fake news produced by governments and political parties in recent British history include the existence of weapons of mass destruction in Iraq, the claim that Brexit would release £350 million a week for the NHS, a stream of official statements about government action to contain Covid, contracts for personal protective equipment, the Partygate issue and the prorogation of Parliament.[19] These reached virtually the entire adult population of the country. According to fact-checking agencies, the 2019 general election was also notable for the amount of fake news produced by official party sources.[20] According to Full Fact, a leading fact check organisation in the UK, 88 per cent of the Conservative Party's advertisements posted in Facebook during the election campaign of December 2019 had already been flagged as containing misleading or false information.[21] A study of 225 statements rated false or misleading by fact checkers and published in English between January and March 2020 found that 'The most powerful spreaders of misinformation were politicians, celebrities or other public figures, who were the source of about 20 per cent of false claims but generated 69 per cent of the total engagement.'[22] The majority of misinformation in social media in this study came from private individuals, but with only a few exceptions most of it had a far smaller reach than that generated

---

[19] Newton, K. 2020. 'Government communications, political trust and compliant social behaviour: The politics of Covid-19 in Britain'. *The Political Quarterly*, 91(3): 502–513.

[20] Goldhill, O. 2019. 'Politicians are embracing disinformation in the UK election'. *Quartz*; BBC. 11 December 2019. 'General election 2019: Row over use of "fake newspapers"'.

[21] Dotto, C. 16 December 2019. 'Thousands of misleading Conservative ads sidestep scrutiny thanks to Facebook policy'. First draft.

[22] Brennen, S., Simon, F., Howard, P. and Nielsen R. 2020. 'Types, sources, and claims of COVID-19 misinformation'. Oxford: Oxford University, Reuters Institute. The authors of this research report are careful to point out its limitations of dealing only with social media posts in English.

by the fake news of public figures. As one writer puts it: 'Real news may be doing more harm than fake news.'[23]

It may seem unlikely, given the attention paid to some of the more eye-catching fake news posted by private individuals in social media, to claim that government and official party sources are responsible for a large proportion of the fake news with the widest reach. If so, consider the following:

Rather than honesty being the driver of content, this election, more than any other, felt like it was fuelled by a political economy of lies. Lies are simply more crowd pleasing, circulate rapidly, are based on intensely affective responses, are mood inducing and therefore are often more commercially attractive.[24]

The lying in the 2019 election has been more systematic than in past campaigns where the problem was more one of voters trying to navigate a stream of spin rather than trying to swim through a torrent of lies.[25]

Lying and cheating are, once again, commonplace in the heart of government ... The alarming truth is that Whitehall integrity is in collapse again. Cameron, who once boasted that he was 'heir to Blair', has taken and refined the techniques of dishonesty that New Labour invented.[26]

All of which raises the question of why the Commons Select Committee of 2019 into disinformation and 'fake news' did not discuss the role of leading politicians in the creation of fake news or the role of the media in reporting it.[27]

The word 'reach' is important and brings us to the second reason why the general public might see so much fake news. It is the job of the mainstream media to report accurately what our political leaders are telling us, and if they are telling us fake news, then mainstream media

---

[23] Leyva, R. 2019. '"Real news" may be doing more harm than "fake news"'. London: LSE, Media Policy Project, Truth, Trust and Technology Commission.
[24] Fenton, N. 2019. 'Delusions of democracy', in Jackson, D., Thorsen, E., Lilleker, D. and Weidhase N. eds., *UK Election Analysis, 2019*. Bournemouth: Bournemouth University.
[25] Gaber, I. 2019. 'Strategic lying: the new game in town', in Jackson, D., Thorsen, E., Lilleker, D. and Weidhase N. eds., *UK Election Analysis, 2019*. Bournemouth: Bournemouth University.
[26] Oborne, P. 29 May 2016. 'Brexit and the return of political lying'. *The Spectator*.
[27] House of Commons Select Committee on Culture, Media and Sport. 2019. *Disinformation and 'Fake News': Final Report*. London: www.Parliament.uk.

reports about it are real news about fake news. The result is that many more people see real news about fake news on their TV and in their newspapers than see fake news online. To complicate matters, it is also the job of the mainstream media to report real news when public figures condemn real news as fake. And to complicate matters still more, depending on their own political views, some users of the mainstream media may regard its real news as fake, and its fake news as real. As if this was not confusion enough there are examples of what has been labelled fake news turning out to be real, and where the conspiracy involved turned out to be not the original claims but the attempt to conceal the real news. The claim that contaminated blood has been widely used in transfusions was initially labelled as fake but then found to be real, though concealed behind a cover-up. Behind all these complications, however, it seems that a lot of fake news is generated by official government sources and this is duly reported in the mainstream media.

The media multiplier effect also works in other ways. Most of the fake news posted on social media comes from private individuals, and would have a small reach but for the mainstream media which is fond of reporting the more outlandish claims, precisely because they are eye catching. This, in turn, may result in a false impression about the amount of fake news and the numbers who believe it. On top of that, some sections of the media and some journalists are famous for inventing their own fake news.

Most in Britain do not see fake news as confined to a few websites. On the contrary, they believe fake news is also generated by the mainstream media and politicians. Two-thirds see fake news as stories where the facts are wrong and 42 per cent say this occurs when politicians and the media pick facts that suit their argument. The same percentage say that fake news is a term used by politicians and the news to discredit stories they don't agree with. When asked why lots of people get things wrong about their country, they assign blame equally to the media (60 per cent), politicians (57 per cent), people being biased (53 per cent) and social media (53 per cent). More than half (56 per cent) believe that politicians and the media lie more than they used to.[28] For the general population, it seems, fake news is not just about

---

[28] Ipsos Public Affairs. Not dated. 'Fake news, filter-bubbles, post-truth and trust'. London: Ipsos.

the unbelievable conspiracy theories and foreign propaganda but is the very stuff of everyday political speeches and newspaper reports.

Fake news, however, is a problem for others. Two-thirds of the British population claim that they can tell real news from fake, but only 28 per cent think their compatriots can; 61 per cent claim that they do not live in a news bubble, but 70 per cent believe that the rest of the country does. Two-thirds believe that others don't care about facts and just want to believe what they want, but 58 per cent believe they are better than average at understanding the social realities of immigration and crime.[29] The Lake Wobegon effect strikes again.

Studies of the volume and reach of fake news are important but they do not tackle the crucial question at the heart of the issue of how much influence it has, if any, on attitudes and behaviour. To the best of this writer's knowledge there is no research that tackles the exceedingly tricky problem of showing that fake news on social media has had an impact on the people who see it, hear it or read it, although assumptions about its strong effect are common. In part this is based on some evidence showing that many people cannot tell the difference between fake and real news. The ability to do this depends heavily on whether the fake news is about an obscure issue or a highly salient and much discussed one, and on whether the source of the news is a trusted or distrusted one.

A recent study found that only 4 per cent were able to pick out which of the following three news headlines was real: 'Putin issues international arrest warrant for George Soros'; 'A baby born in California was named heart eyes emoji'; 'Criminal farts so loudly he gives away his hiding place'.[30] None of these is a major issue about which the public should be well informed, and had the headlines been about Covid, the problems of the NHS or the housing shortage the result would have been very different. Moreover, in the real world people evaluate the reliability of a news item according to whether they trust its source or not, so a news headline such as 'Somali pirates take control of Bournemouth pier' is likely to be disbelieved if it appears on an obscure website or if it appears in the *Guardian* on 1 April. Experiments that take no account of trusted and distrusted sources are likely to produce unreliable results.

---

[29] Ibid.
[30] Van der Linden. 2023. *Foolproof: Why We Fall for Misinformation and How to Build Immunity*. London: HarperCollins.

Lacking direct British evidence about the impact of fake news we have to rely on indirect evidence. If it does have an effect on the beliefs of the general population one would expect it to show up in wrong answers to factual questions of importance that are covered by the mainstream media. A survey of false information in six countries (Argentina, Germany, South Korea, Spain, the UK and the USA) asked questions about the use of social media, search engines, video sites and messaging applications. Most people in each country used one or more these and came across fake news about Covid on them.[31] About a third of social media users said they had seen a lot or a great deal of false information about Covid in the last week. The survey also asked five factual questions about the disease and found that a clear majority in every country except South Korea got three or more questions right. In the UK 86 per cent got three or more right, and the mean figure was 3.77. Education and left political leanings were significantly correlated with the number of right answers, but the use of search engines, social media, video sites and messaging apps were not. They made no difference. So far as we can judge from this research, false information about Covid seems to mislead few people, though the poorly educated and those with right-wing opinions are more likely to believe it. This is consistent with conclusions, mentioned earlier, about the social characteristics of populists and Brexit voters.

A second study focuses on misinformation, political knowledge and Twitter messages in the 2015 UK general election.[32] This asks questions about factual knowledge relevant to election issues (the economy, the EU, immigration and terrorism) and about party policies. It finds that, on balance, social media users became more informed about politics during the 2015 UK general election campaign. Messages from news organisations improved knowledge of issue-relevant facts and party messages improved knowledge about party positions on issues. However, the study also found that partisan messages about highly salient issues can cause knowledge polarisation. It picks out the case of

---

[31] Nielsen, R., Fletcher, R., Newman, N. and Howard, P. 15 April 2020. 'Navigating the "infodemic": How people in six countries access and rate news and information about coronavirus'. Oxford: Oxford University, Reuters Institute.

[32] Munger, K. et al. 2020. 'Political knowledge and misinformation in the era of social media: Evidence from the 2015 UK election'. *British Journal of Political Science*, 52(1): 107–127.

UK Independence Party (UKIP) tweets about immigrants. These did not affect the overall estimation on immigrant numbers but UKIP supporters increased their estimates by 0.25 on a four-point scale. In other words, partisan messages do not have much impact on most Twitter users, but they do on those who are already prepared to believe them.

So far as we can judge from this research, false or misleading information about Covid seems to mislead few people, but it does suggest that social media (1) help to inform rather than mislead people about factual matters and (2) have little effect on most people but can (3) strengthen pre-existing attitudes, especially (4) among those on the right wing of politics. This is consistent with what is known about the legacy news media and the same seems to be true of online news.

Russian and American Bots

There remains the important matter of Russian and American bots used during the Brexit referendum and the 2019 general election. Once again little is known about their effects, partly because neither the government, for its own reasons, nor the intelligence services have revealed any evidence or announced any attempt to discover it. The House of Commons' Intelligence and Security Committee was unable to determine whether Russia had attempted to influence the EU referendum because, it said, the government had not asked any questions or attempted to answer questions about the matter. This in spite of the fact that it has not proved particularly difficult to answer some questions. Reliable research finds concerted Russian attempts to influence the outcome of the Brexit referendum, the general election of 2019 and the Scottish independence referendum in an attempt to destabilise the UK government and society with social media messages about immigration, race and terrorism.[33] Right-wing American interests were also

---

[33] Gorodnichenko, Y., Pham, T. and Talavera, O. 2 June 2018. 'Social media, sentiment and public opinions: Evidence from #Brexit and the #USElection'. London and Paris: The Centre for Economic Policy Research; Llewellyn, C., Cram, L., Favero, A. and Hill, R. 2018. 'Russian troll hunting in a Brexit Twitter archive'. Proceedings of the 18th ACM/IEEE on Joint Conference on Digital Libraries, May 2018: 361–362; Slideshare, 16 February 2018. 'Putin's Brexit? The influence of Kremlin media and bots during the 2016 UK EU referendum'. Sklideshare; Bastos M. and Mercea, D. 20 October 2017. '13,500-strong Twitter bot army disappeared shortly after EU referendum, research reveals'. London: City University of London; Burgess, M. 18 November 2017. 'Here's the

involved in illegal attempts to influence the Brexit referendum in favour of the Leave side.[34] As the House of Commons report says, online Russian influence in British politics has become the new normal.[35] In fact, the ether seems to be full of state and private bots being used to influence and interfere with the domestic politics of other countries.

Interfering in the domestic affairs of other countries has a history going back hundreds of years and there is nothing new about it now, except that the recent activities involved the new media rather than the old-fashioned methods of gunboats, spies, agents provocateurs and Zinoviev letters. How effective are the new methods? Once again, the answer is we do not know because little, if any, research has been done, not least because it is very difficult to do. If the evidence we have about fake news and Covid is anything to go by, the effects will depend on the previous political opinions of those receiving messages, and for the most part attempts to influence or change these opinions are likely to have little success.

Finally, it must be emphasised again that research into fake news is in its infancy and may never advance much beyond that. It is beset by problems of definition, methods and lack of data. Circumstances can, and have, changed quite rapidly in recent years as websites take measures against false information and as consumers learn to deal with fake news and shift to more trusted news sources.[36] Nevertheless, the production and distribution of fake news, however defined, is likely to continue just as the production and distribution of unreliable and misleading news and speculation about fake news is also likely to continue.

At the same time, this is irrelevant to some real and important concerns about fake news. The *possibility* that it may have a small effect on the general population but a large one on a small section of it cannot be taken lightly. Nor can foreign interference in domestic political affairs, whether Russian, American or any other country.

first evidence Russia used Twitter to influence Brexit'. *Wired*; Stukal, D., Sanovich, S., Bonneau, R. and Tucker, J. 2017. 'Detecting bots on Russian political Twitter'. *Big Data*, 5(4): 310–324.

[34] Meyer, J. 17 November 2017. 'New evidence emerges of Steve Bannon and Cambridge Analytica's role in Brexit'. *New Yorker*.

[35] Intelligence and Security Committee of Parliament Press Notice, 21 July 2020. *Russia Report*.

[36] Allcott, H., Gentzkow, M. and Yu, C. 2019. 'Trends in the diffusion of misinformation on social media'. *Research and Politics*, 6(2): 1–8.

Discussion

There is little evidence to suggest that the digital media in general or social media in particular have much of an effect on mass political attitudes and behaviour. The evidence we have is sparse but it is fairly consistent and offers little support for the worst fears about echo chambers, algorithms, political polarisation and populism, at least in the UK. The great majority of individuals still use the legacy media as their main source of news, especially the BBC, and this includes a large proportion of the youngest age groups that are the heaviest users of social media. Users of search engines and of social media and the algorithms they employ get a wider news diet than those who avoid them and go straight to their favourite legacy news, often a newspaper. Ironically, this suggests that partisan newspapers would be more effective promoters of echo chambers than online and social media, but for the fact that newspaper readers also go to other sources of news, mainly the BBC. It is easy to draw false conclusions from studies of one news source that ignore the others that make up the news diets of the great majority of people.

Nevertheless, there is little evidence of echo chambers, radical or alternative websites, or populist politics in the British news media. On the contrary, almost all the evidence suggests that online news is more diverse than the legacy media and that those who go online get a broader and more mixed array of news than those who stick to TV, radio and printed sources. Besides, most of the news accessed online, whether via social media, aggregators or other sources, is that of the legacy media, especially the BBC. Online news is not greatly different from legacy news, since it is mainly legacy news anyway, but it is rather more varied and, perhaps more important, easier to access.

Perhaps this ease of access explains a surprising amount of cross-media use involving a mixture of mainstream, internally pluralist and partisan news. Alternative and radical websites have a small or tiny reach by comparison. As a result, blame for the polarisation of modern politics and the rise of populism cannot be laid at the door of the new media, although they *may* have a role in reinforcing alternative and radical opinion, especially those on the right.

Little is known about fake news, but there seems to be much less of it than is often assumed, and it probably has a much smaller reach than the real news of legacy sources. While many think of fake news as coming from members of the public, the evidence seems to be that the most widely spread comes from government sources that are reported in the mainstream media – real news about government fake news.

The effects of fake news on the general population are barely researched and little is known about them, but widely publicised false information about Covid did not result in a widely misinformed population. On the contrary, social media seem to inform people and have little effect on their political attitudes. Those who believe fake news tend to be the poor, the poorly educated and those with right-wing opinions. As in Chapter 4, the use and apparent effects of the news media are often closely associated with a few demographic variables, including age, education and ethnic and socio-economic status.

The biggest effects of fake news, conspiracy theories and misinformation seem to be a diffuse background mood of political distrust and confusion. They leave people in doubt about what is true or false and about who or what to trust. It is notable, though, that the conspiracy theories and disinformation about Covid did not have this effect. Trust in experts, doctors and the press remained high, while that for government rose with a rally-round-the flag boost at the start of the pandemic, sank as the first and second waves took hold, rose as the vaccination programme got under way, and declined again with the third wave and the Omicron variant. There is little evidence that the media, online or offline, were responsible for these peaks and troughs, but rather they were a response to real events in the country that the media reported.

The last word must be that there is too little work of any kind on echo chambers, fake news, algorithm effects and foreign bots to be able to draw firm conclusions, which leaves plenty of room for plausible and implausible speculation. The commentary that looks only at online news, and not at the main bulk of all news that most people receive, is likely to be implausible, especially when, as is often the case, it is based on assumptions for which there is little supporting evidence.

6 | *Newspapers, Voting and Agenda-Setting*

Before online news and social media, the national papers were the main focus of concern about the power without responsibility of the news media. In the heyday of the popular national press, more than thirty million people were reading a national daily paper, more on Sundays. With such a large market the papers could be party political and not risk their markets, and in the 1970s and onwards their partisan tone grew stronger and shriller.[1] This was a period of attack journalism, especially on the part of the Conservative tabloids which ran harsh and permanent campaigns against Labour and its leaders. In spite of this, in 1979 more Labour voters read a Conservative paper than a Labour one and in 1983 the Conservative circulation was more than three times that of Labour.[2] While this might have been taken as evidence that the Tory tabloids had little influence, there was general agreement that the national press had a great, sometimes decisive, influence over the political opinions and voting behaviour of the British people. Although partisanship became less caustic and circulations declined, the idea of press power without responsibility persists up to the present day and the size and partisan nature of the daily newspaper market makes the UK a good case for testing the power of the press.

This chapter examines the claim that the national press has a strong influence on how people vote on election day. It starts with some general points about newspaper partisanship and the public reaction to it. It continues with a close look at newspaper influences in the 1992 and 1997 elections, which are particularly good test cases of newspaper influence. The 1992 election was the one where the *Sun* claimed to have won it by declaring its support for the Conservative

---

[1] Harrop, M. 1986. 'The press and post-war elections', in Crewe, I. and Harrop, M. eds., *Political Communications: The General Election Campaign of 1983*, Cambridge: Cambridge University Press: 137–149.
[2] Ibid., 138, 145.

Party. In the 1997 election the *Sun* switched to the Labour Party which won by a landslide. Newspapers rarely change sides, and if papers have any influence over voting, this should be revealed clearly by a disproportionate swing of *Sun* readers to Labour in 1997. Consequently, the 1997election has been picked out for in-depth research as an acid test case of newspaper influence.

Since 1992 and 1997 are exceptional elections, the third section of the chapter examines the more normal sequence of elections after that to see if they yield different results. The fourth section of the chapter turns to the question of election agenda-setting over the years in the UK. It has been argued that the media may have little power over what we think, but may have influence what we think about – what we think are the most important issues in elections. If, as many argue, the media have an agenda-setting capacity we would have to conclude that the media have an independent power of their own that is far more significant than a minimal ability to reinforce existing opinions.

Newspapers and Voting

The idea that newspapers influence voting rests on the assumptions that citizens follow the lead of their paper, that their paper is the only or main influence on their voting decision, and that the paper gives clear signals about how to vote, not a mixed and rather jumbled set of cues. Previous chapters show that citizens quite often do not follow the lead of their newspaper or the media in general, and that newspapers are not the only media influence on voting decisions. We now turn to the third assumption: that national daily papers give consistent and unambiguous cues about how to vote.

Readers are not always able to identify the partisanship of their paper correctly. One survey finds that a large majority of broadsheet readers get it right, but small to large minorities of tabloid readers get it wrong, are unsure or do not know.[3] One survey shows that in the case of the *Mail*, *Express* and *Sun* only 37, 44 and 42 per cent respectively understand the party politics of their paper correctly, and that majorities got it wrong or did not know. Confusion of this kind is not limited to the readers of particular papers. When the population as a whole is

---

[3] Lord Ashcroft. 5 July 2012. 'Which party does The Sun support? Do Sun readers know?'. Lord Ashcroft Polls.

asked about the partisan and political positions of the national press there is even more misunderstanding. More than two-thirds are unable to correctly place the *Guardian*, and half are unable to do the same for the *Telegraph* and *Mail*.[4] Similar confusion and misunderstanding is revealed in other surveys.[5] It is difficult to see how newspapers can influence political attitudes and voting patterns of readers who do not know which party their newspaper supports.

Confusion is understandable because although papers are often classified simply as Labour, Conservative or neither, they do not always follow a clear and unwavering party-political line. The *Sun*'s defection to Labour in 1997 is famous but the *Express* did the same in 2001. The strongest of partisan papers are not infrequently critical of the leaders and the policies of the party they normally support, pursuing policies and issues of their own. They are obliged to report hard news about important state matters and decisive political events and policies, including those that reflect badly on their preferred party, even if they try to spin them. Nor do all papers clearly endorse a given party in their election day editions. Some do, but sometimes weakly, sometimes strongly, sometimes with qualifications. Others preserve their neutrality, or suggest who not to vote for. Some have favoured tactical voting to keep a party out of power. Few papers have displayed consistent partisanship in the last eight elections.[6] The *Mail* and *Telegraph* have done so for the Conservatives, and the *Mirror* for Labour. The *Sun* and *Express* have switched from Conservative to Labour and back again. At various times, the *Guardian*, *Times*, *Financial Times*, *Independent*, *Star* and *Record* have offered different advice or none at all.

The editorial lines of newspapers are probably more consistent than their news content, but papers have their own interests, material or ideal, and pursue them independently. Opinion-piece and leader columnists generally stick to their party but are given to urging them to do

---

[4] Ibid.
[5] Kellner, P. and Worcester, R. 1982. 'Electoral perceptions of media stance', in Worcester, R. and Harrop, M. eds., *Political Communications: The General Election Campaign of 1979*. London: Allen and Unwin: 61; Curtice, J. 1998. 'Do newspapers change voters' minds? Or do voters change their papers?'. Paper presented at the American Political Science Association Annual Meeting, Boston.
[6] *The Guardian*. 4 May 2010. 'Newspaper support in UK general elections'. DataBlog.

things differently. Journalists and reporters commonly switch without friction between papers of a different colour, claiming that this does not matter for a professional.[7] The result is what one writer has called the 'chronic instability of editorial opinion'.[8] Consequently, the national papers are rarely either blue or red through and through, but various shades and even mixtures of these colours appear quite regularly on different pages so that the overall effect is a muted set of hues, including a non-partisan white.

It may not matter much if a paper is strong and consistent in its party-political support if it is not trusted and, by and large, trust in the national press in Britain is lower than TV news (BBC, ITV, Channel 4) with the tabloids much lower than the broadsheets. In 2022 the *Sun* was at the bottom of the table with 12 per cent trust. The *Mirror* and the *Mail* were at 22 and 23 per cent respectively and even the BBC, at the top of fifteen news providers, was trusted by only 55 per cent.[9] Since we tend not to believe what we do not trust, this casts some doubt on whether distrusted newspapers have much influence.

This may help to explain why there is not always a close alignment between the politics of a paper and the politics of its readers. In 1997, 28 per cent of Conservative tabloid readers voted Labour as did 22 per cent of Conservative broadsheet readers.[10] On the other side of the coin 6 per cent of Labour tabloid readers voted Conservative, as did 22 per cent of Labour broadsheet readers. In fact, almost as many Conservative tabloid readers did not vote Conservative (41 per cent) as did (43 per cent). While half (51 per cent) of Conservative broadsheet readers voted Conservative, more than a third (36 per cent) did not. Other studies find a fairly loose association between the party allegiance of the national press, and the voting patterns of readers finding that minorities, sometimes quite large, identify with and vote for a party their paper does not support.[11]

---

[7] Chmielewska-Szlajfer, H. 25 October 2017. 'What do journalists writing for right-wing tabloids think about their work?'. London: LSE.

[8] Seymoure-Ure, C. 2001. 'New Labour and the media', in King, A. ed., *Britain at the Polls 2001*. New York: Chatham House: 120.

[9] Kersley, A., 30 September 2022. 'Trust and interest in news falls in UK with Sun, Mail and Mirror bottom of table'. *PressGazette*.

[10] Norris, P., Curtice, J., Sanders, D., Scammell, M. and Semetko, H. A. 1999. *On Message*. London: Sage, 156.

[11] Heath, A., Jowell, R. and Curtice, J. 1985. *How Britain Votes*. Oxford: Pergamon Press; Curtice, J. 1998. 'Do Newspapers change voters' minds? Or do voters change their papers?', Paper presented to the American Political Science

Even if we were to find a closer correspondence between newspaper endorsements and reader voting we would still be left with the chicken-and-egg problem of cause and effect. If papers give their readers what they want to read, and readers select a paper that gives them what they want to read, how can we be sure that the paper is leading and the reader following? That is the tricky question that studies of newspaper effects on voting must answer.

Unravelling the Chicken-and-Egg Problem

The existence of large minorities, sometimes majorities, of newspaper readers who do not understand, care or take any notice of the politics of their newspaper leaves us with its own problem. On the one hand, it suggests that papers have a limited influence over at least some of their readers who go their own way, whatever their paper tells them. On the other, the existence of these readers demonstrates that many people do not self-select their newspaper for its politics and are, therefore, possibly open to political influence by the paper they read.

At the same time, the existence of large groups in the population who read a paper that is inconstant with their own political leanings and voting patterns offers a way of unravelling the chicken-and-egg problem. This involves using the effects of cross-pressures and reinforcement. It may be that people are more likely to follow their own voting inclinations if these are reinforced by the paper they read. Conversely, they may be less likely to follow their own inclinations if they are cross-pressured by their paper. If so, those who are inclined to vote Conservative or identify with the party are more likely to vote Conservative if they are reinforced by reading a Conservative paper. Conversely, if they read a Labour paper they are less likely to vote Conservative. For the same reason Labour voting would be higher among Labour supporters who are reinforced by their paper than those who are cross-pressured.

We also need a control group of people who do not read a paper regularly. Among them, those with a Conservative identification should have a lower Conservative vote than the reinforced, but a

---

Association Annual Meeting. Boston; Hundal, S. 3 June 2010. 'What happens to politics after the Sun dies?'. *New Statesman*; Newton, K. and Brynin, M. 2001. 'The national press and party voting in the UK'. *Political Studies*, 49(2): 265–285, 269.

higher Conservative vote than the cross-pressured. The same patterns should appear among Labour identifiers who read a Labour paper or no paper at all. Thus, we have a set of six expectations for party voting according to party identification, cross-pressures and reinforcement among newspaper readers and non-readers. To make the test more watertight it must also control the characteristics of individual voters that are normally associated with both newspaper readership and voting. In this study the control variables are age, sex, education, income, trade union membership, social class and interest in politics. And since each general election has its own special characteristics, the two in 1992 and 1997 are compared. The 1992 election is the one the *Sun* claimed to have won, and 1997 is the one where it switched its endorsement from Conservative to Labour.

Newspaper effects are unlikely to occur in an election campaign lasting six weeks, and are more likely to build up as a result of a steady drum-beat of reporting and party support over a long period of time. The study takes account of this by using the long-term British Household Panel Study conducted by the University of Essex that has tracked the same sample of 5,500 households and some 8,000 individuals since the study began in 1991. This classifies papers according to their long-term party support, rather than their election day endorsement, and tracks newspaper readership in 1991 against voting in 1992, and newspaper reading in 1996 with voting in 1997. In this way predicted causes precede predicted effects, and it recognises that the causes may take time to have an effect.

The results are wholly consistent with the expectations. Conservatives who read Conservative papers, are more likely to vote Conservative than those who do not read any paper. Socialists who read Labour papers are more likely to vote Labour than those who read a Conservative paper. Socialists who read no paper are more likely to vote Labour than those who read a Conservative paper, but are less likely to vote this way than socialists who read a Labour paper. Unfortunately, there are too few Conservatives reading Labour papers in the panel study to draw conclusions about them, but the results confirm five of the six expectations.

This suggests that there is indeed a newspaper effect on voting, but the conclusion requires three important qualifications. First, the newspaper effect is small to statistically insignificant and heavily outweighed by age, trade union membership and party identification.

These are the main determinants of party voting, not the paper read, which is of little significance. Second, reading a Labour paper is somewhat more important for increasing the Labour vote among Labour identifiers and those with no party ID. Third, though small in both years, the newspaper effect was even smaller in 1997 than in 1992. The reasons for this will become evident later in the chapter.

The conclusions that newspaper effects on party voting are small to insignificant is confirmed by most other British elections. Starting in 1958, when Conservatives papers outnumbered Labour by three to one, Harrop concludes that: 'Although this exercise is not based directly on evidence from the 1983 campaign, the results do strongly suggest that the Labour Party is unable to blame Fleet Street for its debacle in June.'[12] Later studies are able to use time series data to track voting behaviour and newspaper habits over the whole duration of a Parliament, and regression analysis in order to hold constant an assortment of other variables. This enables them to answer the question of whether citizens change their newspaper if they change their voting preference and whether they change their voting preference if they change their newspaper? One study finds that

Neither the *Sun*, nor any other of the pro-Conservative tabloid newspapers were responsible for John Major's unexpected victory in 1992. There is no evidence in our panel that there was any relationship between vote switching during the election campaign and the partisanship of a voter's newspaper.[13]

A second study covers the period from 1992 to 1997. It finds 'little evidence that newspapers had much impact on the aggregate outcome of election ... At best we have found, in line with our previous research, that newspapers have but a limited influence on the voting behaviour of their reader.'[14] A third study states that the effect of the *Sun*'s switch 'was trivial in the overall context of the forces shaping Labour's election victory ... Like the rest of the press, the *Sun* was

---

[12] Harrop, 'The press and post-war elections', 148.
[13] Curtice, J. and Semetko, H. 1994. 'Does it matter what the papers say?', in Heath, A., Jowell R. and Curtice, J. eds., *Labour's Last Chance*. Aldershot: Dartmouth Press: 43–64, 55.
[14] Norris, P., Curtice, J., Sanders, D., Scammell, M. and Semetko, H. 1999. *On Message*. Sage: London: 158–168.

following opinion rather than creating it. In 1997, for sure, it was not "The Sun Wot Won It".'[15] A fourth reports finds that

> [S]ince 1992, many traditionally pro-Conservative newspapers have been highly critical of the incumbent Conservative government, providing a particularly valuable opportunity to study their influence. Panel data collected regularly since 1992 suggest that partisan newspapers have only a marginal influence on the voting preferences of individual readers and that they have little or no influence on overall outcomes.[16]

An Electoral Commission report on the 2005 election also makes the same point that this book has laboured in previous chapters: almost nine out of ten citizens use TV as their main source of news, 50 per cent use the radio and 43 per cent use newspapers, and the influence of partisan papers must be set against that of non-partisan TV, radio and newspapers of record.[17] Studies of, or speculations about, newspaper influence that do not take full account of all the news used by the population may be misleading – indeed, are likely to be so, especially where the low trust rating of many newspapers, especially the tabloids, is concerned.

The Acid Test that Fails, Even as an Acid Test

Because the *Sun* changed its endorsement in a loudly proclaimed way in 1997, and because this is a relatively rare example of a national paper doing so, closer attention has been paid to the possible newspaper effect in that election than in any other. If newspapers influence voting, then this should show up clearly in a larger than average swing to Labour among *Sun* readers. However, the study of cross-pressures and reinforcements discussed earlier tried to uncover a *Sun* effect by testing the effects of Conservative and Labour papers separately from the *Sun* to see if it had a special influence. The figures show that, on the contrary, the swing to Labour among *Sun* readers was even smaller

---

[15] Scammell, M. and Harrop, M. 1997. 'The press', in Butler, D. and Kavanagh, D. eds., *The British General Election of 1997*, Basingstoke: Macmillan: 184.

[16] Curtice, J., March 1997. 'Is the Sun Shining on Tony Blair? The Electoral Influence of British Newspapers'. *The International Journal of Press/Politics*, 2 (2). https://doi.org/10.1177/1081180X97002002003.

[17] Electoral Commission. 2005. 'Election 2005: Engaging the public in Great Britain'. London: Electoral Commission.

than that among the readers of other papers.[18] Another study finds that 'the pattern of vote switching of *The Sun* or any-ex-Tory newspaper proved to be much like that of those who did not read a paper at all'.[19]

What happened in the 1997 election is probably revealed most clearly in a set of simple percentage figures presented by an Ipsos MORI poll. These measure voting intentions according to the swings to the Conservatives and the swing to Labour among newspaper readers and a wide variety of demographic measures. Both swings are helpful because a large number of those who voted Conservative in 1992 did not vote, or did not vote Conservative at all, in 1997, so the overall swing against the Conservatives is larger than the swing to Labour. The results, presented in a brief form in Table 6.1, show three patterns of voting changes among newspaper readers and non-readers alike.

First, the direction of the swings in all cases is the same: against the Conservatives and too Labour. The figures for Sunday papers (not presented here for reasons of space) are, if anything, more uniform, with each category falling within a two to three percentage point range. Second, there is some variation in how much each category moved, but not much. The size of the swing is almost the same for no paper, all papers and other papers, and the swing against the Conservatives was the same for *Sun* readers as for all paper readers. Third, the two exceptions to the general pattern are the slightly larger swings against the Conservatives and to Labour among consistently Conservative paper readers, but these do not suggest newspaper effects. Why would the readers of the loyal Tory papers register the largest swing against the Conservatives and the second largest swing to Labour? Why would the consistently Labour paper register the lowest swing against the Conservatives and a no more than average swing to Labour? If there is a newspaper effect why are the swings among those who do not read a paper identical to those who do?

Part of this might be explained by the difference between net and aggregate swings. If there were large swings in different directions

---

[18] Newton and Brynin, 'The national press and party voting in the UK', 279.
[19] Curtice, J. 1997. 'Is the Sun shining on Tony Blair? The electoral influence of British newspapers'. *Harvard International Journal of Press/Politics*, 2: 9–26.

Table 6.1 *Conservative and Labour swings, 1992–1997 elections, by daily national newspapers*

	Swing against Conservatives (%)	Swing to Labour (%)
Consistently Conservative papers (*Mail, Telegraph, Express*)	16.7	12.7
Consistently Labour paper (*Mirror*)	6	9
Paper that switched from Conservative to Labour (*Sun*)	15	16
Others (*Times, Financial Times, Independent, Guardian, Star, Record*)	12	8.7
No paper	12	9
All papers	13.8	11
Total vote	12	9

Source: Ipsos. 31 May 1997. 'How Britain Voted in 1997', London: Ipsos.

according to party endorsements they might cancel each out, leaving a false impression of no newspaper effect. But this cannot be the case in 1997 because all newspapers register swings in the same direction, so they cannot cancel each other out. The only exception suggesting a newspaper effect in Table 6.1 is the *Sun*'s larger than average swing against the Conservatives and to Labour. This at least suggests a *Sun* effect, so perhaps after all there is a small newspaper effect, but for the *Sun* alone. We return to this possibility a little later.

The suggestion, frequently advanced in previous chapters, has been that the underlying causes of both newspaper reading and voting are the individual characteristics of citizens, especially their age, sex, education, income, social status, ethnicity and religion, plus their political identity. Fortunately, the Ipsos MORI poll that produced the figures in Table 6.1 also presents figures for swings broken down by fifty-eight

Table 6.2 *Conservative and Labour swings, 1992–1997 elections, by selected demographic categories*

	Swing against Conservatives (%)	Swing to Labour (%)
Sex		
Men	10	8
Women	12	8
Social class		
ABC1	15	12
C2DE	11	10
Work		
Full time	13	11
Unemployed	10	13
Housing		
Outright owners	12	5
Council tenants	9	9
Private tenants	7	8
Trade union membership		
Members	13	11
Non-members	12	9
National average	12	8

Source: Ipsos. 31 May 1997. 'How Britain Voted in 1997', London: Ipsos.

demographic categories covering sex, age, social class, region, phone ownership, work status, housing tenure and trade union membership.

If demographic characteristics are the key, then substantial variations between different groups in the electorate would be expected. The Ipsos MORI poll finds the complete opposite. Every one of its fifty-eight categories is within a percentage point or so of the national average. Not only does every single category swing against the Conservatives and to Labour but every swing is within a few percentage points of all the others. Table 6.2 presents a few of the figures as examples.

Irrespective of demographic features and irrespective of the paper read, every group in the population acted in much the same way in the 1997 election. Neither the press nor the usual social and economic characteristics of voters made much difference to the way that many deserted the Conservatives and rather fewer opted for Labour. In the 1997 election the great majority of the electorate behaved as one.

This presents us with a new puzzle. Party voting in the 1997 election did not vary according to either the newspaper read or demographic groups. What explains this highly unusual state of affairs that resulted in a Labour landslide? The answer is simple and obvious. Elections are political events and, curious though it may seem, the result was the outcome of political circumstances.[20] The polls had shown a clear Labour lead ever since Black Wednesday, 16 November 1992, only a few weeks after a new Conservative government had taken office after the 1992 election. Black Wednesday was the day the government was forced by economic pressure to withdraw the pound sterling from the European Exchange Rate Mechanism. It cost the country an estimated £3.4 billion and its cost the Conservative government its priceless reputation for economic competence. Its opinion poll ratings dropped almost overnight and remained low for the next four years. It was unprecedented for a party and its leader (Blair) to sustain such a high level of approval for such a long and unbroken time. Many voters formed their voting decision in 1992 and stuck to it to the last. As one journalist put it, 'this was never going to be the kind of election in which the press could sway'.[21]

On top of that the government added to its unpopularity with scandals, internal rancour, indecision, incompetence and an uncharacteristically poor campaign that revealed deep splits over the EU. Labour managed an unusually slick campaign led by the young and charismatic Blair and a group of wily campaign managers. In retrospect and with the advantage of 20:20 vision the 1997 election was a foregone conclusions because a great number of voters had made up their mind four years earlier.

This does not explain the slightly larger than average swings, shown in Table 6.1, to Labour among readers of the consistently Conservative press (16.7 per cent) plus a larger than average swing to Labour (12.7 per cent). In contrast, the *Mirror*, a faithful Labour paper had a smaller than average swing against the government, and an average swing to Labour. In Table 6.2 the ABC1 social status group had the largest

---

[20] See, for example, Harrison, M. 1997. 'Politics on the air', in Butler, D. and Kavanagh, D. eds., *The British General Election of 1997*. Basingstoke: Macmillan: 133.

[21] McKie, D. 1998. 'The tabloid press and the 1997 general election', in Crewe, I., Gosschalk, B. and Bartle, J. eds., *Political Communications: Why Labour Won the General Election of 1997*. London: Frank Cass: 15–130.

swing against the Conservatives and the second largest swing to Labour. Does this show that true-blue papers are good at manufacturing Labour voters, or that the upper social strata are ripe for conversion to the socialist cause? Of course not.

The answer to these, and other anomalies in the figures, is simple. Tory papers have a larger than average proportion of Conservative readers and, therefore, a larger pool of voters who could turn against the party in the right circumstances. With few Conservative voters among *Mirror* readers, there is less room for change and so the paper records a slightly smaller swing against the Conservatives and only an average one to Labour. The social class of ABC1s are similarly Conservative in most elections, with a large pool of potential switchers who could do what the rest of the country was doing by deserting the Conservatives and voting Labour. But because it is a big leap from not voting Conservative to voting Labour, some of the Tory faithful could not bring themselves to vote at all, or voted for the half-way house Liberal Democrats. The variations from average swing figures in the tables reveal not newspaper or social and economic effects but a simple ceiling effect that sets limits on how many were available to swing.

It is possible that the few election studies that do find significant, even very large, newspaper effects in 1997 are actually measuring not a newspaper effect but a ceiling effect. But it takes exceptional political circumstances to produce a collective mood that produces the same swing to Labour and from the Conservatives. That is why the 1997 election turns out to be a very bad case to estimate a newspaper effect, least of all a natural experiment that provides us with an acid test of such effects.

The 1992 election is a better test, but close analysis of that shows, as already demonstrated, that it was not the *Sun*, or any other paper, that won it.

Newspaper Effects in Normal Times

If 1997 is a particularly bad year for a test of newspapers effects what about more normal times? Fortunately, there is plentiful evidence about them because the *Sun*'s claim to have won it in 1992, followed by the landslide victory for Labour in 1997, promoted new interest in newspaper influence. Starting with 2000 (not an election year), an Ipsos article investigates the question: 'Do readers believe what the editors want them to?' It concludes

Table 6.3 *Conservative to Labour swings election to election, by national newspapers (%)*

	1992–1997	1997–2001	2001–2005	2005–2010
Express	+10.5	−2.0	−3.0	−5.0
Mail	+15.5	−5.5	−2.0	−4.0
Mirror	+7.5	+1.0	−2.0	−6.5
Record	+2.0	+3.0	−1.5	+2.5
Telegraph	+12.0	−6.0	−1.5	−5.5
Financial Times	+14.5	+0.5	0.0	–
Guardian	+9.5	−6.5	−5.0	+0.5
Independent	+9.5	−2.5	−2.5	−1.5
Star	+14.0	−7.0	−1.0	−10.0
Sun	+15.5	+0.5	−5.5	−13.5
Times	+17.5	−1.0	+0.5	−8.0
Evening Standard	–	+2.0	−8.0	–
No paper	+10.5	+2.0	−4.0	−6.0
All adults	+10.5	−2.0	−3.0	−5.0

Source: Ipsos, 24 May 2010, 'Voting by Newspaper Readership 1992–2010', London: Ipsos.

In general, then, there seems little evidence at the moment that editors are influencing the views of their readers, although of course the argument is a purely negative one. But if it is true that the influence of the Press has been overstated, this should not necessarily be surprising. Poll after poll has shown in recent years that journalists are among the least trusted of professions (ranking with or often below politicians).[22]

We can judge this from swing figures, obligingly provided by Ipsos MORI again, for the election to elections of 1997–2001, 2001–2005 and 2005–2010 compared with the figures for 1992–1997 (see Table 6.3).

The first column of the table repeats what we already know about the 1997 election: the swing to Labour is much the same for all papers, irrespective of their partisanship, and most figures cluster around the non-reader and total adult averages, give or take a few percentage

[22] Ipsos. 6 October 2000. 'What the papers say: Do readers believe what the editors want them to?'. London: Ipsos.

points. The same is true of the uniformly small swing against Labour in 2001–2005 and 2005–2010, when almost all papers saw the same fairly small leakage of Labour support over time and away from the landslide victory of 1997. Once again, most newspaper readers move in the same direction and to the same degree, whatever party their paper supports.

The largest figure in the 2005–2010 column is the *Sun*'s swing of 13.5 per cent to the Conservatives, which happens to coincide with its return to the Conservative cause after the previous three election with Labour. Does this indicate a strong *Sun* effect, after all? According to MORI polls, it does not.[23] Their figures show that *Sun* reader support for Labour fell from 45 per cent (actual vote) in the election of 2005 to 29 per cent (intended vote) in September 2009. But this happened *before* the paper officially declared its support for David Cameron and the Tories on 30 September 2009. Once again, the paper seems to have followed its readers rather than leading them. From September 2009 the paper hammered Labour and presented the Conservatives in the best light on its front pages. In spite of this, reader support for the Tories increased by 3 per cent – two percentage points *lower* than the national average.

This leaves the 1997–2001 column in Table 6.3 where there is a mixture of plus and minus signs. But it is difficult to see how newspaper partisanship accounts for this variation. The *Telegraph* swings 6 per cent to the Conservatives but the *Guardian* also swings this way by 6.5 per cent. The *Sun*, still on Labour's side, had a smaller swing to the party than those who did not read a paper. The *Express*, converted to the Labour cause after unbroken support for the Conservatives in fifteen consecutive elections from 1945 to 1997, registered the same swing against Labour as the country as a whole. Like the *Sun* in the previous election, it seems to have no measurable effect on its readers' voting choice.

What the figures in Table 6.3 show is not a newspaper effect but, in spite of the best efforts of the partisan press, a slow drift back to more normal voting after the Labour landslide of 1997. This is typical of any government that sooner or later runs into problems and loses support, and of oppositions that rejuvenate themselves with new leaders,

---

[23] Worcester R. and Herve, J. 10 June 2010. 'Was it the Sun (and the Times) wot (nearly) won it?'. London: Ipsos.

policies and public images. After such a large swing to Labour in 1997 it was likely that voters would gradually return to their normal voting patterns as time passed, especially the Tories who had voted Labour in 1997. In the case of the *Telegraph*, *Express* and *Mail*, the size of the swing back to the Conservatives was larger than average because the size of the swing to Labour in 1997 was larger than average.

By 2017 the huge swing of ten years earlier had been erased but commentary on the general election of that year was still referring to the *Sun*'s claim of twenty-five years earlier. In that election Temple points out, with some disbelief, that '[o]f course, the use of the phrase "it's the Sun wot won it" and the seriousness with which academics treated the claim, implies extraordinary power to our newspapers and their hold over their diminishing readership'.[24] Once again, however, the verdict on that election was that '[t]his was a campaign, in other words, that showed both the determination of powerful gatekeepers in the mainstream media to foster a pro-Tory agenda and the enduring ability of ordinary voters to ignore these voices'.[25] Is the continuing belief in newspaper effects yet another example of belief preservation, or more simply an unawareness of the weight of research to the contrary?

Reinforcement

It has been argued that the newspaper effect is not a strong one but a weaker one of reinforcement in which the partisan press can simply shore-up and stiffen the pre-existing opinions of their leaders. Tables 6.1 and 6.3 do not present strong evidence of reinforcement. On the contrary, the consistently Conservative papers show an average or greater swing to Labour in 1997 followed by fairly average swings back to the Conservatives in the following three elections. It might be

---

[24] Temple, M. 2017. 'It's the Sun wot lost it', in Thorsen, E., Jackson, D. and Lilleker, D. eds., *UK Election Analysis 2017: Media, Voters and the Campaign*. Bournemouth: Bournemouth University, Centre for the Study of Journalism, Culture and Community: 52.

[25] Freeman, D. 'Media bias hits a wall', in Thorsen, E., Jackson, D. and Lilleker, D. eds., *UK Election Analysis 2017: Media, Voters and the Campaign*. Bournemouth: Bournemouth University, Centre for the Study of Journalism, Culture and Community: 48.

argued that the swing to Labour would have been even larger in the case of the Tory press had it not reinforced the views of some of their readers, but this introduces the complications of a counterfactual and some rather unconvincing arguments about why larger than average numbers of voters defected from their paper's endorsement.

However, the reinforcement effect has not been much researched. It has usually been an unresearched fallback position to salvage at least some media effects when nothing stronger has been found. It may be that reinforcement effects are as elusive as direct effects on voting, but it is also possible that reinforcement has an effect on the strength of party-political opinions and identity of the party faithful, rather than on those who contemplate changing their voting choice. We do not know, but lacking this knowledge we are left with little evidence of newspaper reinforcement effects.

Agenda-setting

Agenda-setting theory states that the media cannot tell us what to think but has a powerful influence on what we think about. In modern times this theory originates in the empirical work of Maxwell McCombs, who summarises forty-five years of research by stating that the media are like teachers who repeat their lessons over and over again so that when 'citizen students' are asked what are the most important issues facing the country they repeat the lessons they have learned from the media.[26] As a result, he writes, 'the news media set the public agenda'.[27]

The evidence for this is variable and inconclusive. One study of sixteen countries using a big data approach finds that agenda-setting varies from one country to another and is contingent on the economic, political, social and media contexts of the countries and of individuals in the population.[28] This seems to suggest that agenda-setting is

---

[26] McCombs, M. 2014. *Setting the Agenda: Mass Media and Public Opinion*. Hoboken, NJ: Wiley: 47–51.
[27] Ibid: 2
[28] Vu., H. et al. 2019. 'What influences media effects on public perception? A cross-national study of comparative agenda setting'. *International Communications Gazette*, 81(6–8): 580–601. See also Vliegenthart, R. et al. 2016. 'Do the media set the parliamentary agenda? A comparative study in seven countries'. *European Journal of Political Research*, 55(2): 283–301.

dependent on a total context of almost everything. Nevertheless, we are fortunate to have evidence about agenda-setting in the context of the British general elections of 1987, 1997, 2001, 2005, 2015 and 2019.

The first systematic attempt to investigate the matter in the UK was Miller's panel study of television and elections in the 1987 general election.[29] He selected TV because it was the most popular source of election news but found little correspondence between the main items of its news and what electors were mainly concerned about. TV news focused on defence, terrorism and crime but voters were mainly concerned with the daily bread-and-butter issues of unemployment, health, education and social services, which had relatively little news coverage. When TV gave defence more air time in the third week of the campaign, viewers did not follow. Miller concludes that 'Overall, therefore, the agenda set by television was miles away from the agenda of issues that the electorate rated important and wanted discussed.'

In the light of the *Sun*'s switch to Labour in the next election, there was more interest in agenda-setting, but a MORI poll found that the media and the public agendas went their own ways with little overlap.[30] Another study at that time found that the priorities of most electors were fairly constant from one election to the other and there was little indication that any shift in these depended on media exposure.[31]

A fourth study of the 1997 election conducted a more intensive two-pronged research strategy.[32] A carefully planned and analysed experiment involved 474 participants, divided into a control group and six experimental groups, who were shown a set of videos dealing with tax, employment, health, pensions, Europe and overseas aid to see what effects these had on the participants' election priorities. The second strategy used an analysis of 6,072 news articles in national daily and

---

[29] Miller, W. 1991. *Media and Voters*. Oxford: Oxford University Press: 62; Gavin, N. T. 2018. 'Media definitely do matter: Brexit, immigration, climate change and beyond'. *British Journal of Politics and International Relations*, 20 (4): 827–845.

[30] Ipsos. 6 October 2000. 'What the papers say: Do readers believe what the editors want them to?' London: Ipsos.

[31] Curtice, J. 1996. 'Do the media set the agenda?'. European Consortium for Political Research, Joint Sessions of Workshops, Oslo.

[32] Norris, P., Curtice, J., Sanders, D., Scammell, M. and Semetko, H. 1999. *On Message*. London: Sage.

Sunday papers published during the election campaign period, tracing the main items of focus and how they changed in the six-week period. These were compared with the agendas of a large national sample of voters and the ways in which those agendas changed during the campaign period.

The results of both exercises were the same: the public followed its own agenda. The priority given by experimental subjects to tax, health, employment and pensions were unaffected by the news videos. In the national sample of voters the priority given to health, education, employment, law and order and taxation changed by barely a percentage point or two during the campaign. This despite extensive coverage in the media of membership of the European Union, splits in the Conservative Party and political corruption (sleaze), all of which remained the concerns of small minorities in the population. The single exception was a greater priority attached to foreign affairs in the experimental study as a result of the video shown.

The authors put the media failure to set the agenda down to issue salience. It seems that voters are not much influenced by the media agenda where their own personal experience and knowledge is involved, and where the issue is an old and much discussed one that is also attached to party identification: tax, employment, health, education, pensions or social services, for example. These are salient issues of immediate concern. New issues that have not yet impacted on the public consciousness, and abstract and remote technical matters and events in distant parts of the globe, are less salient and may be more amenable to media influence and agenda-setting. Their appearance on the public agenda may also be more fleeting, precisely because they are not matters relating to daily, household existence.

An account of agenda-setting in the 2001 election compares news article in six main national papers, a similar content analysis of the press releases of the Conservative, Labour and Liberal Democratic parties and data about the public agenda conducted by two public opinion polls at the beginning and end of the campaign.[33] All three were disconnected from each other. The media did not follow the agenda that the parties tried to set in their daily press conferences, and the public did not follow

---

[33] Harris, P., Fury, D. and Lock, A. 2006. 'Do political parties and the press influence the public agenda? A content analysis of press coverage of the 2001 UK general election'. *Journal of Political Marketing*, 5(3): 1–28.

either the press or party agendas. The end result was that that the short-term agenda-setting impact of the press on the public appears to have been limited, as was the impact of the parties and public opinion on press coverage. The qualification 'in the short term' is important because McCombs specifies 'the recent past' to be the period during which the medias agenda-setting capacity operates.[34]

Norris's study of agenda-setting in the 2005 election goes beyond the media as possible influences on the public's election agenda to include people-intensive channels (local party contact activity) and new technology channels (internet campaign information). But this widening of channels of political communication produces no evidence of media agenda-setting effects:

Contrary to the media agenda-setting hypothesis, the results indicate that none of the uses of campaign communications generated a significantly greater propensity for the public to alter their issue agenda ... the issue agenda followed by the media in their daily headlines, by parties in their daily press briefings, and by the public, appear to operate independently during British general elections, without the gradual convergence predicted by agenda-setting theory.[35]

The public agenda, it seems, is generally immune to outside influences whether coming from the national mass media, local party activities or internet content.

For the 2015 election Moore and Ramsay collected a large body of data about the content of sixteen mainstream mass media news sources, the communications of the two main parties and also, for the first time in British agenda-setting studies, social media content. The study concludes that

Despite the party and media focus on the economy, health and immigration remained, for the public, two of the most important issues facing Britain during the campaign. Immigration was considered the most important issue facing Britain in 4 out of 5 months between January and May 2015. In contrast, it was the fifth most covered issue in mainstream media, and the ninth most discussed by political actors and influencers on Twitter.[36]

---

[34] McCombs, Setting the Agenda, 47–51.
[35] Norris, P. 2006. 'Did the media matter? Agenda-setting, persuasion and mobilization effects in the British general election campaign'. *British Politics*, 1 (2): 195–221, 214.
[36] Moore, M. and Ramsay, G. 2015. 'UK Election 2015: Setting the agenda'. London: Kings College London, CMCP Policy Institute: 4.

Table 6.4 *Top media and popular agenda topics in the final week of the 2019 general election (%)*

Key issues, TV and press		Most important issues facing the country	
Electoral process	32	Brexit	63
Brexit/EU	13	Health	46
Business/economy/trade	8	Environment	31
Health/health care	7	Economy	26
Standards/scandals	7	Immigration/asylum	23

Sources:
Key Issues: D. Deacon, 2019. 'What Was All That About, Then? The Media Agenda in the 2019 General Election', in D. Jackson, E. Thorsen, D. Lilleker and N. Weidhase, eds., *UK Election Analysis, 2019*, Bournemouth: Bournemouth University.
Most Important Issues Facing the Country: YouGov Tracker Poll, December 2019. 'The most important issues facing the country.'

Table 6.4 compares media and popular agendas in the final period of the 2019 general election. The figures in the two columns are not exactly comparable, coming from different sources with different categories. The first column is the content analysis of TV and the press conducted by the University of Loughborough in the last week of the election campaign and the second is the YouGov tracker poll of the popular agenda in that week. There is some overlap of media content with the public agenda if we assume that business/economy/trade is the same as the economy, that health and health care is the same as health and Brexit is the same as Brexit/EU, but even here the percentage figures attached to these items in the two columns do not correspond closely. The other agenda items in the two columns come from different planets, signifying a wide gap between the media and the public agenda.

Discussion

Perhaps it is not surprising that the best research using the best methods and data find little evidence of a newspaper effects on voting decisions. Few papers are always completely loyal to their party all the time and most have delivered mixed and qualified messages. Quite a few tabloid readers mistake or do not know which party their paper supports. And, in any case, they are not generally trusted. If you read the *Sun* because it's cheap and cheerful, because it is easy to read and a bit of a laugh, you are not likely to take its voting advice very seriously.[37] Besides, most people, including tabloid readers, get most of their news from public service TV and BBC radio, so the fact that most daily papers have a conservative and/or Conservative bias and favoured Brexit may not count for much.[38]

On top of this, a vast amount of experimental psychology has uncovered powerful psychological mechanisms that individuals use to preserve their beliefs and opinions. This literature shows that pre-existing beliefs usually, although not always, triumph in the face of opposing views. In fact, opposing views can have a boomerang effect of embedding beliefs more firmly. And lastly, the simple idea that people believe what they read in the papers and that it was 'the *Sun* wot won it' underestimates the serious difficulties encountered in trying to pin down media effects when readers choose their paper and papers are pushed by market forces to provide their reader with what they want to read. It has been argued, though we do not know for sure, that the *Sun* has switched its endorsement in order to be on the side of most of its readers.

A few studies do find a statistically significant impact in 1997. How can this be explained? One possibility is that research covering a short period before and during the official election campaign miss the fact that the great majority of the population changed their voting intention after Black Wednesday, four years before polling day. Another possibility is the larger pool of voters reading Conservative papers who were available to swing against the Conservatives and to Labour, compared with the much smaller pool who read Labour papers. This would explain why readers of the faithful Conservative press (the *Mail*, *Telegraph* and *Express*) swung more to Labour than readers of Labour papers and the electorate as a whole.

When the figures are disaggregated there is also little evidence to support the idea of reinforcement. The *Mail*, *Telegraph* and *Express* did not prevent a larger than average desertion from the Conservative cause in 1997 and an even larger swing in that direction compared

---

[37] Digital Spy, Forums. Not dated. 'Why do so many people read the Sun, the Mirror and the Mail?'.

[38] See, for example, Gavin, N. 2018. 'Media definitely do matter: Brexit, immigration, climate change and beyond'. *The British Journal of Politics and International Relations,* 20(4): 827–845.

Discussion 119

with those who did not read a paper. Once again this is likely to reflect the fact that these three papers had a large proportion of readers who could swing this way, compared with the *Mirror* with its larger proportion of Labour readers. None of this will become evident without disaggregating by newspaper, classifying them correctly according to their partisan or neutral political stance and conducting a comparison with non-paper readers.

A clearer example of the limits of press power is provided in the 2016 American presidential election. In that year more than three-quarters (76.6) of the 653 newspapers and magazines that reported the news endorsed Hilary Clinton, 12.6 per cent endorsed no candidate, 3 per cent were for Trump and 4.9 per cent recommended not voting for Trump. Of the 100 papers with the largest circulations, over half (57 per cent), with a total circulation of 13.1 million, were for Clinton, and two with a circulation of 36,000 supported Trump.[39] In 2020 Biden was endorsed by 45 per cent of the top 105 papers, including of eight of the biggest ten, Trump by 7 per cent, and yet Trump won 46.9 per cent of the vote.[40] Newspaper endorsements count for little in the national elections of both the USA and the UK.

Agenda-setting theory fares no better when tested against British national elections. In none of the elections of 1987, 1997, 2001, 2005, 2015 and 2019 did the public agenda follow those of the media. Perhaps this should not surprise us either. Because they live in close proximity in the Westminster village, journalists and politicians develop their own particular interests and short-term obsessions with the faults of leading politicians, political scandals, the electoral horse race, most recent polls and issues that flare up and die.[41] The electorate

---

[39] American Presidency Project. 2016. '2016 general election editorial endorsements by major newspapers: Top 100 newspapers based on daily circulation'. Santa Barbara, CA: UC Santa Barbara. See also Democracy in Action. Not dated. 'An expanding, evolving media universe'. https://www.p2016.org/media/index.html.
[40] Solender, A. 2 November 2020. ' Biden trounces Trump in final tally of major Newspaper endorsements: 47 to 7'. *Forbes*.
[41] Deacon, D. et al. 2019. 'What was all that about, then? The media agenda in the 2019 general election', in Thorsen, E., Jackson, D. and Lilleker, D. eds., *UK Election Analysis 2017: Media, Voters and the Campaign*. Bournemouth: Bournemouth University, Centre for the Study of Journalism, Culture and Community: chapter 64.

may sometimes be interested in reading about these things but there is little evidence that they affect voting.

Why, when agenda-setting has been confirmed often in the USA, is there so little trace of it in the UK? We do not know and can only speculate. One possibility is the importance of public service news in the UK and its small role in the USA. The more the electorate uses and trusts the balanced, impartial and accurate news of the public services, the less influential the press is likely to be. The possible irony here is that the more impartial and accurate a news source, the more it is trusted but the less it will exercise a partisan influence. The more partisan a news source, the less it is trusted and less it can exercise a partisan influence.

A further point emerges from these conclusions about voting and agenda-setting in British elections. There is now a disconnect between the political science of voting, political attitudes and behaviour, on the one hand, and media impact studies, on the other. Few election studies now use media variables in their explanations of voting, and studies of attitudes and behaviour almost never do. For example, the broad-ranging British Election Study of 2001 has little to say about the media, having found them to be of little importance in the previous elections.[42] Similarly, the twenty-seven chapters of *The Routledge Handbook of Elections, Voting Behavior and Public Opinion* barely touches on the media, and the one essay that does states

> There seems to be little question that the media matter in politics in general and in elections in particular. Despite what seems to be this accepted truism, researchers have been hard pressed to demonstrate without question that media influence political attitudes and behaviors.[43]

And this in spite of the fact that the study of political attitudes and behaviour is a data-rich and widely investigated field of research.

There is also a disconnect between media studies finding large or massive media effects and the experimental psychology of belief preservation. Very little of the media effects literature refers to this vast

---

[42] Clarke, H., Sanders, D., Stewart, M. and Whiteley, P. 2004. *Political Choice in Britain*. Oxford: Oxford University Press.
[43] Banducci, S. 2018. 'The role of the mass media in shaping public opinion and voting behaviour', in Fisher, J., Fieldhouse, E. and Franklin, M. eds., *The Routledge Handbook of Elections, Voting Behavior and Public Opinion*. London, Routledge: 305.

body of literature stretching back over six decades, in spite of the fact that the literature is virtually unanimous about the great difficulties of trying to change opinions.

All this raises the question, if the news media do not determine voting behaviour or election agendas, what does? The answer from the research is clear and consistent. In the election of 2019, for example, the variables most closely associated with party voting were age, sex (for the 18–24 age group) and education.[44] In the EU referendum voting ran most clearly along age and education lines and, to a lesser extent, employment status and income.[45] These are among the usual social, political and economic variables that form the standard model that emerges from most election studies and from the large volume of research on other forms of political attitudes and behaviour. They are also the underlying variables that explain how much news individuals get, from what sources and how they react to that news. The media are minor players; the driving force is provided by the demographic variables of the standard model.

This may be true but it still does not explain what determines the attitudes and beliefs that underlie both the choice of news media and their supposed effects. The answer that it is the variables of the standard model are part of the answer but not the whole answer. Age in and of itself, for example, cannot explain why older people prefer to get their news from TV and papers. There is nothing about age, as such, that leads people to make these choices. Nor can age explain why older people were much more likely to vote for Brexit or for the Conservative party in 2017. But the life circumstances typical of older age groups can explain a lot. They tend to have ingrained habits, are more likely to have developed lasting political attitudes, have a rather different set of life experiences than other cohorts, are less computer savvy and many have more time to watch TV and read newspapers. They live on pensions, not wages or salaries, and they are more likely to have paid off their mortgage and to have health issues, all of which might affect their voting behaviour.

Age, in other words, is important not in itself but because it stands for and is a shorthand way of referring to a range of other things that

---

[44] McDonnell, A. and Curtis, C. 17 December 2019. 'How Britain voted in the 2019 general election'. London: YouGov.
[45] Guardian, A. 24 June 2016. 'How Brexit vote broke down'. *Politico*.

do have an impact on voting behaviour. Similarly, income in and of itself cannot explain attitudes and behaviour but the life circumstances of the rich and the poor can. When income is used as an explanatory variable it is assumed that it is not money pure and simple that counts, but all the things that go with it or the lack of it. There are many middle-class socialists and working-class Tories. Money, class, sex and minority status are indicators of (proxies for) a whole set of social, political and economic features that are often tied to them. What the variables of the standard model stand for, and how these condition media effects, is revisited in Chapter 8.

7 | *Media Malaise and the Mean World Effect*

Although the news media have been praised in the past as the fourth estate of the realm – a cornerstone of democracy that informs the public about public matters and holds the powerful to account – it is now more commonly treated as a fifth column that undermines democracy and corrupts its citizens and procedures. The list of criticisms levelled at the news media is long and varied. It is said that the huge volume of news that is available every hour of the day, and the speed with which items of interest come and go, creates public confusion, ignorance and news fatigue. Too little effort is given to helping the public understand events and the connection between them. Journalism is charged with reducing complex matters to simple two-sided issues and preferably to conflict between them. If there is no conflict, reporters will try to generate it and if this does not work, they will invent it. News, it is complained, has been reduced to the lowest common denominator of infotainment and, in any case, one argument is that television, by its very nature, can do nothing but amuse us. The focus on bad news and conflict is said to create a mean world effect of distrust and political cynicism about politicians and democratic institutions. The tabloids undermine their own credibility with their cheque-book journalism, their illegal hacking and their own fake news. Even the broadsheets distract attention from the important policy issues by filling column inches with horse race coverage of who is winning and who is losing in election campaigns. In between, the insatiable search for new news and breaking news creates a volatile fast-forward effect which cuts short the time for serious debate and makes it difficult to follow stable, long-term policies. Similarly, some claim, the media build up politicians only to tear them down with attack journalism and investigative journalism.

Malign media effects are not thought to be limited to the news. It is claimed that the vast increase in entertainment media diverts citizens from civic duties and participation, with the result that communities are hollowed out, election turnout is decreasing, party membership declining and social solidarity and civic responsibility are eroded. TV has also been the object of widespread criticism. Its murder, crime and horror films are said to make people indifferent to violence, crime and bloodshed and contribute to a lack of social trust. Soap operas turn drama and personal conflicts into normal parts of daily life. A great deal of television and most advertising glamorise the rich and famous, and promote possessive individualism, greed and selfishness. The obsession with celebrities creates a 'wannabe' and 'wannahave' world in which everyone is young, rich, beautiful and famous. If any of this is true, it works by invisible and insidious stealth under the radar of conscious awareness by cultivating the worst in human behaviour rather than promoting the best.[1]

There may well be much more than a grain of truth in some of these claims, but at the same time, some statements are contradictory, some have little or no evidence to back them up and some are based on cherry-picked evidence. For example, one claim is that the modern media create powerful presidents and prime ministers (even turning prime ministers in to de facto presidents) by focusing the limelight on them and allowing them to appeal directly to voters and over the heads of their party and parliamentary colleagues. Against this, others claim that the media cut political careers short by relentless news coverage that reveals the human weaknesses of leaders and highlights their deficiencies and failures. Can the media do both? Perhaps, but this raises a new aspect of the matter that is not explained. All politicians fall from grace sooner or later and for one reason or another, and while there is little doubt that the media have helped to bring some careers to an abrupt halt, it is not clear whether this has been the media's doing or the failings of the individuals concerned. Even so, some politicians have been described as survivors who seem to be unaffected by adversity and criticism that bring others down. Far from cutting careers short, Thatcher and Blair clocked up more than twenty-one years in Number 10 between them, Merkel was chancellor for sixteen years, Obama,

---

[1] For a fuller account of media malaise see Norris, P., Curtice, J., Sanders, D., Scammell, M. and Semetko, H. A. 1999. *On Message*. London: Sage: 97–99; Newton, K., 1999. 'Mass media effects: Mobilization or media malaise?'. *British Journal of Political Science*, 29(4): 577–599; Schuck, A. 2017. 'Media malaise and political cynicism'. *The International Encyclopedia of Media Effects*. Wiley Online Library.

Clinton and George W. Bush all survived their maximum of eight years, and Trudeau and Macron are still going in their eighth year of leadership.

This chapter looks, first, at the role of the news media in creating a general mood of political disaffection and dissatisfaction – something frequently referred to as media malaise. In the second part, the effects of watching TV in general, not just the news, are examined to see if this is a source of political alienation, cynicism, distrust and lack of political interest and understanding. The third part looks at the main causes of the decline of democratic satisfaction to see what this can tell us about the effects of watching TV news and other programmes.

Media Malaise

An Ofcom survey asks regular users of the news how they rate what they get from TV, printed papers, radio, magazines, social media and other websites. In every case, except social media, clear majorities and often large ones say that news 'Is important to me personally', that it 'Helps me understand what's going on in the world today', that it 'Offers a range of opinion', that it 'Helps me make up my mind' and that it has 'A depth of analysis and content not available elsewhere'.[2] Political magazines have a consistently high score on these items followed by TV news. The same survey finds that seven major TV channels have the same qualities. It should be added that these are not figures for the adult population as a whole but only for those who use it a news source at least weekly, so they do not include news avoiders, who may have different opinions. However, there are few who do not get TV or radio news at least weekly. Nor do these figures for self-rating understanding tell us anything about how much people actually do understand of the news they get. But that is not the point. The media malaise argument is that people *feel* alienated, confused and disengaged by the news, but the evidence here is that they do not. On the contrary, they find it important and helpful and come back regularly for more. But only up to a point. We have already seen how news avoiders feel overwhelmed by too much news, and more recently

---

[2] Jigsaw Research, 13 August 2020. *News Consumption in the UK: 2020*. London: Ofcom, figures 11.4, 11.5.

how some have been angered or depressed by bad news and Brexit news. It is not clear whether this is a media effect or a real-world effect.

The most thorough, extensive and intensive analysis of the role of the media in British elections triangulates on the subject of media malaise with a cross-sectional survey, a campaign panel study and an experimental study of TV news.[3] The panel study began with a first-wave questionnaire a year before the election, with two further waves during the official campaign and a fourth just after polling day. They find that those who make most use of both TV news and newspapers are the best informed about politics and have higher levels of civic engagement. Nor is attention to the news in newspapers or on TV associated with changes in political trust, subjective efficacy or political participation. And, as we found in Chapter 6, the media had no measurable impact on the public's election agenda or voting patterns. On the contrary, the electorate made up its own mind about which party to vote for in the same way that it set its own agenda. British Election Studies from 1964 to 1997 show that most voters make up their minds about who to vote for 'a long time' before the election, although those who leave it until the campaign have increased from 12 to 27 per cent.[4] This leaves little room for campaign effects, unless it is a permanent campaign between election periods.

The experimental part of the study found little influence of TV on party preferences, and even exposure to predominantly negative news, often claimed to be the guilty party in turning citizens against politics and participation, had no effect on the propensity for voting. Positive coverage of a party did have a powerful effect of strengthening party support, although no sign of this was evident in opinion polls in the real world. The authors suggest that this is because the experiments fed their participants with clearly negative videos, whereas impartial BBC News in the real world has a neutral effect. The experiments also find that while TV news had no effect on the importance attached by the public to the domestic political issues of taxation, unemployment, the NHS and pensions, they did increase the significance of foreign policy issues of Europe and the developing world, in the short run at least. In the long run, however, effects of this kind have been found to wear off, as experimental effects tend to do.

---

[3] Norris et al., *On Message*.   [4] Ibid., 179.

The study concludes that the news media are more likely to mobilise and inform than to induce a mood of distrust, alienation and apathy:

> Those most attentive to news on television and in the press, and regular viewers and readers, were considerably more knowledgeable than the average citizen about party policies, civics and the parliamentary candidates standing in their constituency. They were also more likely to turn out. ... Far from producing cynicism and turning-off voters, as critics charge, this evidence suggests that the British media largely succeed in their public service role.[5]

The strongest associations with attitudes and behaviour in the study do not involve media measures but, as usual, those for income, age, sex, identification with the government of the day and, above all, education. Education is strongly and positively correlated with all the measures of knowledge, understanding, efficacy and trust, and equally strongly and negatively correlated with political cynicism.

A second study, a comparison of the UK, the USA and New Zealand, examines how attention to the media during election campaigns results in changes in support for the political system. The UK part of the study is based on British Election Study data for the 1997 election. Its conclusion is that

> [M]edia coverage during the campaign, if it has any effect, has a mobilization effect. In most instances, the campaign has a positive influence on levels of trust and efficacy. While the content of the media has not been systematically linked to the survey data, the overall conclusion is that attention to the campaign in the media positively influences level of system support ... In all cases, newspaper reading had a positive effect on levels of system support.[6]

These conclusions are strongly supported by another test of the mobilisation versus media malaise theories in the UK. This uses British Social Attitudes data to examine the associations between media use and measures of media malaise. Media use is covered by newspaper reading habits and the use of television (terrestrial, cable and satellite), home video recorders and cinema attendance. Media malaise is measured by

---

[5] Ibid., 113.
[6] Banducci, S. and Karp, J. 2003. 'How elections change the way citizens view the political system: Campaigns, media effects and electoral outcomes in comparative perspective'. *British Journal of Political Science*, 33(3): 443–467.

a set of twenty measures of political knowledge, self-rated political interest and understanding, trust in public officials, political cynicism, subjective (personal) efficacy and confidence in British democracy. The study compares broadsheet readers, tabloid readers and those who do not regularly read a newspaper, and because it takes time for newspaper influence to build up, it takes account of newspaper reading the year before the survey. Because there may be a difference between watching TV news and TV in general, the study also compares these as well. The control variables in the study are the usual suspects of age, income, education, social class, party ID, economic activity/inactivity and unemployment.

These individual characteristics are closely connected with media consumption. Broadsheet readers are notably better educated than tabloid readers and likely to be older, male and with a higher income and social class. The higher the income, education and class, the less general TV people watch, and also the less TV news they watch. In fact, tabloid readers watch more TV news than broadsheet readers, because for them watching the news is part of a pattern of high TV consumption. The highest educational groups watch much less general TV than others, and watch slightly less TV news, although they are heavy users of broadsheet papers, suggesting, again, that the educated prefer reading their news to watching it. Age cuts across income, education and class because while older people have only a slight tendency to be hard-copy broadsheet readers, they watch a lot of TV and they especially watch a lot of TV news. Economic activity is another cross-cutting factor. The economically active are marginally more likely to be broadsheet readers, are much less likely to watch a lot of TV, but are significantly more likely to watch the news.

These patterns are the result of an interaction between political interest (associated with education, income and class) and time available for use of the media (associated with age, retirement and economic activity). In other words, how much and what kind of news people get from which sources are related to, and are conditioned by life cycle effects, personal characteristics of sex, class, income and education, and the amount of time available. Thus, there is a tangled three-way set of interrelationships between individual characteristics, media use and a wide array of political attitudes and behaviour, making it difficult to sort out causes and effects.

Holding the most important individual characteristics constant, however, shows that broadsheet readers are better informed, rate their interest and understanding comparatively highly, are more trusting politically and are less cynical. They are more mobilised than alienated by the news they get from their papers. Perhaps this is not surprising given the nature of broadsheets and their readers. However, media malaise theories suggest that tabloid readers are more likely to suffer from their news diet than broadsheet readers and non-readers of any kind of paper. But the evidence of the survey suggests that there is little difference between tabloid readers and non-newspaper readers. Both have the same scores for political knowledge and neither shows signs of political alienation. Nor do they show any signs of mobilisation. Reading a tabloid or not reading a paper at all makes little difference to political knowledge, attitudes or behaviour.

Television makes a difference, however. The more individuals watch TV news the more they know about politics, the higher they rate their own interest, information and understanding of politics, and the greater their confidence in the democratic system of the country. There is no evidence here that TV news watchers suffer from media malaise any more than those who avoid it. At the same time, there is a tendency for tabloid readers to watch TV news, and their TV habit has the effect of informing them about politics, not as much as reading a broadsheet paper, but more than those who avoid papers and watch little TV news.

The strong effects of the broadsheets and weaker effects of TV news have different impacts on the total population because 10 per cent read the papers but 90 per cent watch TV news. In addition, the neutral effect of the tabloids must be set against the relatively weak but positive effect of the TV news they watch. Most of those who do not read a paper watch TV news and are influenced by its relatively weak but positive effects. For the population as a whole, therefore, media effects are small to negligible, but where they are statistically significant they are positive and not consistent with media malaise theories.

A third, major test of the media malaise thesis is Norris' *Virtuous Circle*, an extensive examination of the effects of political communications across Europe.[7] This is an important work because it makes use

---

[7] Norris, P. 2000. *A Virtuous Circle: Political Communications in Postindustrial Societies*. Cambridge: Cambridge University Press.

of a vast amount of evidence drawn from different sources, covers twenty-four different Western countries with different political and media systems, and uses cross-sectional and time series data, plus an experimental study. The result is that, even after holding constant education, age, sex, income and a set of political attitudes, exposure to the news media in the UK contributes to knowledge about abstract and distant issues of party politics in the EU. Use of the news media was also associated with higher levels of confidence in democratic principles, evaluations of EU institutions and performance and voting turnout in European elections in 1989 and 1994. On the other hand, it was not associated with attitudes of trust between the populations of EU member countries, nor with support for national political leaders.

Norris concludes her in-depth and broad comparative study in this way:

> Successive tests have established that those most exposed to the news media and party campaigns consistently proved the most knowledgeable, not less; more trusting towards government and the political system, not less, more likely to participate in election campaigns, not less. These positive associations were found in a succession of models, in Europe and the United States, despite a battery of structural and attitudinal controls for factors that could plausibly affected media use and political engagement.[8]

These conclusions apply to the UK among the other countries, as does an important qualification she adds to the overall conclusions: 'The association between use of the news media and civic engagement often was only modest.' Throughout her study, as in many others, the control variables, of age, sex, income education and political identity and interest are usually more powerful than media measures, sometimes considerably more powerful.

General and Entertainment TV

We have found evidence of small but positive news media effects and little evidence to support media malaise theories. But perhaps it is not the news that matters but TV in general. After all, almost everyone watches TV during the week, many watch it for several hours a day and most spend much more time with soap operas, films, sitcoms,

[8] Ibid., 314.

sport, reality shows and nature programmes than with the news. Perhaps there is something about TV in general that breeds ignorance of and negative attitudes towards politics, especially if the TV diet includes a great deal of films and drama about crime, murder, violence, horror, disaster and political corruption. The problem here is that we have little evidence about what kinds of entertainment TV are most likely to induce media malaise or how much time people spend with them.

There are, however, ways of estimating the association between watching a lot or a little entertainment TV and measures of political knowledge and media malaise. The first is to compare the evidence of malaise among broadsheet readers, TV news watchers and total TV watching, holding constant the powerful variables of income, education, political ID, sex and age. The British Social Attitudes survey, discussed earlier, shows that those who watch a lot of TV in total do indeed have a slight but statistically significant tendency towards poor knowledge of politics, a low self-rated understanding of them, poor subjective efficacy and a degree of political cynicism. There is no association with political trust or views about the quality of British democracy. Education and gender have a stronger and more statistically significant association with political knowledge and understanding, and identification with the party of government has stronger and more significant associations with internal efficacy, trust, faith in democracy and lack of political cynicism. Once again, it is the demographic variables of the standard model background variables that count much more than media measures.

It would seem that watching a lot of TV is patchily and weakly associated with some measures of malaise and poor knowledge, but the analysis can be pushed a bit further by examining the different combinations of media use that make up individual news diets. It might be expected that those who watch a lot of TV in total will also tend to watch a lot of TV news, simply because the TV is on, but how these two are combined depends on particular social groups in the population. Older age groups watch a lot of TV in total, especially a lot of TV news, whereas higher class, income and education groups watch little TV in total but a slightly more than average amount of TV news – they mainly get their news in print form. The economically active watch relatively little TV overall, but a lot of TV news. Higher socio-economic groups tend to be broadsheet readers who watch little TV in general but slightly more TV news than average. Sex and unemployment are not associated with either total TV or TV news although women and the unemployed are less likely to be broadsheet readers. The result is a jumble of patterns of TV and newspaper reading that cut across each other.

One result of this is that the negative effects of watching a lot of TV are likely to be offset to some degree by the stronger and positive effects of reading a broadsheet paper and watching TV news. In which case we have a possible explanation for the weak and patchy results of watching hours of TV. Some support for this suggestion is provided by a comparison of different combinations of media use and political knowledge and a self-rated understanding of politics. Compared with the rest of the population, the highest levels of knowledge and self-rated political understanding are found among those broadsheet readers who watch a lot of TV news *and* a lot of general TV. Their trust and internal efficacy is also higher than average and cynicism lower. Whatever their combinations of TV consumption, the broadsheet group is always better informed and with more positive attitudes towards politics.

At the other end of the continuum the lowest levels of knowledge and understanding are found among those who watch a lot of entertainment TV combined with either reading a tabloid or not reading a paper regularly. In particular, watching a lot of entertainment TV does seem to be associated with the indicators of malaise, though not strongly and not in the case, just mentioned, of broadsheet readers who watch a lot of TV news *and* a lot of entertainment TV.

This leaves us with a puzzle. If it is the case that watching hours of entertainment TV is associated with media malaise, albeit weakly and patchily, what is it about TV that has this effect? This aspect of media malaise theory has not been much investigated, and it is not obvious what the answer could be. Audience ratings show that the most popular programmes are sport, nature, comedy, sitcoms and romcoms, soap operas and reality shows such as *Strictly Come Dancing*, *Britain's Got Talent* and *The Great British Bake Off*. Do these inspire fear and loathing? More likely it is crime, mystery, political thriller, horror and disasters films, but why should they have this effect when the news, frequently said to be depressingly full of bad news, is a more likely candidate for producing malaise? And, in any case, we have the old problem of cause and effect. Which is more likely: that crime, disaster and horror films produce political cynicism, insecurity and distrust or that those who are secure and trustful are more likely to enjoy this kind of entertainment?

If Not the Media, then What?

This section takes a little detour to consider what does underlie political malaise if it is not media induced. This will bring us round to an important point about the role of the media in the formation of mass political opinion.

There is nothing new about political disaffection, distrust and cynicism in the UK and the rest of the world, and it has been carefully tracked and investigated over the past fifty or sixty years.[9] Extensive study by the Bennett Institute's Centre for the Future of Democracy shows that dissatisfaction with the democratic system in the UK can fluctuate substantially, but from 1970 it followed a general downward trend to hit a low point of 33 per cent in 2005, after which is started to climb again particularly steeply after 2017. By 2020 it had reached 62 per cent, the highest in fifty years.[10]

In searching for explanations for this it is necessary to exclude some possibilities. Many other countries in the Western world are also experiencing a notable decline of confidence in the way their country is run, so the particular and special features of the British system cannot explain the whole of the story, though they may explain part of it. And part of that may be media related, although it is notable that research on the decline of political satisfaction in the UK only mentions them in passing, if at all – another example of the disconnect between general political science and media research.

---

[9] See, for example, Dinic, M. 4 December 2020. 'How democratic is the UK?'. London: YouGov; Wike, R., Fetterolf, J., Schumacher S. and Moncus, J. 21 October 2021. 'Citizens in advanced economies want significant changes to their political systems'. Washington, DC: Pew Research Center; Wike, R. and Fetterole, J. 7 December 2021. 'Global public opinion in an era of democratic anxiety'. Washington, DC: Pew Research Center; Dunleavy, P., Park. A, and Taylor, R. eds. 2019. *The UK's Changing Democracy: The Democratic Audit – 2018*. London: LSE Press, Hansard Society; Institute for Public Policy Research. 5 December 2021. 'Revealed: Trust in politicians at lowest level on record'. London: IPPR.

[10] Klassen, R., Slade, A., Rand, M. and Collins, R. 2020. 'The Global Satisfaction with Democracy Report 2020'. Cambridge: Centre for the Future of Democracy: 21.

Nor is the malaise diffused throughout the UK. It is stronger in some parts of the population and in some parts of the country than in others. Trust in politicians and political leaders has declined sharply, much less in doctors, judges and teachers. Trust in the BBC remains substantially higher than trust in tabloids. A majority of the population believes that devolution on the mainland is improving but not in Northern Ireland. The further from London you get, the higher the level of dissatisfaction with the way that British government and politics work. Yet so far, the great majority continue to believe that democracy is the best form of government, even if they believe that British democracy falls short of what they expect of it. By and large, those who support the government are more satisfied with politics and government than those who favour opposition parties.

The population discriminates by picking out some things and not others for disapproval. And the things they pick are, as the Bennett Institute's report puts it, largely responses to 'objective circumstances and events: economic shocks, corruption scandals, and policy crises. These have an immediately observable effect on the average levels of civic dissatisfaction.'[11] The institute's list of global and regional objective circumstances includes the economic crisis of 2008, the eurozone crisis beginning in 2009, the European refugee crisis and Brexit in the UK. Other studies add economic pessimism, poor handling of Covid, austerity policy and growing income inequality. The view is growing that the country needs major economic, political and social reform but that this is not possible because of political divisions in the country and within the parties and Parliament. This, in turn, is linked to an unfair electoral system, and the view that those in power do not run the country for the benefit of the general public.

We can argue about this list of problems but the point is that they all refer to objective trends and events, not to constructions of the media. Of course, the media report these trends and events, as they should, and consciously or unconsciously, willingly or inevitably, they can exaggerate, distort and spin them according to their own views. But no matter how biased they are, they cannot conceal the fact or importance of Brexit, economic problems, social and political divisions, global warming, government performance, party leadership, austerity

---

[11] Bennett Institute. 29 January 2020. 'Global dissatisfaction with democracy at record high'. Cambridge: Cambridge University, Bennett Institute: 42

and the state of the country's social services. To quote the Bennett Institute again:

[I]f satisfaction with democracy is now falling across many of the world's largest mature and emerging democracies – including the United States, Brazil, the United Kingdom, and South Africa – it is not because citizens' expectations are excessive or unrealistic, but because democratic institutions are falling short of the outcomes that matter most for their legitimacy, including probity in office, upholding the rule of law, responsiveness to public concerns, ensuring economic and financial security, and raising living standards for the larger majority of society.[12]

In other words, it is not media malaise that is responsible for democratic dissatisfaction but the objective conditions of government, the economy and society.[13]

Discussion

Chapter 6 found little evidence of media influence on voting behaviour and mass political agendas, but this chapter finds evidence of positive effects on political knowledge and background dispositions towards politics – what people know about politics, whether they feel they have some influence in the system, whether the democratic system works well or poorly, how much they feel they understand and their trust in the government and public officials. Another way of saying this is that the media have few, if any, effects on voting behaviour or on public election agendas, but they do have a small but positive effect on public knowledge and understanding of politics, and on general attitudes towards the political system and their own place in it.

Reading seems to be more important than watching, but TV news is also associated with higher levels of knowledge and political confidence.[14] In his influential book, *Amusing Ourselves to Death*, Postman claims that TV can do nothing but entertain us, and that it is reading

---

[12] Ibid., 42.
[13] See also van der Meer, T. 25 January 2017. 'Political trust and the "crisis of democracy"'. Oxford: Oxford University Press, Oxford Research Enclyclopedias.
[14] On learning more from reading than watching see also Sundar, S. 2000. 'Multimedia effects on processing and perception of online news: A study of picture, audio, and video downloads'. *Journalism & Mass Communication Quarterly*, 77(3): 480–499.

that educates and informs us.[15] He is half right. Reading a good newspaper is highly informative and has a positive impact on our political dispositions, but TV can also inform us and is, in Britain, the most important single source of news for most of the population. The qualification 'in Britain' is important because most people tune in to public service news. TV may play a different role in countries with only, or predominantly commercial TV.

The fact that large numbers tune into TV news, although they are not particularly interested in politics, suggests that many watch the news because the TV is on. It is a convenient, generally undemanding medium compared with reading a good newspaper, and the news is available at regular intervals on different channels. So those who are not particularly motivated to keep up with the news watch it nevertheless, and absorb information and hear different opinions about it. Because they are not a self-selected audience for news, and fall into it rather than seeking it out, they offer a way into the problem of cause and effect created by self-selection. In their case we can be more confident that it is TV news that informs them and motivates them politically, rather than the other way round in which the politically informed and motivated turn on the news.

There is no evidence in this chapter that those who fall into the news are confused and alienated by it; on the contrary, the evidence suggests small but positive media effects on political knowledge and attitudes. If anything, it is the total amount of TV watched, not news consumption, that provides evidence of media malaise, although the evidence is weak and patchy. A satisfactory explanation of this is hard to find, given that by far the most popular forms of TV entertainment (sitcoms, romcoms, reality shows, sport, soap operas, gardening/cooking/housing, comedy, nature programmes) seem to be politically neutral and harmless.

However, even the strongest media effects we find are small, compared with the individual characteristics of media audiences – age, income, socio-economic status, sex, political interest and identity, and especially education, party identification and political interest. Compared with the variables of the standard model, media effects are weak or non-existent.

[15] Postman, N. 2005. *Amusing Ourself to Death*. Harmondsworth: Penguin Books.

Discussion

The evidence in this chapter reinforces the point that studies focusing on one medium to the exclusion of others are in danger of drawing conclusions that are incomplete, only partly right or possibly wrong. People get their news from different outlets that can reinforce or counteract each other. It is not enough to focus exclusively on the tabloids, overlooking the fact that tabloid readers tend to watch a lot of TV news. Similarly, those who watch a lot of entertainment TV are generally less well informed than those who do not, unless they also happen to read a broadsheet *and* watch a lot of TV news. The fact that most people get most of their news from TV has great significance for the effects of tabloid newspapers and, as we saw in Chapter 5, for those who go online for news.

And last, in contrast with media malaise theories, studies of declining political support in the UK and other countries rarely see the need even to mention the news media, because they find that the moods of political satisfaction and dissatisfaction are a clear response to objective events and developments. In the UK in the last decade or so, they have picked out economic shocks, political corruption and incompetence, growing inequality, the decline of social services and Brexit. Of course, these are reported in the news media, as they must be, and perhaps priming, framing, biasing and spinning the news has its effects, but the evidence is that people react more strongly to events and developments in the political world than to the way they are reported. This is not to deny that the modern media play a role in communicating and spreading ideas, beliefs and moods about politics, but there is little evidence to suggest that they create them. They are, if anything an ancillary influence, much less of a creative force.

This leads us into Chapter 8, which deals with first-hand personal experience and face-to- face conversation as important sources of political information and influence that may reinforce, complement or counteract the news that people get from the media.

8 | *Personal Experience as a Reality Check*

It is commonly assumed that we are largely or wholly dependent on the news media for information about current political events and developments. This seems to be a reasonable claim and some media textbooks state it in so many words. Few of us walk the corridors of power, have ever sat in the Visitors' Gallery in the Commons, are not admitted to the meeting rooms where important decisions are made, do not take part in press conferences, do not have any first-hand contacts with national or even local politicians, rarely even see them briefly in person and do not have any special knowledge of most technical issues of modern government or of countries on the other side of the world. Most people are not particularly interested in politics so they sensibly take short cuts and rely on trusted sources of news.

If the news media are our main or only source of political information, this would explain why they are said to exercise such a strong influence on what we know, what we think and what we do about politics. Indeed, a good deal of research on the news media is based on the unquestioned assumptions that they have (1) a monopoly of political information and opinion, and (2) that this gives them great power over mass attitudes and behaviour.

And yet common sense or not, there are grounds for questioning these two beliefs. Previous chapters show that the great majority of people in Britain do not follow the general election agendas of the mainstream media or of the main political parties. Most voters have their own agendas, and when the mass media and the parties are embroiled in their own interests the electorate blithely ignores them. Nor do newspaper have much, if any, effect on voting. Even the fallback position of reinforcement, which would count as a form of minimal power, fails to find convincing evidence, though it is not much researched.

This leaves us with a vacuum where explanations of mass political attitudes and behaviour as well as the role of the media are concerned.

If not the media, then what? This chapter explores a possible answer to this question based on the substantial weight of evidence in previous chapters that find the variables of the standard model of the social sciences are closely association with media consumption and with political attitudes and behaviour. The first part of the chapter discusses what the variables of the standard model stand for. The next, main part of the chapter is divided into two sections. The first of these discusses the importance of everyday life in formation of political attitudes and behaviour. The second part considers political talk as one aspect of everyday life that has been found to have a strong influence on political attitudes and voting behaviour and which may have a strong influence on how people interpret and understand the news they receive.

The Variables of the Standard Model Are Proxies

Previous chapters find that the standard model of the social science that explains a wide variety of social and political attitudes is also associated with both the news diets of individuals and the ways they react to the news they get. In other words, news media use and news media effects are not a special case for social science study but one part of a general pattern of social and political behaviours and attitudes that are associated with the general model. The model consists of demographic variables such as age, sex, income, education, social status, religion, ethnicity and, where politics is concerned, political interest and identity. Different combinations of these demographic variables are usually found to be associated more or less closely with different kinds of attitudes and behaviour with the implication that they are causes of them.

However, demographic variables are not, in and of their nature, causal variables. Age does not determine whether people vote or who they vote for. Most people do not decide to vote or not, or to vote for this party rather than another, because they are eighteen or eighty years old. Age, in this case, is a compact, convenient and easily measured proxy for the things that are commonly associated with age. Older citizens have ingrained habits, they have their own generational backgrounds and experiences, they generally know more and understand more about politics than younger age groups and they tend to have more time to give to the news. They live on pensions, not wages or salaries, and they are more likely to have paid off their mortgage and to have health issues and they are generally better off, all of which might affect their voting behaviour. The young often have a different set of political attitudes because they are at a different point in the life cycle and/or because they have a different set of life experiences.

Similarly, education in and of itself cannot explain voting behaviour. What is there about a physics degree, or an A-level in maths, or ten rather than two GCSEs that leads people to take more or less interest in politics and to vote for this or that party? Education is a proxy for the things commonly associated with it, including income and status, media literacy, a stronger interest in and knowledge of politics, an ability to understand how politics might have an impact on the life of individuals and political values. An education in the arts or humanities may encourage a more liberal and humanistic outlook, one in science and engineering may lead to a more technocratic approach to life, but this has nothing to do with voting or not voting and only a tenuous connection to the left–right dimension of voting.

In short, the variables of the standard model are indicators or proxies for the kinds of lives people live, the kinds of material and ideal interests they might have and the kinds of social and economic problems and advantages they might have. They also tell us something about the kinds of news media they are likely to attend to and the kinds of political attitudes and behaviour they are likely to have. Standard model variables are shorthand references to a large number of social and economic characteristics that tend to cluster around them in everyday life.

This is all vague, general and lacking in detail so what follows is an attempt to put some flesh on the bones by exploring what sorts of experiences matter and how they are associated with media use and effects.

Everyday Life

In the elections of 1987, 1997, 2001, 2005, 2010 and 2015 the main concerns of the electorate were different combinations of the economy and jobs, taxes, health, education, social services and sometimes housing and law and order. These are the main bread-and-butter issues citizens face in their daily lives. They involve the core public policies that affect them directly and the public services they use most

Everyday Life

frequently. Consequently, they are the issues by which government performance is mainly judged on polling day. This despite the emphasis placed at various times by the mainstream news media and the main political parties on the EU, corruption, internal party disputes, terrorism, overseas aid and occasional controversies about special events that flared up during the campaigns. Voters stuck to their main personal concerns and what they knew about first hand and valued the most.

Small wonder that an exhaustive study of the 2001 general election, *Political Choice in Britain*, barely mentions the media and concludes that

In Britain, as in other mature democracies, a strong economy characterized by vigorous growth, coupled with low rates of inflation and unemployment, universal access to high quality, affordable health-care and education, safe and efficient transport, a sound national defence, and low crime rates are prominent examples of things that virtually everyone values.[1]

Most adults have a strong and ever present concern with their household finances and family well-being. Some 11 million households have mortgages, another 5 million are private renters and 4.4 million are in social housing. More than 30 million pay income tax and 4.5 million self-employed people manage their own tax affairs. There are 12.5 million state pensioners. Officially there are 1.3 million unemployed people in UK, although 1.7 million say they want a job, 1.9 million are on employment and support allowance, 3 million on housing benefits and 5.9 million on Universal Credit. The total number of people claiming social benefits of one kind or another is 22.8 million. In the labour force, 197,000 are employed by the armed forces, 5.8 million are employed in the public sector, 3 million in central government, 2 million in local government and 450,000 are civil servants. The NHS employs roughly 1.5 million people.

There are 9 million school children in the UK of whom 1.5 million have special educational needs, but 7 per cent of the total population has been privately educated. In 2020, official sources reported 2.44 million children (aged 0–19) in absolute low income and 2.99 million in relative low income. In 2020 one million children lived in long-term

---

[1] Clarke, H., Saunders, D., Stewart, M. and Whiteley, P. 2004. *Political Choice in Britain*. Oxford: Oxford University Press: 326.

workless households. This means that there are millions of adults in the UK with first-hand experience of the living conditions of these children. According to research by Heriot-Watt University, 3.6 million people live in overcrowded homes, 5 million can't afford where they live or live with their parents against their wishes and 1.4 million live in substandard conditions. In 2020, 23 per cent of the privately rented housing sector failed to meet the Decent Homes Standard set by the government's Department for Communities and Local Government (14 per cent of owner-occupied homes). There are 14.6 million disabled people, 7.2 million on the hospital waiting list and a growing hidden backlog of individuals who would normally be referred for medical care. More than a million people live more than a mile from a bus stop. In 2020–2021 the police recorded 5.8 million crimes in England and Wales and in the UK that year adults (aged sixteen and over) experienced 9.1 million offences. Total household debt (excluding mortgages and equity releases) in the UK exceeds £120 billion. In 2021 there were approximately 111,000 personal insolvencies.

People in their millions pay taxes, depend on wages, salaries, pensions or state support, know about housing costs and rely in one way or another on social services and public facilities. They have all been to school and many now have, or have had, their own children or grandchildren in full-time education. Most have first- or second-hand experience of medical, dental and hospital services. Many know about unemployment, part-time employment or self-employment. Some are hit hard by inflation, interest rates, a rise in mortgage costs or negative equity. Most encounter potholes, the homeless, public transport, urban congestion, pollution, boarded-up shops and inner-city decay. Some have first-hand experience of police, fire, ambulance and pest control services. Most come across, or are aware of, dangerous roads and street crime. They get their passport and driving licence renewed, come into contact with street-level bureaucrats, their refuse is collected or not, their children or grandchildren use public playgrounds and they walk in public parks. The homes of some have been flooded. They come across expensive houses with luxury cars in the drive, and decaying row houses with wheelie bins and rubbish outside. They see collection points for food banks in their supermarkets and people selling the *Big Issue* in the streets. Millions are employed in public services and the military and know about working for them and the services they provide. If individuals have no first-hand experience of these things, they are highly likely to have someone in their close social circle who has and talks about how they really are.

Broadcast news about these matters is not projected onto blank screens devoid of previous knowledge and opinion. On the contrary, such matters are so deeply embedded in normal life that it is a rare individual who is not well acquainted with a range of them, is unconcerned about them and does not bring a lifetime's experience to the news about them. First- or second-hand experience of them provide a background knowledge of the state of the nation and for a basis for judgements about the effectiveness and efficiency of government and public services.

Personal experience is a benchmark by which to judge the news. It is said that everyone is an expert on education because they went to school and probably have children in the family there now. Similarly, millions are all 'experts' on health, housing, family finances and public services of many kinds because they use them to a greater or lesser extent. Some of us are 'experts' on unemployment, inflation, Universal Credit, the gig economy, minimum wage, dangerous streets, poverty, levelling up, rented accommodation, high-rise flats, urban blight, discrimination, pollution and austerity.

Although there is no UK research to turn to, it is possible, perhaps likely, that people prick up their ears about news items if they have close personal knowledge and experience of them. Teachers pay attention to news items about education, doctors about health and medicine, businesspeople about commerce and finance, shopkeepers about consumer trends, older people about pensions, students about university costs, people waiting for medical treatment about waiting lists, and so on. Those with a special interest in issues – global warming, social equality, animal rights, the EU, government and democracy – are likely to seek out news about them, take note when they come across them in the news media and accept or reject news about them according to their own views of the matter. In this way, everyday life has a power over what sort of news people get and how they evaluate it.

A study of how citizens acquire political information in the USA states that

[Voters] can and do apply to political decision making a great deal of information that they have acquired in their daily lives ... political information acquired when making individual economic decisions and navigating daily life: shoppers learn about inflation of retail prices; home buyers find out about trend in mortgage-loan interest rates; owners of stocks follow the Dow-Jones averages; people learn where it is safe to walk; and they learn about health and drugs. How and when this information is used remains to be shown.[2]

The last sentence in this quotation is an important sting in the tail. Thirty years after the publication of this book we still know little more about how, when and to what effect this information is used in the USA or the UK. But there are some hints.

Most people in the UK know whether inflation is rising, falling or constant, and know what the rate is within a few percentage points. For example, in December 2007 the British public thought inflation was 3.2 per cent and the actual figure was 2.08 per cent. Fast forward to May 2021 when the public thought inflation was running at 2.5 per cent and it was actually 2.1 per cent. In that year, 7 per cent thought costs had fallen in the previous twelve months, 66 per cent thought, correctly, that they had risen. They can learn about inflation from the media, of course, but it is unlikely that they could be this close to accuracy on any given random month if they depended only on the news media for their information, rather than getting a general feeling from the weekly changes in their household finances.[3] Time series analysis shows that higher inflation rates are associated with lower government approval ratings and reduced vote intentions for incumbent political parties.[4]

Official figures show a decline in crime in the UK over the past decade or so, and while most people generally overestimate the amount of it, the numbers overestimating it have declined from 84 per cent in 2009 in to 60 per cent in 2016. The accuracy of public perception of crime rates is far closer to the official figures when people are asked about local rather than national trends, perhaps because they have personal experience and knowledge of their own locality. Those with personal experience of crime are more likely to believe that crime is on

---

[2] Popkin, S. L. 1994. *The Reasoning Voter: Communication and Persuasion in Presidential Campaign.* Chicago and London: University of Chicago Press: 22, 24. I am grateful for an anonymous reviewer for pointing this book out to me.

[3] Official figures and mass opinion about inflation can be found in Rate Inflation, United Kingdom Inflation Rates: 1989 to 2023. www.rateinflation.com/inflation-rate/uk-historical-inflation-rate; Bank of England/Ipsos Inflation Attitudes Surveys.

[4] Scheve, K. Not dated. 'Public attitudes about inflation: A comparative analysis'. London: Bank of England.

the rise than those who have had no experience.[5] The point here is that people use their personal experience as a basis for judgements about government performance, not that these judgements are correct.

A British study of political culture confirms the importance of personal experiences of racial or sexual discrimination in raising commitment to the principles of liberty and equality. Similarly, those with negative experiences with the police are more likely to support the principle of liberty and to have a reduced confidence in the judicial system.[6] There is also evidence in other countries that everyday experience can supply us with information and impressions about national economic trends and developments. These are, by definition, aggregate phenomena about which individuals can have no direct, first-hand experience so it might be argued that they must rely on media information about gross national product and national unemployment and inflation rates. And yet, an American study finds that the performance of the national economy is a 'doorstep' issue that people come across without necessarily realising it, in the same way that we move from room to room across doorsteps without thinking about it.[7] This research finds that Americans who do not get any economic news are able to form a judgement about national economic performance and, moreover, their impressions are much the same as those who do get such news from the media. Those without economic news use their own household economies and what they see around them to form their impression. Those who attend to economic news use it and their own household economies to arrive at their judgements. There is not much difference between the two because information about the state of the national economy is all-pervasive and unavoidable.

In Sweden, personal experiences of public services have a direct impact on attitudes towards the welfare state and on more general matters of ideology and democracy.[8] What happens in other countries does not necessary occur in the UK, but it is worthwhile trying to find

---

[5] Office for National Statistics. Not dated. 'Public perceptions of crime in England and Wales: Year ending March 2016'. ONS.gov.uk.

[6] Miller, W., Timpson, A. and Lessnoff, M. 1996. *Political Culture in Contemporary Britain: People and Politicians, Principles and Practice*. Oxford: Oxford University Press: 330–363.

[7] Haller, H. and Norpoth, H. 1997. 'Reality bites: News exposure and economic opinion'. *Public Opinion Quarterly*, 61(1): 555–575.

[8] Kumlin, S. 2004. *The Personal and the Political: How Personal Welfare State Experiences Affect Political Trust and Ideology*. Basingstoke: Palgrave.

out whether it does and whether citizens are as dependent on the news media as is generally assumed.

Everyday life has a powerful effect precisely because it is everyday, because it is in-your-face and unavoidable, and because it involves the things closest to most people's hearts – family, friends, home, health and happiness. Political scandals may be interesting and amusing to read but they do not displace the immediate concerns and worries of the voters at election time. This helps to explain why the media do not set election agendas and do not have much influence over voting patterns, and why newspaper readers not infrequently nurture beliefs and values at odds with the paper they read. It also helps to explain why so many in the population are able to ignore or reject the messages they receive from the news media, unless those messages agree with their own material and ideal interests.

Everyday life is the background muzak of politics that is largely overlooked and ignored as a mediator of the news media and a force that conditions media effects, although it may be more important than the news media and deserves more research attention. It is, of course, accounted for in the standard model of political science in so far as variables such as age, sex, income, education, social status, political interests, partisanship and minority/majority group membership provide insight into the kinds of lives that people live.

Political Talk

Talking about politics with others is an integral part of everyday social life and it has consequences for political attitudes and behaviour as well as media effects. For present purposes, political talk involves the occasional and informal exchanges of comment, information and opinion that crop up from time to time in a spontaneous and disorganised fashion among networks of families, friends, neighbours and work colleagues.[9] This can take the form of face-to-face meetings or, increasingly, online communication.

An interest in the importance of political talk is not new. It goes back at least to the work of the French sociologist Gabriel Tarde and the

---

[9] Conover, P. and Miller, P. 2018. 'Taking everyday political talk seriously'. *The Oxford Handbook of Deliberative Democracy*. Oxford: Oxford University Press: 378–391.

British academic and statesman Lord Bryce, at the end of the nineteenth and the beginning of the twentieth century. They came independently to the view that conversation is vital to the process in which individuals first take information and opinion from newspapers, form an opinion about it, and then talk about it with friends and colleagues. This helps them clarify and organise their own thoughts and, by sharing them with others, helps to create public opinion. For this sifting and sorting of opinion to happen, Tarde believed that newspapers had to be compatible with the aims and principles of their readers, and Bryce was of the opinion that newspapers should be acceptable to the predilections of their readers. Both believed that newspapers were important for kicking off the process in which public opinion was formed but did not determine the outcome. Tarde and Bryce's accounts of the role of political talk comes close to Darnton's study of news dissemination in eighteenth-century Paris (Chapter 4).

An interest in political talk is also found in the Frankfurt School's writings on the public sphere but differs in that the public sphere is formal and public, discussion circles informal and usually private. The public sphere is more limited, probably to the chattering classes of educated, middle- and upper-class males; discussion circles and networks are more inclusive of friends, family and work colleagues. According to Habermas: 'A portion of the public sphere comes into being in every conversation in which private individuals assemble to form a public body.'[10] Discussion networks are not assembled but occur when individuals in private social circles meet and happen to talk about politics. In which case, they are probably far more frequent and more widespread than assemblies in the public sphere and are likely to involve much larger numbers of people drawn from more varied social backgrounds. Whereas the public sphere tends to be restricted to a minority of those with strong political interests, political talk is a fragmented, intermittent form of personal mass communication. If so, it may be more important than the public sphere for the sifting, sorting and consolidation of opinions and the creation of public opinion.

The importance of political talk is also at the heart of the work of Lazarsfeld and Katz in 1955, but differs from their work as

---

[10] Ginsborg, P. 2005. *The Politics of Everyday Life: Making Choices, Changing Lives*. New Haven, CT: Yale University Press: 135.

well.[11] They investigate the top-down flow of communication from opinion leaders who pass on their knowledge and opinion to the less politically interested and involved. Forty years later the pioneering work on discussion networks of Huckfeldt and Sprague investigated not a vertical, top-down process but a horizontal exchange between citizens as equals.[12] Political talk may include opinion leaders but they are not dependent on them and many may not have them.

Political talk is quite common in Britain. Studies conducted in 1987, 1992 and 2015 found that almost half the respondents to the surveys reported talking to their partner or spouse about politics, a quarter mentioned other family members and 30–40 per cent mentioned friends, neighbours and work colleagues.[13] A Hansard Society study in 2019 found that 30 per cent never talked to others about government and politics but 10 per cent do so every day, 22 per cent a few times a week and another 19 per cent a few times a month.[14] Another survey conducted during the EU referendum campaign found that three-fifths (61 per cent) said they had discussed the referendum with family members, 54 per cent had done so with friends, 27 per cent with colleagues, 18 per cent with others in their social circle and 8 per cent with others outside their social circle. One in five said they had not talked to anyone about the referendum.[15]

During the 2015 election campaign, four out of five respondents named at least one political discussant and two out of five named three, and the most frequently cited discussants were spouses, friends and relatives.[16] An in-depth study using interviews, a survey and diary-keeping comes to much the same conclusions. It finds that 85 per cent regularly talk politics with friends, 72 per cent with family and 55 per

---

[11] Katz, E. and Lazarsfeld, P. 2017. *Personal Influence: The Part Played by People in the Flow of Mass Communications*. London: Routledge.

[12] Huckfeldt, R. and Sprague, J. 1995. *Citizens, Politics and Social Communication: Information and Influence in an Election Campaign*. Cambridge: Cambridge University Press.

[13] Pattie, C. and Johnston, R. 2016. 'Talking with one voice? Conversation networks and political polarisation'. *The British Journal of Politics and International Relations*, 18(2): 482–497.

[14] Hansard Society. 2019. *Audit of Political Engagement No 16: The 2019 Report*. London: The Hansard Society: 27.

[15] Helm, T. 21 May 2016. 'Tory EU referendum voters are switching to remain, says poll'. *The Guardian*.

[16] Fieldhouse, E. 10 December 2014. 'Are we influenced by how our friends vote?'. britishelectionstudy.com.

cent with work colleagues.[17] Ofcom's *News Consumption Report 2022* states that 'word of mouth' was a source of news for 31 per cent of adults, placing it between radio (40 per cent) and printed newspapers (24 per cent), but far below TV (74 per cent).[18] Word of mouth is especially important for the 12–15-year-olds for whom talking with family was the most common way of finding out about the news (65 per cent) followed by TV (59 per cent). For this young age group, family, radio and TV are perceived as the most truthful news sources, while social media and friends are perceived to be the least. The young rely on their parents to indicate what is true and not true and what news sources to trust.

The central place of the family in political talk is consistent with what is known about political socialisation. In the words of Ginsborg: 'To a large extent they [families] shape the way in which individuals connect to the wider world.'[19] They are the place where information is exchanged, where political issues can be discussed safely and in private, and where political opinions can be shaped, tried and tested. They are also the central locations of the class, education, income, gender, ethnicity and political identities which are so important for political attitudes and opinions, as well as what news sources are used and how individuals react to them.

A problem with the survey figures for political discussion is that they rely on self-reported memory and what respondents include and exclude from the term 'politics'. Nevertheless, different surveys using different questionnaire wording on different groups in the population come to generally consistent conclusions. They show that the British talk to one another quite often about politics, as they do in other Western countries.[20] There are those who refuse to engage, but they seem to be a large minority, not the majority.[21] Most political talk occurs between people who know each other quite well and in private

---

[17] Couldrey, N. and Markham, T. 2006. 'Public connection through media consumption: Between oversocialization and de-socialization? *Annals of the American Academy of Political and Social Science*, 608(1): 251–269.

[18] Jigsaw Research. 21 July 2022. *News Consumption in the UK: 2022*. London: Ofcom: tables 2.4 and 13.2.

[19] Ginsborg, *The Politics of Everyday Life*, 91.

[20] Conover, P., Searing, D. and Crewe, I. 2002. 'The deliberative potential of political discussion'. *British Journal of Political Science*, 32(1): 21–62.

[21] Eliasoph, N., 1998. *Avoiding Politics: How Americans Produce Apathy in Everyday Life*. Cambridge: Cambridge University Press.

places, or among private groups in public places such as pubs. More important, discussion networks are usually mixed in their political composition. Pattie and Johnston's research covering surveys in 1987, 1992 and 2014 found that an average of 34 per cent over the three years included no party-political partisans, 16 per cent contained Conservatives, 14 per cent Labour, 3 per cent Liberal Democrats and 32 per cent were of mixed partisanship.[22] Another study finds that 72 per cent of Labour supporters had a fellow Labour supporter to talk to, while 66 per cent of Conservatives and 47 per cent of Liberal Democrats were similarly supported, compared with 38 per cent of UKIP voters.[23] On the whole it seems that some discussion circles are closed politically but most are open and mixed – another indication that many people live in a fairly pluralist world in which they get a fairly mixed political diet of news and opinions. As Pattie and Johnston put it: 'Despite the tendency for conversation networks to converge on similar positions, disagreement and political diversity persist.'[24] Most citizens get a fairly mixed news diet from the mainstream media and from their political talk as well.

Much of the research on discussion networks and politics is centred on voting in general elections, but the EU referendum campaign was a significantly different event. It was an issue that cut across party lines and involved complex economic issues, speculation about the future and no small amount of fake news. One might have expected the news media to have played a more important part in helping people make up their minds about such a controversial, unsettled and unclear issue, but the reverse seems to be true because voters relied somewhat more on their personal networks. Three out of four adults said that they based their voting decision primarily on discussion with family or friends, and those under twenty-four were twice as likely to be affected this way than the over sixty-fives.[25] It is possible that close family played a much larger role in the EU referendum, since casual observation

---

[22] Pattie, C. and Johnston, R. 2016. 'Talking with one voice? Conversation networks and political polarisation'. *The British Journal of Politics and International Relations*, 18(2): 482–497.
[23] Fieldhouse, 'Are we influenced by how our friends vote?'.
[24] Pattie and Johnston, 'Talking with one voice?', 496.
[25] Stamp, G. 1 May 2010. 'Election: How do friends and family influence votes?'. BBC, politics/election.

suggests that discussion between Brexiteers and Remainers was closed off by the reluctance of Brexiteers to talk with Remainers.

Conover, Searing and Crewe's comparison of the USA and the UK finds that most face-to-face discussion in the UK is about national political topics, rather than local or international ones, and that discussion circles mainly involve people who know each other well.[26] They are most likely to take place in the home but they are not infrequent at work, in church gatherings, with neighbours and in bars and pubs. Although money, social status and education do not affect who participates in political talk, women, the poor and the old tend to be excluded. The social norms of discussion are also important because while most people like hearing stories about the experiences of others and their opinions, argument about issues and the reasons for holding opinions are generally avoided. More than half (58 per cent) of political talk in Britain involves moderate disagreement but fewer than one in eight is highly contested.

Discussion increasingly takes place online and one study examines the content of three websites – Netmums, DigitalSpy and MoneySavingExpert – an approach that has the advantage of covering a large number of website members (3.6 million) over a four-year period that involved 115 million individual posts linked into 5.3 million threads of discussion.[27] None of the three websites were set up as dedicated political forums but politics emerged naturally out of other topics. Some of them were reactions to particular news items but they also arose out of personal experiences, demonstrating the main point of this chapter about the links people make between their everyday personal experience and the politics of the country as a whole. Compared with dedicated political websites, the discussion was less macho and competitive, more helpful and supportive. Almost a quarter of the threads of political discussion went beyond the passive discussion of public policy to propose solutions for action.

Political talk has consequences, two of which are of relevance to this book. First, the direct political consequences. According to Pattie and Johnston, in the 1992 election campaign 'social networks were indeed important influences on voting decisions. In particular, political

[26] Conover et al., 'The deliberative potential of political discussion'.
[27] Graham, T., Jackson, D. and Wright, S. 2015. 'From everyday conversation to political action: Talking austerity in online "third spaces"'. *European Journal of Communication*, 30(6): 648–665.

conversations formed a distinct context within which people evaluated the parties and decided who to support.'[28] Those without someone in their discussion circle to support their party choice are more likely to defect, and conversely, those with friends and family who support that choice increases the reinforcement effect.[29] Equally, the more homogeneous the politics of a discussion group the greater the tendency towards polarisation, the more their members shift towards radical views and the greater they see their differences from other parties. But it is important not to exaggerate the effect. It applies to a minority of the homogeneous groups and the effect is small. 'It polarises a bit but does not produce ideological ghettoes.'[30] Political talk can also result in political action, including signing petitions, consumer activism, writing to MPs, starting a campaign or protest and writing to the media.[31]

The second set of consequences concerns the ways in which news reports interact with discussion networks. Political talk supplies citizens with an alternative source of information and opinion that may complement or contradict the news they get from the media. They can use their own experience and those of others to form a grassroots impression of how well the government is performing. They can also compare what they know about their own lives and those around them with news reports and government pronouncements about the state of the nation. This is not to say that the impressions are accurate or that they apply to the country as a whole, only that news does not fall on empty minds or on individuals who have no other way of knowing what is going on. On the contrary, daily life and daily chat supplies individuals with information and opinion through which news reports are filtered and evaluated, accepted or rejected, absorbed or forgotten.

Research on the associations between discussion circles and media use and effects is relatively sparse in the UK, but American research suggests that interactions between the two are a fruitful line of research. One notable large-scale study of a presidential election finds that the influence of discussion circles was second only to partisanship

---

[28] Pattie and Johnston, 'Talking with one voice?', 62. See also Pattie C. and Johnston R. 2001. 'Talk as political context: conversation and electoral change in British elections, 1992–1997'. *Electoral Studies*, 20(1): 17–40.
[29] Fieldhouse, 'Are we influenced by how our friends vote?'.
[30] Pattie and Johnston, 'Talking with one voice?', 26
[31] Graham, 'From everyday conversation to political action'.

as an influence on voting.[32] Political parties and personal discussion were the most important carriers of partisan messages, and compared with them the influence of newspapers and TV news were weak and mixed. The study concludes that the powerful effects of personal discussion networks was one of its most significant findings.[33] The weakness of the media effects should not now be surprising.

Discussion

The politics of everyday life is a subject that falls neatly between the gaps between political science, sociology and media studies. Besides, everyday life is mundane and boring compared with the *Sturm und Drang* stirred up by fake news, the transformative powers of digital technology, the malign influence of social media, the dangers of algorithms, the power of a daily paper to swing an election and the attempts of foreign interests to influence British elections and referendums. Yet the indications are that commonplace personal experience and political talk may be powerful influences on political attitudes and behaviour, as well as powerful filters that condition media effects. They may help to explain why previous chapters have often found weak media effects on mass politics.

It is said that where politics are concerned, where you stand depends on where you sit. In which case, where you stand may depend on your view of the outside world when you sit and look through the window. What you see may be another run-down, multi-occupied building, a pleasant suburban garden or the rolling hills around your country house. The things encapsulated by these views are part of everyday life that are ever present, immediate, demanding of attention and inescapable, not something that can be switched on or off at will, like TV news, or like the paper that can be tossed aside, or the computer that shows something more agreeable at a click. What you see from your window will likely depend on your social grade, age, occupation, income, education, social background and ethnicity. In turn these

---

[32] Beck, P., Dalton, R., Greene, S. and Huckfeldt, R. 2002. 'The social calculus of voting: Interpersonal, media, and organizational influences on presidential choices'. *American Political Science Review*, 96(1): 57–73.

[33] See also Druckman, J., Levendusky, M. and McLain, A. 2018. 'No need to watch: How the effects of partisan media can spread via interpersonal discussions'. *American Journal of Political Science*, 62(1): 99–112.

determine the daily experiences that shape political attitudes, opinions and behaviour. Daily experience also exercises a strong influence on whether individuals access the news, how much they get, where they get it from and how they react to its reports.

Discussion circles, like daily life, may have both positive and negative effects. They can pass on information, misinformation and disinformation but they may also help people to learn the difference between them. They can help people sharpen up their ideas and bring them into contact with alternative ideas, but they may also confuse and complicate matters. They may highlight some issues but repress others. They may prompt action but equally their cross-pressures may demotivate as well. They may be inclusive of varied opinions from different people or exclude unwelcome ideas and certain sorts of people. They may bridge social and political divides but they may also polarise. Whether their effects are positive or negative seems to depend on whether they are politically mixed or homogeneous, political or non-political (of course), cross-pressuring or reinforcing.

There seems to be a contrast, perhaps a contradiction, between the influence of discussion circles in shaping and changing opinions and the conclusions of the belief preservation literature of experimental psychologists. Discussion circles research suggests that opinions are confirmed or modified by talking about them. Psychologists usually claim that beliefs are usually preserved. The difference is that discussion circles involve face-to-face talk with known others, the experiments usually involve written material in the form of made-up or real news and opinion pieces. There is a growing awareness of the importance of personal interaction by parties in election campaigns – doorstep campaigning rather than leafleting. Perhaps first-hand discussion can reach parts that written material cannot?

This chapter does not claim that we can do without the news media and rely wholly on personal experience and political talk, but it does argue that we are not totally dependent on the news media for political information and opinion. More than that, it may be that personal experience and talk are, as in the USA, a more important influence on public opinion than the news media. This is not to say that the opinions shaped by political talk are right or accurate or acceptable, only that political talk can play a part in their formation.

Discussion

Therefore, to understand citizen politics, ask not what paper is read or what websites are frequented, ask instead what is seen from the windows of the places people live in. This will say a lot about how individuals feel about politics, government and democracy, and how they feel will tell you a lot about whether they engage with politics or not and about how they react to the news they get. But a lot of research has yet to be done to be reasonably confident of that conclusion.

9 | *Pluralism and Democracy*

This chapter pulls together the findings of the previous chapters about the political effects of the British media. The empirical statements found here are based on the evidence produced in previous chapters, and, if necessary, the reader should refer back to them if the conclusions appear to be speculation produced like a rabbit out of a hat. First, the chapter examines the classical theory of a pluralist media which is the main, perhaps the only, general prescriptive theory of how a news system should be organised in a fully functioning democracy. For the past 150 years or so, pluralist theory has been the ideal by which to judge the democratic credentials of the news media system, but during this period, and especially since the emergence of a huge and diverse amount of online news, it has become increasingly clear that pluralist theory is no longer an adequate account of what an ideal news system should look like. At the same time, in the last half of the twentieth century it was increasingly claimed that the British news system failed to measure up to pluralist criteria, but it turns out that the media system, as a whole, is better at its job than is generally recognised. The task of this chapter is, first, to update pluralist theory and expand it to cover the things it neglects, and second, with these modifications in mind, to examine how well the British news system measures up to the ideal according to pluralist theory.

One serious obstacle in the second part of the chapter is lack of evidence. On the supply side there is now a countless and diverse number of news sources and little is known about many of them. On the demand side there are fifty-five million adults accessing different news from different sources and reacting to it in different ways, and there are big gaps in our knowledge of the choices they make and the effects of the media upon them. The result is that it is not possible to arrive at a grand theory of media effects or to produce a neatly tied parcel of cut-and-dried generalisation. But it is possible to arrive at a set of observations based on evidence, some of it well documented in many sources, some of it based on fewer but reliable studies

Pluralist Theory

Pluralist theory is the classic account of what is required of the news media in a democracy dating back at least to John Stuart Mill's defence of free speech in *On Liberty*. In the USA the theory took root with Justice Oliver Wendel Holmes statement that 'the best test of truth is the power of the thought to get itself accepted in the competition of the market'.[1] Pluralism's central tenet is that in a free society with free speech there should be many competing sources of news that present the public with different accounts of events and express a variety of political opinions about it. In this way an array of political interests will have a voice in the system and individuals will be presented with the information and a range of political opinion that enables them to make up their own minds. Free and open debate will allow truth to emerge from the push and pull of public discussion.

The essential feature of pluralist theory, therefore, is that the news media should be in many independent hands and not controlled by a monopoly or oligopoly of power, whether political or economic. Few would argue against that. But a closer look at pluralist theory shows that it is curiously underdeveloped in some respects, makes highly questionable assumptions and is silent on some important matters. One of the things it does not specify is how many news sources make a pluralist system, but this question has been outflanked by modern technology that has generated not a mere pluralism of news sources but a hyper-pluralism. The issue now is not how to guarantee the minimum number of different news sources necessary but how to deal with hundreds of thousands of them.

A more serious problem is that pluralist theory does not consider or mention the importance of reliable and trustworthy news. It assumes that events will be reported accurately, although they will be interpreted differently. The theory was born in the mid-nineteenth century, a time when misinformation was much more of a problem than

---

[1] Schultz, D. and Hudson, D. June 2017. 'Marketplace of ideas'. *The First Amendment Encyclopedia*. https://mtsu.edu/first-amendment/page/first-amendment-encyclopedia.

disinformation, and it argued that truth would somehow be clarified by the competition of ideas. In this respect, classical pluralist theory has a lot in common with the classical free market economic belief that competition between many producers is the most efficient way of producing the goods and services that consumers demand. Indeed, according to the Nobel Prize–winning, Chicago School economist, Ronald Coase, there is no difference between the market for goods and the market for ideas and they should both be organised along free market lines.[2]

Unfortunately, it is not possible to move so easily from classical free market economic theory to a pluralist free-speech contest for truth. The virtue of a free market, it is claimed, is its efficiency in satisfying consumer demand, which means that if people want junk food the supermarkets will produce it at a price that consumers are able and willing to pay. Similarly, if people want junk news in a pluralist system then commercial news organisations will produce it. And as quality news is often labour-intensive and expensive to produce, there are strong financial incentives to produce quick and dirty, if not junk, news. Since facts are expensive and opinions cheap, there is also an economic incentive to produce opinion rather than information. Perhaps that is why British tabloids are often more focused on opinion and persuasion than news and information, and since ideologues are often happy to give you their opinions for free, that is why the web is a hyper-pluralist domain of free market opinions, some of which are strongly contested, some misinformed and some almost certainly wrong. This does not clarify the truth but feeds people who do not want to hear it and confuses some of those who do. It is not possible to use the theory of free market economics as a model for a pluralist news media system that produces truth out of the competition of ideas.

There are other reasons why free market pluralist theory does not work. The free market economy is a way to allocate scarce goods and services and it is built around calculations about marginal costs and utilities. How do you calculate the marginal utility of reliable news compared with junk news? How do you compare the marginal utility of news that is free of government control with the state propaganda of a totalitarian dictatorship? Besides, scarcity plays a crucial role in

---

[2] Coase, R. H. 1974. 'The market for goods and the market for ideas'. *The American Economic Review*, 64(2): 384–391.

Pluralist Theory

economic theory whereas ideas, theories, information and news are not limited by scarcity. They are limitless in principle and, unlike raw materials, will continue to grow, probably exponentially.

News and opinion in the modern world are also fundamentally different from goods and services in another way. According to the Nobel Prize winner Paul Romer, ideas and information are different from physical goods in that they are 'non-rival', or shareable without limit.[3] If I buy a newspaper, a car or a house no one else can use them unless I sell, rent, lend or give it to them, and hence there is a market for scarce commodities. But if I 'consume' news on TV or online I am not limiting any number of people from doing the same thing. My watching TV news does not prevent ten or ten million others from watching it as well. In this respect, free-to-air news on TV, the radio and open-access websites are not scarce commodity goods and services that need markets to allocate resources and adjust supply and demand. What happens instead, in the absence of a Tim Berners-Lee, who gave away his idea of the World Wide Web, is that those who control non-rival resources turn them into market commodities by placing them behind licensing laws, cartels, pay walls, membership fees and patents. Once something becomes non-rival, Romer argues, imperfect competition becomes the norm when the creator of an idea, invention or information erects rules, laws and practices that turn them into a commercial entity.

Ideas, information and theories are also different from physical goods because in the digital era the cost of distributing and storing them have fallen steeply, sometimes close to zero. A TV show may be viewed by one or one million people for virtually the same production cost. The costs of producing quality news are rising but the costs of online distribution are falling, which is why it is in the interests of the print media to get everyone online. It is also why the number of political blogs, home-made websites and YouTube videos have escalated at a hitherto unimaginable speed. But the cost of closing down a TV studio or channel can be very high, whereas websites can be opened up, closed down or fall into disuse at little or no cost, so the result is a

---

[3] Romer, P. 1990. 'Endogenous growth and technical change'. *Journal of Political Economy*, 98(5), part 2: S71–102.

large turnover, which helps to explain why there are some 1.14 billion sites but only around 200 million active ones.[4]

Finally, the UK is a prime example of why pluralist theory, on its own, does not accurately describe the conditions of a democratic news system. Pluralism argues that a democracy requires a free market of many news sources because this is the only way of producing a diversity of news. This confuses pluralism (which refers to the number of news producers) with diversity (which refers to a range of political opinion). A common complaint about the national newspaper market in the UK is that it is dominated by Conservative papers and by a large market for four or five tabloids that are similar in content and style. A plurality of newspaper owners does not guarantee a diverse news content.

Nor can pluralism be measured simply by counting the number of independent news outlets. To count heads in this way is to treat the BBC as the equal of the *Daily Star* ('The home of fun stuff') and the *Sun* as the equal of the *Financial Times*. The difference between them is not only the amount of news they carry but also the way that they treat the news. Chapter 2 shows that public service TV and radio news in Britain are internally pluralist in the sense that they are required by content regulation in the public interest to be balanced, accurate and impartial. Maintaining balance, impartiality and accuracy is a tall order in a world of tight deadlines and dwindling resources, but even those who accuse the BBC of bias will probably recognise that its bias is of a different order to that of the tabloids and that its reporting is generally accurate and trustworthy. This makes BBC and ITV news the most highly trusted in the country. Critics of the broadsheets will similarly recognise the difference between them and the tabloids. In short, a pluralism of news does not guarantee a diversity of news and a diversity of news can be produced by relatively few internally pluralist news sources.

This not to say that a democracy can manage well enough with only one or two internally pluralist public service to provide the news, but it does say that pluralist theory is wrong to assume that (1) citizens can only get an overall perspective of news and opinion from a competitive

---

[4] Huss, N. 16 February 2023. 'How many websites are there in the world?'. siteefy.com.

commercial market, and (2) that a pluralism of news sources will produce a diversity of news.

The commercial market in the UK also supports a set of newspapers of record, a phrase that implies internal pluralism and reliability even when it is mixed with a degree of partisanship. It is possible to separate news and opinion. Critics of the broadsheets will probably recognise that for all their 'faults' they are different from the tabloids. The existence of broadsheet papers shows that a commercial market does not necessarily or inevitably produce news that is biased in the interests of the business class that controls it. There is a demand for impartial news and the broadsheets are one way of trying to satisfy it. Critics of the commercial sector are wrong to assume that it only produces biased news.

The UK's newspapers of record are an important part of the mixed public–private system because, although they have comparatively small circulations, they probably punch above their weight among decision makers and the politically interested and active. This is partly because of their trustworthy news, and also because of their investigative journalism that produces stories of national importance that are followed up in other parts of the news. Their significance is also recognised by online news aggregators who use them to curate their own material.

Overall, the British news system approaches the ideal of pluralism at least on the supply side, but not for the reasons that either pluralist theory or classic free market theory suggests. Its pluralism lies in its mixture of partisan and internally pluralist content, in a mixture of public service and commercial media, and in a mix of these in the TV, radio, print and online sectors that results in a vast number of news producers of many kinds and content.

This brings us to the main oversight of pluralist theory which has nothing to say about the demand side of news consumers. In the same way that the theory of perfect competition assumes that consumers have a full knowledge of the market, so pluralist theory assumes that individual citizens will use the pluralist news system to acquire all the necessary information and understanding of politics to play their role as engaged citizens. This is plainly utopian. Most people are not greatly concerned with politics and do not devote much time to informing themselves about them. Most take short cuts, work with gut feelings rather than knowledge and understanding and rely on a few news sources they trust or trust more than others. Given this reality, what many members of the public want is not a hyper-pluralist system but one or two reliable and impartial sources that provides them with what they want to know for the lowest cost and least time and effort.

There is a further problem. The idea that truth will emerge from a free market for ideas ignores all that we know about belief preservation and the way in which individuals can accept, ignore, reject or avoid any given media message according to their pre-existing beliefs and opinions. Truth does not necessarily emerge from the free competition of ideas and the fact that this idea persists, contrary to a great weight of evidence, is another example of belief preservation. As Frederick Schauer, a distinguished professor of law at the University of Virginia and a leading scholar of the First Amendment of the Constitution of the United States, puts it: 'Indeed, the persistence of the belief that a good remedy for false speech is more speech, or that truth will prevail in the long run, may itself be an example of the resistance of false factual propositions to argument and counter example.'[5]

The British Media and Democracy

How does the British news system measure up to the demands of pluralist theory and, more to the point, how does it measure up to the demands of a news system in a democracy in the digital age with a huge mixture of commercial and public service news? In answering this question it is as well start with what the system does not do, given all the myths about it. At present there is a strong feeling that the British media are a powerful force that undermines democracy. This is often asserted by politicians, public intellectuals, members of the general public and media researchers alike, and their list of complaints is long: the media have a monopoly of news and thereby exercise a powerful influence over what ordinary citizens know and think about politics and how they behave politically; the commercial mass media are biased in the interests of the big businesses that own and control them; by concentrating on bad news the media are responsible for a mean world effect in which trust in politicians, democratic institutions and democracy itself is eroded; the result is a decline in political interest and

---

[5] Schauer, F. 2012. 'Facts and the First Amendment'. *UCLA Law Review*, 57 (4): 910–911.

participation and spreading alienation and disillusionment; the growth of radical and extremist opinion on the web is helping to polarise political opinion; the media are aiding and abetting the spread of populism; online news and social media are assisting the fragmentation and instability of politics; social media spread disinformation, conspiracy theories and fake news; the hyper-pluralism of the modern news system makes it easy for individuals to create echo chambers of opinion for themselves. The next section deals with these claims.

What the News Media Do and Do Not Do

A large body of commentary and research of media effects is based on the claim or assumption that the news media exercise a great deal of influence, or outright power, over the hearts and minds of the population. The first and most general point is that a large body of evidence shows that neither the mainstream media in general, nor the news media in particular, have strong or negative effects on the political attitudes and behaviour of the population. While some absorb and act upon media messages, large numbers and sometimes majorities of the population ignore or reject these messages. At the same time large numbers, often large majorities, nurture beliefs for which there is little, if any, support in the mainstream media. Can we continue to believe that the mainstream media wield a powerful influence over popular beliefs and behaviour when, contrary to a steady drum-beat of information issued over decades, large numbers are obese, fail to take healthy exercise, smoke, abuse alcohol and drugs, and believe in conspiracy theories of many different kinds. And how can we reconcile the idea of a powerful media with the beliefs of millions in ghosts, telepathy, a secret cabal that controls the world, communication with the dead, contact with space aliens, voodoo science, fake history and quack medicine when such things are rarely mentioned in the mainstream media, never mind supported by them. These observations suggest some modification, at least, of the claims made for media power.

Evidence shows that different people can and do draw different conclusions from the same media message. Some accepted their newspaper's views on the EU referendum, others rejected it. Some agree with their newspaper's party-political endorsement on election day, others do not. Some believed that leaving the EU would mean an extra

£350 million for the NHS, but that entailed ignoring or denying evidence reported in the news that it was not true. Equally, the same person can draw different conclusions from the same message found in different sources. They might believe something stated on BBC News or in the paper they choose to read, but disbelieve it if it appeared in a paper or website they do not trust. Others may reject the mainstream news in favour of alternative websites. These observations suggest, at the very least, that a large part of media effects turn on how audiences respond to the messages they receive – that media effects are not media effects alone, but the result of an interaction between the media and their audiences in which individuals choose to avoid, ignore, reject or agree with any given media message.

Substantial support for these conclusions is found in an accumulation of experimental psychology research that explores what is variously called belief preservation, heuristics or motivated reasoning. This finds that individuals have a capacity to persist with their beliefs even if they are presented with evidence, argument and simple logic showing they are false. Some of the mental mechanisms that enable individuals to protect their beliefs are discussed in previous chapters, including confirmation and disconfirmation bias, selective perception, the boomerang effect, the Lake Wobegon effect, the Dunning–Kruger effect and the hedgehog effect found among expert political advisers. In ordinary language we give examples of belief preservation when we say that people are in denial, that they will not listen, that it is like talking to a brick wall or that they are as stubborn as a mule. Somehow, however, most media effects research has managed to overlook, ignore or deny both the voluminous experimental research and the commonplace observations about others, although to its credit, it has made its own contribution to belief preservation literature with the hostile media effect that allows partisans to reject impartial news because they believe it to be hostile to their own beliefs.

Trust is another overarching factor that can either enhance or diminish media effects. It varies between TV, radio, print and online news, being relatively high for public service TV and much lower for online and social media news. If trust in a news source is an essential precondition for its influence, as psychologists claim, then public service TV and radio and the newspapers of record are likely to be more influential than the tabloids and distrusted social media. The irony is that the most trusted news sources are those that present the most accurate, balanced and impartial accounts of events, and the least trusted are those that are the most partisan in their presentation of the news. It seems that the more a news source tries to persuade the less successful it is likely to be, unless it is preaching to the converted.

It is not uncommon for individuals to preserve their partisan attachments and political beliefs while reading a paper that supports an opposing camp. There is little evidence that the *Sun* had much effect on the 1992 election when it claimed to have won it for the Conservatives, and no more evidence that it had any effect in the next election when it swung its support from the Conservatives to Labour. For that matter, repeated attempts by the country's best experts on voting behaviour have failed to find much, if any, evidence of a newspaper effect on party voting, although they have found other effects discussed later. A second irony is those most of those interested in politics are likely to have stronger opinions about them and are the least likely to be persuaded otherwise by the news and opinion they get from the media. Those least interested in politics do not seek out the news and are unlikely to be much influenced by it. Or perhaps it is the other way round for them: the less interested and knowledgeable are more likely to be influenced by whatever news they might come across. We do not know.

Research on newspaper effects has sometimes fallen back on the argument that they might have a reinforcing effect on party identifiers. In the much-studied 1997 election there is no evidence of reinforcement, but on the contrary the *Mail*, *Telegraph* and *Express*, the only faithful Conservative papers in that election, registered a larger than average swing against the Conservative Party and a larger than average swing to Labour. This appears to be the result of the papers having a larger than average pool of Tory voters who could, in line with the country as a whole, swing against an unpopular Conservative government and to Labour.

Nor is there evidence that the news media are able to set election agendas for British voters. In the general elections of 1987, 1997, 2001, 2005, 2015 and 2019 electors stuck to a common and fairly consistent set of concerns of their own. They remained unaffected by deviations from these on the part of the press and the parties, of which there were quite a few.

At various times the British media have been held responsible for the Brexit vote, for party voting in general elections and for the rise of populist politics, but there is little hard evidence to support these claims. Leavers and Remainers were divided mainly along the lines of age and education, not the papers they read. Similarly, voting patterns in the 2019 general election followed demographic contours, not newspaper positions, and the same is generally true of populist and non-populist sympathisers. In fact, voting patterns in the referendum, the 2019 election and the distribution of populist beliefs follow similar demographic lines, not the newspaper read.

In recent years attention has switched from the legacy media to new digital media. New media technology in the past has often produced exaggerated speculation about its impacts, and this is especially true of the massive explosion of digital communications. In its early days, digital optimists believed that the web would introduce the young and previously apolitical to news and opinion, create a new group of citizen journalists and act as an open and democratic forum for political discussion. That has now been submerged by concerns about fake news, alternative websites, conspiracy theories, populism, self-reinforcing echo chambers of political opinion, algorithms, foreign bots and social media. These are assumed to have a powerful effect on some individuals, especially the young and impressionable, and to have a general effect of fragmenting and destabilising the political system with their populist and extremist politics.

This is mainly speculation because there is little information about the political content of most alternative online news, and virtually no hard research on its effects on individuals. What we do know suggests that, in most cases, the amount and reach of mainstream news heavily exceeds those of fake news and alternative websites. There is also little evidence of a spread of echo chambers but, on the contrary, robust evidence in the UK and the USA of a surprisingly large amount of cross-media traffic involving a mixture of different partisan news sources. Also surprising, and inconsistent with claims about echo chambers and the effects of algorithms, is the finding that people who go online for news come across more news sites than those who go straight to the favoured, trusted newspaper or TV news. Some tread the straight and narrow path from the *Times*, *Guardian* or *Telegraph* to the BBC, ITV or Channel 4 and back, but those who use search engines, news aggregators and shared online news come across more news sites and more diverse ones.

Given this, and the online reach of the legacy media, the evidence that the new media are contributing to political fragmentation, polarisation and destabilisation looks remarkably thin. Radicals and extremists do use digital technology to organise themselves, as do other political groups and parties, but so far there is a lack of evidence that individuals are converted to their points of view simply by viewing YouTube material or coming across webpages. It seems more likely that those with radical and extremist tendencies are seeking out alternative sources of opinion that confirm their opinions. Radical and alternative websites are more of a symptom than a cause of politicisation, conspiracy theories, populism and extremist politics.

Even the youngest age group in the population still gets most of its news from the BBC and older groups get much more from the BBC and other mainstream TV channels governed by public service rules. This helps to explain why, in spite of the publicity given to fake news and disinformation about Covid, the great majority of the population was correctly informed about it and acted accordingly. A minority seems to have drawn the wrong conclusions from the information, and others believed the disinformation despite the daily bombardment of information from the mainstream media.

It does not follow that there is no need for concern about fake news, conspiracy theories and disinformation, but it does mean that this concern should be set in the context of widespread distrust of social media news on alternative websites, the vastly larger amount of mainstream news that reaches the public and the weight of research showing that opinions are not readily influenced by information and opinions that appear in the news, whether mainstream or alternative.

Last, there is little evidence to support theories of the mean world effect and media malaise. Those who pay the most attention to the news do not generally show signs of alienation, political distrust, cynicism, fear, low personal competence, disengagement or disillusionment with democracy or its institutions or its leaders. If there is a mean world effect it is associated, if anything, with entertainment TV, but it is not clear which, of the many different kinds of entertainment TV, are responsible for this. It is unlikely to be the most popular programmes, which are soap operas, sport, romcoms, reality shows, sitcoms, drama and nature programmes. It is possible that crime, war, disaster, mystery and supernatural films might do the damage but, as in all media effects research, there is the cause-and-effect problem: does this sort of content provoke mean world effects or do people who are not afraid, distrustful or alienated seek it out as harmless entertainment? We are left with the conclusion that the mean world and bad news effects are mainly the product of the real world and the different ways in which it impacts on different individuals.

There is no question that the digital media has had a huge impact on many social patterns, from the number of times that people check their iPhones to the almost instantaneous communication of the latest news to tens of millions of individuals. There is no question that the web and social media contain deeply disturbing content, but content and effects are different matters and this book is about political effects. The best research we have about online news at present is that its political effects are most likely to be heavily outweighed by the legacy media of TV, radio and printed matter, much of which can be found online. Such media effects that have been found are mainly rather small, but positive rather than negative.

If Not the Media, then What?

So far, we have found few indications of media power or influence. This is not the end of the story and the rest is picked up later in this chapter, but meanwhile it is reasonable to ask the question: if it is not the media then what is it? The answer is that there is a coherent alternative explanation of mass attitudes and behaviour that fits the facts, so far as we know them at present.

We can start with the British agenda-setting research on a series of six general elections since 1987. This finds that the items most frequently found at the top of voter agendas are not those of either the media or the parties but relate to the individual and family concerns of taxes, education, health, housing and the economy, with Brexit and immigration/asylum seeking appearing in recent years. When attention is turned to party voting in elections, we find that it is not associated with newspaper reading but with individual demographic variables, often those of age, sex, education, income, social grade and ethnicity. These, plus a few others closely associated with them, have been found so often in other research on a wide variety of attitudes and behaviour that they have become the default *modus operandi* of behavioural studies – its standard model. When the standard model is applied in media effects research one or more of the variables in the standard model usually outrank media and usually (not always) reduce media variables to statistical insignificance.

A third approach complements the conclusions of agenda-setting and voting research. It suggests that the knowledge and experience accumulated in ordinary, everyday life have a direct effect on political attitudes and behaviour. This topic is largely unexplored at present, but what there is indicates that first-hand experience of a wide range of public services and government policies provides individuals with a strong impression of how well the government is performing. Personal knowledge and experience of this kind acts as a reality test of what politicians and the media are saying and creates the foundation for attitudes towards politics and the political system and an evaluation of the parties and their leaders. In most cases, the most important concerns are those of individual and family life – health, education, housing, income, social services, taxes and the state of the national economy – but daily life also brings people into contact with a wide range of other issues and public policies ranging from potholes and public parks, to pollution and playgrounds.

Many have regular personal knowledge and experience of these matters, and those who do not will probably know someone who does and talk about them in normal interactions with friends, colleagues, neighbours and family members. Political talk of an occasional and random nature has been shown in both American and British studies to have a direct impact on voting behaviour. The fact that it is first hand, rather than processed second-hand through the media, may reinforce its influence.

Agendas, voting and a wide variety of political attitudes and behaviour can all be traced back to the standard model of demographic variables. The variables in and of themselves are not important but they serve as useful indicators of a set of social and economic circumstances in everyday life. Income on its own tells us little about a person's politics, but it is often a powerful variable in research because of the things that usually – not always – go with wealth or poverty and the graduations in between. Similarly, age, as such, is independent of politics, but older groups probably worry less about education, mortgages and wages, and more about pensions and health. Those with young families are likely to focus on education, childcare, wages, taxes and inflation. Ethnic minorities are concerned about discrimination and equality, and the young are often more worried about global warming and Brexit than older age groups. In short, the variables of the standard model are important because they are general indicators of the everyday living conditions and circumstances that are generally associated with political attitudes and behaviour. The news does not fall upon blank minds. It is received by people with backgrounds that are layered with impressions, memories, encounters with the hard facts of routine life and the stories and comments of others, upon which they build a view of the political world.

What the Media Do

The first thing to note about the British news is the large role played by public service TV and radio. Audiences for TV news are declining but BBC 1 remained the most important single source of news in the country in 2021, with a 53 per cent reach across the adult population. The next largest was ITV with 35 per cent. The BBC News Channel, BBC website, Channel 4, BBC 2 and Channel 5 are all in the top-twenty news sources in the country. Public service radio also figures largely in the news landscape, with BBC 1, 2 and 4 featuring in the top twenty. Sizeable proportions of the population also watch BBC and ITV local and regional news.

Compared with the commercial sector, public service differs in the amount and content of the news it delivers. It broadcasts news more frequently throughout the day, sometimes in brief news headlines, sometimes with in-depth programmes and sometimes at peak viewing and listening hours when commercial channels are more likely to feature popular entertainment programmes. It contains more hard information and less soft news than the commercial sector. Public service TV news is also the most highly trusted source of news in the country, which helps to explain why it is the most widely used. Trust and ease of access via TV, radio and the web help to create a news-rich environment that enables people to fit the news into their daily routines. It also means that many who are less interested in politics will fall into the news because the radio or TV is on. This helps to explain why most of those who rely on only one source of news get it from the BBC.

The result of this news-rich environment is a smaller knowledge gap between the well informed and poorly informed. It has also been found that the kinder, gentler and more inclusive content of public service TV in Europe helps to create a more trusting and inclusive civic culture. Whereas the audiences for most other news sources are divided along demographic lines, the BBC reaches a large cross-section of the entire population, thereby contributing (as it was set up to do) to social integration rather than fragmentation and division. The effects are not strong compared with the demographic variables of the standard model but they have been found consistently across the public service systems of western Europe. How well informed about politics citizens are is not just a function of their individual characteristics but also of the media system they live in.

The second thing to note is that, while they seem to have little if any effect on party-political attitudes, party voting and popular election agendas, the news media have small but positive associations with some political attitudes and behaviour. Other things being equal, those who pay most attention to the news are likely to be better informed and more positive in their attitudes towards political leaders, governments, political institutions and democracy. They are also more likely to engage in political life and to vote in elections. The effects are rather stronger for newspapers than TV, but contrary to some suggestions, they also apply to those who fall into TV news as well as those who seek it out.

The American writer Neil Postman believed that TV can only amuse us to death and that only by reading can we learn and understand. He was half right. People learn more from reading than watching, and they learn more from a quality paper than a tabloid, but they also learn, though less, from TV news. In part this is because the more highly educated prefer to read than to watch, but holding education constant there is still a newspaper effect and, as one would expect, a stronger broadsheet than tabloid effect. Nevertheless, *Sun* readers claim to watch more TV news than *Guardian* readers, and the TV habit shows in their political knowledge. Once again, we can only understand *Sun* effects in the context of its readers' broader news diets.

According to Marshall McLuhan, it is not the content of a medium that matters but the kind of medium it is, which means that 'the medium is the message'. Research shows, however, that how much is learned from newspapers depends on whether it is a broadsheet or a tabloid – same medium, different content. Similarly, how much is learned from the TV or radio depends on whether it is from brief headline news or long, in-depth discussion and analysis – same medium, different amounts and different content. Radio news is probably the same as TV although much less is known about it. All three mediums are similar in that they help people learn about and understand politics, but how much is learned depends not so much on the medium as on its content and how much news it provides. In other words, the medium is not the message: the message is the message. Since it is also the case that individuals have their own way of interpreting and reacting to any given message, we can add a rider to the statement that the message is the message. This now reads: 'The medium is not the message; the message is the message and the message is what people make of it.'

The main political effects of the media, therefore, seem to be informing people and encouraging positive attitudes towards the political system, rather than the more common assumption that they influence voting and party-political attitudes. The positive effects include political attitudes and behaviour that are the opposite of those posed by mean world and bad news theories.

The third main thing to note about the UK's news media system is more speculative than the previous two. In general, individuals with strong partisan views about politics are least likely to change their views in response to media influences. They are more likely to demonstrate belief preservation and the hostile media effect because they are strongly attached to views about matters of importance to them – sometimes about other matters as well. In which case the media may exercise more influence on new issues that have not yet become clear-cut matters of public opinion and which are not clearly attached to party-political beliefs and policies. The same may also be true of technical and scientific news that are different in kind from the ideological issues that divide the parties. These might include such things as economic theory, fiscal policy and trade deals, the organisation and funding of the NHS and the pros and cons of foundation and grammar schools. They are also likely to include matters of foreign policy that are remote from everyday domestic life and concern countries about which most people know little. In this respect there is an important difference between opinion formation and opinion change. The news media are much less likely to change opinions that are already well formed, and more likely to form opinions about new and technical matters that are not sifted, sorted and mulled over by public opinion. Since research finds that people are inclined to stick with the first information they receive, even if it is subsequently found to be false, the media may exercise more influence at the very beginning of a public debate rather than later on.

Trust also plays a part. It involves taking a risk that a news source is likely to be accurate and impartial in its reporting on any given issues. If so, individuals who know nothing about the issue and have no personal experience of it may be willing to take a short-cut and accept the reports of news sources they trust. This is an example of the interaction between news producers and audiences in that it may result in media influence, but only if the audience is prepared to trust the source. The evidence is that they are most likely to trust the public services and broadsheet papers because they have proved themselves to be trustworthy. Influence depends on trust and trust has to be earned. This suggestion is supported by the finding that the economic news of broadsheet papers, which are more highly trusted, can exercise a modest but persistent influence on their readers than the distrusted tabloids.[6]

Discussion

It must not be forgotten that there are problems with media effects research that are not easily overcome. The difficulties of isolating causes and effects, a lack of clarity about what exactly is meant by news, the possibility that questionnaires about news consumption produce unreliable and inflated responses, and a severe lack of data about many aspects of the news media all contribute to a research area that requires great caution in drawing firm conclusions. Unfortunately, a lack of evidence seems to encourage strong views about the news media and much speculation, plausible or implausible, about their effects.

The phrase 'media effects' is itself a bit of a booby trap because it encourages broad generalisations about 'the media', whereas there is no such thing, only a vast and sprawling array of different news providers sending out mixed, contradictory and confusing messages. Nor is there such a thing as mass opinion, but a multifarious assortment of different and conflicting opinions. This means that any

---

[6] Gavin, N. and Sanders, D. 2003. 'The press and its influence on British political attitudes under New Labour'. *Political Studies*, 51(3): 573–591.

statement about 'media effects' is likely to be wrong, at least in some respects if not in all of them. Research that considers the effects of any one part of the landscape to the exclusion of all the others is likely to be misleading, and research that considers only one side of the supply and demand equation, not how they interact, is likely to be similarly misleading.

It is usual to finish a research publication by saying that it raises more questions than answers and that 'more research is needed'. That is certainly the case with this book, given that one of its constant refrains is lack of evidence. It is possible, however, to take the next step and point out areas of research that might be productive. First, news diets are crucial for an understanding of what news people get from what kinds of sources. This is the core of the demand side of pluralist theory, and with a few notable exceptions it is an area of research that has been largely neglected.

Second, there are indications (little more) that the experiences of daily life play an important role in the formation of political opinion about both particular public policy issues and more general beliefs about the value of democracy, the effectiveness of government institutions and abstract issues of equality and justice. More is known about the impact of political talk, but there are still many unanswered questions about that.

Third, survey research needs to sort out the matter of what 'news' means in the minds of respondents and be clear when they are talking about political or other news. For that matter, what does it mean when people say they read a paper? Do they glance at the headlines before turning to sport? When they watch TV news are they really waiting for the latest scores or the weather to come up, or perhaps flicking though their iPhones, or talking to someone?

Fourth, radio and the web are black holes in research. We know little about how much or what kind of news is broadcast on the radio, although we know that large sections of the population listen to it as part of their daily routine. Some trust it highly as a source of information. And then there are tens of thousands of political webpages and online blogs and videos with an unknown content and an unknown audience.

The answers to these questions are not merely of importance to academics who are said to live in ivory towers. They are of real importance for practical politics as well, as we will see from Chapter 10.

10 | *Practical Lessons*

The power of the news media is one of those old myths that keep on coming back no matter how much evidence is piled up against it. It is a recurring myth because it is easy, convenient and satisfying to blame the media for anything that troubles modern politics. It is easy because the media are always there to play the part of scapegoat and because the conduct and content of sections of the British media invite blame and criticism. In 1991 the national heritage minister, David Mellor, was so angered by the way that parts of the press had behaved that he announced they were 'drinking in the last chance saloon', and that the 'sacred cow' of press freedom should be controlled in order to limit their extreme – and, as it turned out, illegal – activities. They had been drinking freely in that saloon for decades before and they continued to drink there unhindered afterwards. It is made easy by the media themselves because tabloid headlines are designed to attract attention and because blaming the media is so common that blaming them one more time is just repeating conventional wisdom.

It is convenient to blame the media because it requires no further thought about the real causes of problems. TV, the tabloids and social media are responsible, it is confidently stated, for obesity, football hooliganism, poor English grammar, dumbing down, copycat crimes, violence, materialism, fake news, road rage, loss of social capital, right- and left-wing extremism, conspiracy theories, terrorism, sexism, racism, populism, political alienation and apathy, Brexit, fear and the young and impressionable being led astray in multifarious ways. Those with minority political beliefs find it is especially convenient to blame the media. They need to explain why their own beliefs are not shared by a large majority of others, and the easy answer is they are fooled and brainwashed by the media. The irony is that those in the mainstream of politics blame alternative websites, fake news and social media for political extremism, while those with alternative views blame the mainstream media for hoodwinking the masses.

It is satisfying to blame the media because this massages the ego. The assertion that others believe what they read in the paper is a self-congratulatory way of stating that the speaker is so much better than others who are too stupid and ignorant to do anything else. An Ipsos MORI poll in 2018 found that 70 per cent of the population agreed with the statement that others live in internet bubbles because they were looking for opinions they already agreed with. Only 30 per cent agreed that they did this. While 28 per cent believed that others can tell real news from fake news, 66 per cent were confident about their own ability to do so and 56 per cent admitted that they were better at spotting fake news than the average person.[1] These are more examples of the Lake Wobegon effect.

'People have a basic desire to feel good about themselves.'[2] What better way of doing this than pointing out how defective others are, but to do so is to evade the real causes and, therefore, ignore real solutions. As long as we blame the media for the things that are rooted in social, economic and political conditions we will never be able to tackle those conditions in a constructive way. Chapter 7, for example, shows that the decline of political trust, confidence and participation and the rise of political cynicism, alienation and disengagement are linked not to the media but to real economic and government trends in this country and globally. Blaming the media in this case is simply a distraction from real problems.

Another example, by way of illustration, is the way that social media are blamed for all sorts of things, including the troubles of young people in the UK with bullying, self-harm, poor health, worry about studies and exams, poor mental health, difficulties with friends and family, body image anxieties, uncertainty about the future and even suicides. Harmful social media effects may well play a part in explaining some of these, but they are not the whole story or even the most important part of it.

UNICEFS's most recent study, 'Worlds of Influence: Understanding What Shapes Child Well-being in Rich Countries', shows how poorly Britain's young fare compared to similar countries.[3] Using thirty-one

---

[1] Ipsos. 2018. 'Fake news, post-truth and filter bubbles'. London: Ipsos.
[2] Mlodinow, L. 2012. *Subliminal: The Revolution of the New Unconscious and What It Teaches Us about Ourselves*. London: Penguin: 19.
[3] UNICEF Innocenti. 2020. 'Worlds of influence: Understanding what shapes child well-being in rich countries'. Florence: UNICEF Office of Research, Innocenti Report Card 16.

indicators of well-being, it finds that Great Britain ranks 27th of forty-one countries on all these measures, just below the Republic of Korea and Hungary. It ranks 39th on life satisfaction, 34th on the social context of well-being, 29th on mental well-being, 28th on obesity, 26th on academic proficiency and social skills and 19th on physical health. There is no evidence that these rankings are associated with social media effects in Britain or that British children are affected by social media any more than the children of other rich countries. However, Britain is also well below average or towards the bottom of the forty-one country rankings for its public policies relating to social, educational and health matters and none of these are associated in any direct way with social media content. Nor are Britain's above average figures for poverty and inequality, the percentage of 15–19-year-olds out of school and parents who work long hours and have difficulties meeting their responsibilities for their children attributable to social media effects.

Poverty is a key matter associated with a broad spread of long-lasting problems that persist across generations. According to official statistics for 2019–2020, the estimated percentage of children in Britain living in absolute poverty before housing costs are taken into account was 17 per cent, and after housing costs are included it rises to 26 per cent.[4] These statistics must be put down to economic and political causes, not the media or social media. The longer this is not recognised the longer the problems will persist.

Political Leaders and the Media

Politicians have their own special reasons for believing in media power. They cannot control most of the things that affect their political plans, policies and careers because these are directed by global economics, natural disasters, foreign governments, the previous governments in their own country and by the vagaries of public opinion. Asked what he thought were the biggest challenges for statesmen, Harold Macmillan was reputed to have replied: 'Events, dear boy, events.' One of the few things they believe they can control is how they are

[4] Department for Work and Pensions, 25 March 2021. 'Households below average income: For financial years ending 1995 to 2020'. London: Gov UK, National Statistics, Welfare.

presented in the morning papers, but only if they spend a lot of time, trouble and taxpayers' money on press releases, spin doctors and damage limitation.

In his book *Who Governs Britain*, Anthony King writes: 'Why do party leaders take newspapers – especially the *Mail* and the *Sun* – and some other media so seriously, sometimes to the point of appearing craven in their dealings with them?'[5] The word 'craven' stands out, presumably as intended, in a book that is balanced, detached and analytical. A large part of the answer, perhaps the most part of it, involves the fact that if people believe that something is true, it will have real consequences, even if it is untrue. So it is with our political leaders. Their belief that the media are powerful leads them to think and behave as if the media are powerful.

In January 1981 the prime minister, Margaret Thatcher, had a meeting with the *Sun*'s owner Rupert Murdoch at Chequers just three weeks before Murdoch made his successful bid to buy the *Times* and the *Sunday Times*. The meeting was secret at the time and flatly denied for the next thirty years, but was revealed in 2012 when documents released by the Thatcher Archive Trust contained a note about it written by the prime minister's press secretary, Bernard Ingham.[6] Murdoch's purchase was controversial, because of his reputation and because he already owned the *Sun* and the *News of the World*, both national titles with large circulations. Owning two more would give Murdoch control of 40 per cent of the national press and was, therefore, a matter for the Monopolies and Mergers Commission. Thatcher cleared the way for Murdoch's purchase by avoiding the Monopolies and Mergers Commission and manipulating the political system.[7] Her deal with Murdoch guaranteed the Conservative Party the support of two more national papers.

Just as Thatcher took great care to keep her meeting with Murdoch secret, Tony Blair did not disclose his flight half way around the world to Australia to meet Murdoch in an attempt to get him onside for the Labour Party before the 1997 election. Since the *Sun* had attacked the

---

[5] King, A. 2015. *Who Governs Britain:* London: Pelican Books: 152
[6] McNally, P. 25 April 2012. 'Rupert Murdoch: Thatcher meeting over Times was "quite appropriate"'. Brighton: Mousetrap Media.
[7] For a detailed account of the meeting and the political machinations used by Thatcher to secure the deal see Evans, H. 2013. *Good Times, Bad Times*. London: Bedford Square Books.

Labour leaders Michael Foot and Neil Kinnock without mercy in previous elections, the decision to attend the meeting raised eyebrows in Blair's inner circle. He explains in his memoirs, *A Journey*, that not to go would have sent the signal to Murdoch to carry on doing his worst, and his worst was very bad indeed. A close relationship between Blair and Murdoch followed, with frequent social events arranged between them, ending with Blair becoming godfather to one of Murdoch's children. Cabinet Office documents reveal that there were six telephone discussions between Mr Blair and Mr Murdoch in twenty months, all at crucial moments of his premiership.[8]

A series of distinguished journalists have since provided insights into the relationship between Murdoch and Blair. According to Hugo Young, a leading political columnist at the time, Blair's office usually took Murdoch's view into account before making any big move. Andrew Neil, a *Sunday Times* editor, writes that the relationship was almost incestuous and the line between the state and the press became so blurred that it was difficult to tell one from the other. A third says that Murdoch's presence in Number 10 was so strong that he was almost like a 24th member of the Cabinet, on some issues more influential than the prime minister.[9] The Cabinet Office revealed three phone calls between Murdoch and Blair in the nine days before the start of the Iraq war in 2003. Murdoch was keen to get the UK involved.[10] Blair and Murdoch also spoke on the day that the Hutton Report into the death of Dr David Kelly was published.[11]

Less is known about Gordon Brown's relationship with Murdoch, and requests for information were turned back by the Cabinet Office because, they said, there were no minutes of meetings or any other interactions. It may not be significant that there are no official records of meetings involving Murdoch and his people with Brown and other prime ministers because a lot of business was conducted by 'networking, negotiating, wine drinking, canape quaffing, villa visiting and

---

[8] Press Association. 19 July 2007. 'Blair and Murdoch spoke days before Iraq war'. *The Guardian*.
[9] Young, H. 2003. *Supping with the Devil: Political Writing from Thatcher to Blair*. London, Atlantic: 60–61; King, *Who Governs Britain*, 150.
[10] Grice, A. 22 July 2011. 'Labour accused of hypocrisy over Murdoch contacts'. *The Independent*.
[11] Sabbagh, D. 5 September 2011. 'How Tony Blair was taken into the Murdoch family fold'. *The Guardian*.

yacht boarding'.[12] It is known, however, that Murdoch visited Chequers in October 2007 during a weekend when Brown decided not to call an election, and that Brown attended the wedding of Rebekah Brooks, Murdoch's favourite editor. This was to no avail, because at that time Murdoch was in the process of switching his support back to David Cameron and the Conservatives.

As the 2010 election approached, Cameron did everything he could to get and keep Murdoch on his side. Ken Clarke, a senior member of the cabinet, states that Cameron may have done some sort of deal to get Murdoch's support and that as a result the Murdoch empire was suddenly back on the Conservative's side in the 2010 election.[13] Andrew Coulson, editor of Murdoch's *News of the World*, was appointed director of communications for the government, and normal relations were resumed with Murdoch's people with parties, personal contacts and meetings. Cameron provided the Leveson Inquiry with a list of 1,400 meetings he held with media proprietors and editors during his time in opposition, plus a list of meetings with James Murdoch (fifteen), Rupert Murdoch (ten) and the former News International chief, Rebekah Brooks (nineteen).[14] Official figures show that Mr Cameron met Mr Murdoch and executives of his companies twenty-six times in his first fifteen months as prime minister.[15] Cameron's successor, Theresa May, also took care to meet Murdoch, despite a promise to keep the media at arm's length.[16]

At one point Cameron arranged a meeting between Ken Clarke and Rebekah Brooks at which 'I found myself having an extraordinary meeting with Rebekah who was instructing me on criminal justice policy from now on, as I think she had instructed my predecessor, so far as I could see, judging from the numbers of people we had in prison and the growth of rather exotic sentences … Rebekah Brooks

---

[12] McSmith, A. 1 October 2009. 'How Cameron cosied up to Murdoch and Son'. *The Independent*.

[13] Waterson, J. 23 November 2017. 'Ken Clarke says David Cameron did "some sort of deal" to win Rupert Murdoch's support'. *BuzzFeed News*.

[14] Tataro, P. 15 June 2012. 'Cameron admits ties between British MPs and press became "too close"'. *The Sydney Morning Herald*.

[15] Channel 4 News. 6 September 2011. 'David Cameron admits he was too close to media'.

[16] Martinson, J. and Mason, R. 29 September 2016. 'Theresa May had private meeting with Rupert Murdoch'. *The Guardian*.

described herself as running the government – now in partnership with David Cameron.'[17]

According to Lance Price, a director of communications for the Labour Party, the deals between British prime ministers and Murdoch comprised an unwritten understanding that if they did not interfere with his business interests he would not attack them in his newspapers.[18] Murdoch said that he never asked any prime minister for anything, but the unwritten understanding was that Thatcher would help him buy the *Times*, that Blair's government would not join the euro without going to a referendum first, that Blair would help him with his BSkyB dealings and that Blair would join the USA to go to war with Iraq. A former Labour minister states that Murdoch asked for Brown's help to quell the inquiry into the *News of the World* hacking charges.[19] Giving evidence to the Leveson Inquiry into the culture, practices and ethics of the British press, John Major said that Murdoch had asked him to change his policy about the European Union at a dinner they had before the 1997 election, and that if he failed to do so his papers would not support him.[20]

Further evidence is provided by Seymour-Ure, who writes that 'Blair was diligent, too, at schmoozing with media barons and editors'. He was in regular contact with Murdoch personally and is reported to have intervened on Murdoch's behalf with the Italian prime minister, Romano Prodi, over BskyB's interest in a deal with Italian TV. Seymour-Ure also recounts how Blair read a lesson at Lord Rothermere's (the *Mail*'s owner) memorial service in 1998, and how he invited Richard Desmond, the new owner of the *Express*, to a welcoming tea at Downing Street. The *Express*, a Conservative paper of long standing, came out in support of Labour in the 2001 election.[21] Applications under the Freedom of Information Act also document

---

[17] Vaughan, R. 23 November 2017. 'Ken Clarke: David Cameron did "a deal" with Sun tycoon Rupert Murdoch'. *iNews*.

[18] Price, L. 2014. *Where Power Lies: Prime Ministers v the Media*. London: Simon and Schuster.

[19] Greene, R. 20 April 2012. 'Rupert Murdoch admits phone-hacking "cover up"; apologizes'. CNN.

[20] BBC News. 12 June 2012. 'Leveson Inquiry: John Major reveals Murdoch's EU demand'. BBC.

[21] Seymour-Ure, C. 2001. 'New Labour and the media', in King, A. ed., *Britain at the Polls*. New York: Chatham House: 131.

three phone calls between Blair and Desmond between 29 January 2003 and February 2004.[22]

When he resigned from office, Tony Blair complained that '[t]he fear of missing out means today's media, more than ever, hunts in a pack. In these modes, it is like a feral beast just tearing people and reputations to bits. But no-one dares miss out.'[23] Out of office, Blair spoke more frankly about his relations with the press. In his evidence to the Leveson Inquiry in 2012 he said that his meeting with Murdoch in 1995 was to prevent his papers 'tearing us to pieces' and to get the *Sun* on board, because '[y]ou were in a position where you were dealing with very powerful people, if they were against you, they were all-out against'.[24] At the Leveson Inquiry he acknowledged that his relations with Murdoch were unhealthy, but that if you are pursuing something you believed and they did not, you were in for a big fight – you feel their intense power and need to deal with it. He decided as a political leader that he was going to manage it, not confront it.

For his part, Cameron admitted to a House of Commons committee that he had allowed himself to get too close to media proprietors and editors, that the relationship between politicians and the media needs resetting and that he had spent too much time trying to win the support of newspapers and broadcasters. He also stressed that he had contacts with a wide range of media organisations, besides Murdoch's News International.[25] The Cabinet Secretary Lord O'Donnell said 'I think the Prime Minister himself, the current Prime Minister, has said that he felt his relationships had got too close, and I agree with that.'[26]

A World with a Responsible not a Powerful Media?

What would happen if it was recognised that the influences of the news media are widely and greatly exaggerated and that their influence on

---

[22] Press Association. 19 July 2007. 'Blair and Murdoch spoke days before Iraq war'. *The Guardian*.

[23] De Michelis, L. 2010. 'Preaching to the "feral beast": Tony Blair's farewell speech to the press'. Milan: University of Milan Faculty of Letters and Philosophy, Essays N. 3 – 03/2010.

[24] CBS News, 28 May 2012. 'Tony Blair: I ducked fight with the UK media'. www.cbsnews.com/news/tony-blair-i-ducked-fight-with-uk-media/.

[25] Channel 4 News. 6 September 2012. 'David Cameron admits he was too close to media'.

[26] Hickman, M. 15 May 2012. 'David Cameron "too close to media" says ex-civil service chief Gus O'Donnell'. *The Independent*.

voting and public agendas is not at all strong? We would have to search for real causes not imaginary ones, and the main thrust of this book is that real causes are found in the daily lives that people live – in the things that concern them most and usually appear at the top of their election agendas. For most, politics is a sideshow in daily life and the news media are a sideshow of that. The news forms a small part of the total output of the mass media, and most people access only a tiny part of the news available to them. Education, health, welfare, taxes, housing, the family economy, crime and public services are centre stage of political concerns and for some discrimination, the environment, the EU and the ideal interests of liberty, justice and equality join the list.

The result is that if we want to know why people have their political opinions and vote the way they do we should look at the lives they live, not the news they get. The news media do not explain why they voted Remain or Leave, why Labour voters in the red wall turned blue, why members of the Conservative Party voted for Liz Truss, why Boris Johnson's approval ratings fell so steeply or why Jeremy Corbyn's initial support also declined.

All of this is to simply to state the obvious that people live different lives that lead them to respond in different ways to political events, just as it leads them to respond in different ways to news reports about those events. They respond in different ways according to their own life circumstances and experiences, and because political events and policies affect different people in different ways. This says nothing about whether their response is reasonable, rational or realistic and it says nothing about whether we should agree or disagree with them. The point is that in trying to understand beliefs and behaviour, blaming the media will not do. It deflects from an understanding of the real causes and therefore prevents any attempts to solve real problems.

To take just one example, those who rejected scientific and expert views about the dangers of Covid did so for different reasons, among which were a deep suspicion of big pharma, big government and the nanny state and libertarian opinions about individual rights. They failed to comply with social-distancing rules and isolation when infected because it was inconvenient, they didn't care, because they had to go to work to earn a living, because it was impossible to do so at school or work or because they were young and unlikely to be much affected by the disease. The mainstream media message did not condone or recommend any of these reasons for not social distancing, not wearing a face mask and not getting vaccinated. If individuals found webpages to support this behaviour it was probably because they sought them out, not because they happened upon the web pages by accident and were convinced and converted by them.

If we think that the media, either mainstream or alternative, is responsible for those who refused to comply with public interest messages about Covid then the same problem will arise next time there is a pandemic. If we recognise the real reasons then there is a chance of dealing with them and minimising the danger. The same is true of many other features of political life – racism, sexism, populism, misogyny, violence, anti-democratic politics, immigration and asylum seeking, nationalism, patriotism, xenophobia and dissatisfaction with the way democracy works in the country. Some elements in the media system may well prop up and reinforce some of these problems, but the media are not the fundamental cause of such things.

This is all very abstract and 'what if' but there is a concrete example of how things can be done if we realise that the media are not the main problem, though they could be part of the solution. In the 1960s and 1970s, Finland held the record for the Western country with the worst health. It had a particularly poor diet of high fat and alcohol, and a large and early death rate among men from cardio-vascular diseases and lung cancer caused by smoking and a lack of a physical activity. By the turn of the century it was one of the fittest countries in the West, with men living seven years longer and women six years longer than in the 1960s. The country achieved this with an outstanding example of social engineering. According to the pioneer of the experiment, Pekka Puska: 'We didn't tell people how to cut cholesterol, they knew that. It wasn't education they needed, it was motivation. They needed to do it for themselves.'[27] So a programme was set up to change dietary and smoking habits by implementing a plan to get people involved in physical activities that they enjoyed and was cheap and easily available. The programme did that in many intelligent ways that ranged from cleaning out swimming pools to buying men beer in pubs so long as they talked about what sport or activity they would do if the facilities were available – and then made the facilities available.

The Finns recognised that there was no sense in repeating ad infinitum a public information campaign telling people what to eat, what to

[27] Ask Dr. Stoll. 14 August 2917. 'Fat to fit: How Finland did it'. Stoll Foundation.

drink and not to smoke. They knew that there was no sense in simply telling people to take up a sport or get some exercise unless there were tracks to ski, paths to walk, pools to swim in and pitches to play on. The national and local media were brought in as an essential part of informing people about grassroots action plans. The media are good at informing people and not good at getting them to think and act differently, and in Finland they were used to inform and encourage people to get involved in the physical activity facilities that were provided.

In Britain we deal with the obesity and bad health problems in a different way. Over the past decades we have been telling people again and again to eat and drink sensibly and exercise moderately, and now we are selling school playing fields.[28] The media campaign about obesity has been running for several decades and has not worked because it has not got to the roots of the problem. Insanity is said to be doing the same thing over and over again and expecting a different result.

How would British politics change if it were accepted that media owners are emperors who have no clothes when it comes to the voting behaviour and agenda-setting of their readers? First, political leaders and aspiring leaders would spend less valuable time and money cosying up to the editors and owners of the tabloids. Second, they would not have to trim their sails when trying to curry favour before elections. Third, they would not have to waste their time trying to second-guess the wishes of media masters when they are making policy decisions. Fourth, newspaper owners would not waste their time asking British politicians to do them favours. Fifth, prime ministers would then be responsible to the electorate and not to unelected and sometimes irresponsible power brokers. Sixth, the overall effect would be a more democratic system of British government in which there was less power without responsibility. Seventh, rules for the regulation of the media market and for proper conduct of journalism – some already in place – could be applied as they were intended. Eighth, politicians might even take steps to reset the relations between them and the press, as Cameron said they should. And ninth, when asked by a journalist

---

[28] Santry, C. 17 February 2017. 'Exclusive: Councils to sell hundreds of acres of school playing field land'. *Times Educational Supplement*.

why he was so opposed to the EU, Murdoch is supposed to have replied: 'When I go into Downing Street, they do what I say; when I go to Brussels, they take no notice.'[29] Murdoch denies saying this, but whether or not he did, the effect of recognising the true limits of media power would be that British politicians would also take no notice. They could take back control.

[29] Ponsford, D. 19 December 2016. 'Rupert Murdoch denies saying he was anti Europe because at Downing Street, not Brussels, "they do what I say"'. *PressGazette*.

Index

accepting but ignoring media messages, 14, 55–62, 72
accepting media messages, 14, 62, 69
  according to personal beliefs, 72, 75, 76, 77, 162, 163
  and daily life and talk, 143, 152
  and trust and partisanship, 173
agenda-setting, 3, 6, 44, 113–117, 119–120, 126, 168–169, 185, *see also* priming
algorithms, 78–81, 95, 153, 166
amusing ourselves to death, 135
attack journalism, 4, 6, 15, 97, 123
avoiding the news, 14, 24, 38, 51, 56, 69, 148, 149, 164

bad news effect, 4, 9–10, 123, 126, 168, 172, *see also* mean world effect, media malaise
Bail, C., 75
Bartels, L., 5
Baudrillard, J., 2
BBC
  criticism of, 27, 28, 69
  government hostility towards, 28
  in the news landscape, 18–19, 21–22, 35, 170–171
  and commercial TV, 26, 28, 30
  wholesale and retail news, 35
  in news diets, 38, 42, 48, 51, 80–81, 83, 85, 95, 118, 167
  trust and distrust in 22–27, 48, 75, 95, 134, 164–166
  online, 45, 48, 80
  and voting, 26
  and pluralism, 160
  in the news system, 26, *see also* public service, internal pluralism, commercial media: regulation of in the public interest

belief preservation, 14, 68–77, 112, 120, 154, 162, 164, 172. *See also* disconfirmation bias, beliefs of conviction and convenience, hostile media effect
beliefs of conviction and convenience, 65
Berners-Lee, T, 159
bias in individuals, 69, 75, 164
  and preference for unbiased news, 24, 81, *see also* massive and minimal effects, belief preservation, cognitive bias
bias in the news media
  in commercial and public service news, 14, 24–28, 35–36, 125
  and newspapers of record, 24
  and the preference for impartial news, 24, *see also* priming, framing and internal pluralism.
Black Wednesday, 108
blaming the messenger, 9–10
boomerang effect, 70, 71, 118, 164
bots, 1, 79, 93, 94, 96, 166
Bourdieu, P., 2
Brown, R, 68
Bryce, Lord, 147

causes and effects, problems of, 7, 8, 128, 173
ceiling effect on vote swings, 109
Channel 4, 23, 28, 30, 42, 44, 46, 80, 85, 100, 166, 170, *see also* public service media
Chomksy, N., 3, 4
Coase, R., 158
cognitive bias. *See* belief preservation, hostile media effect, beliefs of conviction and convenience, confirmation bias

commercial media
  market restraints upon, 12, 24, 26
  concentration of ownership and control, 19, 21–22, 34–35
  and pluralism, 19, 23, 157, 161
  and public services, 26, 33
  social and political effects of, 94–122, 123, 133, 135, 137, 162, 168
  news content of, 35, 36
  in the news landscape, 18–36, *see also* bias in the news media
  in the news system, 26, 34
  in news diets, 44, 49, 80, 83
  and populism, 86. *See also* mass media, bias in the news media
concentration of media ownership and control, 19, 21, 23, 35
confirmation and disconfirmation bias, 69, 73. *See also* belief preservation
conspiracy theories, 1, 17, 46, 59–60, 66, 70, 72, 76, 79, 81, 90, 91, 96, 163, 167
convictions and behaviour with little or no mass media support, 62, 68
Cross-media traffic, 46, 47, 81, 84, 104, 166

Darnton, R, 67
de Botton, A., 2
demographic variables
  explanatory power value of, 31, 121, 131
  and news diets, 39, 42, 47, 48
  and fake news, 96
  and voting, 121
  and the standard model, 139–140
  and agenda-setting, 168, 169
  and BBC audiences, 171, *see also* standard model
denying media messages, *see* rejecting media messages
discussion circles, *see* political talk
Dunning-Kruger effect, 14, 72, 73, 164

echo chambers, 1, 14, 37, 53, 78–81, 84, 95, 96, 166
Elections and voting, 6, 8, 88, 97, 122, 126, 130, 135, 141, 165, 166
  the Murdoch Press 24–25, 178–183
  and rejecting newspaper advice about voting, 60, 62

and fake news, 88, 89, 92, 93
and agenda-setting, 113–117, 119, 135, 146
and political talk 120
entertainment TV, 29, 170
  and news avoidance, 38, 78
  and avoidance of civic duties, 123, 124
  political effects of, 15, 123–124, 130–133, 135–137, 167–168

Facebook
  as a news source, 22, 44, 46, 53, 82–84
  and populism, 85
  and fake news, 87–88
falling into the news, 30, 32, 136
  and self-selection of the news 136
Fine, C, 68
Fox news, 18, 25, 84
framing, 137, *see also* agenda setting, priming

hard news, 29, 54, 99
Harrop, M., 103
hedgehog effect, 74, 164
Herman, E, 3
hostile media effect, 14, 27, 69, 72, 164, 172
Huckfeldt, R., 148
hyper-pluralism, 22, 23, 34, 52, 157, 163

ignoring or rejecting media messages about matters of general belief and behaviour, 14, 56–77, 143, 162, 164
  and voting, 60, 62
  and everyday life and political talk, 143, 146
infotainment, 12, 123
internal pluralism, 14, 27, 52, 160–162
issue salience, 115
ITV
  government pressure on, 28
  public service regulation of, 26
  criticism of 27–28.
  news content of, 28, 29
  in news diets, 34, 40, 43–49, 166, 170
  political effects of, 29–34

Index

online in social media, 45–46, 80
and populism, 85
trust in, 100, 160, *see also* public service news

Kahneman, D., 68
Katz, E., 147
Klapper, J., 5
knowledge gap, 31, 34, 170

Lack of evidence about the media and their effects, 8, 9, 13, 14, 15, 22, 156, 167, 173, 174
Lake Wobegon effect, 14, 72, 91, 164, 176
Lazarsfeld, P., 147
legacy media
  misleading nature of the term p. 22, footnote 13, 53.
  online legacy media, 21–22, 34, 52–53, 78, 79, 95, 166
  in the news landscape, 18–21
  and news diets, 39–49, 52–53, 93, 95, 168
  and echo chambers, 81–84, 93.
  and populism, 85, *see also* mainstream media, TV, radio, newspapers
Leveson Inquiry, 180

magazines, 20, 21, 40, 42, 48, 49, 54, 125
mainstream news
  and minority groups, 20, 40
  In the digital age, 34, 38
  and pluralism, 35, 36, 95
  and news diets, 53, 79, 89, 150, 167
  in the news landscape, 18, 21
  in the news system, 23
  and attitudes and behaviour, 55, 68, 70, 73, 79, 92, 112, 138, 141, 163, 164, 167, 175
  and populism, 84–85
  and fake news, 87, 166
  and political agendas, 113, 117
  and reinforcement, 112, 117. See also legacy media, TV, radio, newspapers, mass media
Mann, C., 67
market for news and ideas, 158, 160.
market pluralism, 14, 19, 157–163

massive and minimal media effects, 1, 7, 120, 163
mass media, *see* mainstream media, commercial media, legacy media
McCombs, M, 3
McGuire, W., 5
McLuhan, M., 171
meaning of 'news', 174
mean world effect, 4, 9, 10, 15, 123, 136, 167, 168, 172, *see also* media malaise, bad news
media and democracy in Britain, 37, 155
  fears about, 1, 5, 123, 133
  and media pluralism, 12, 15, 36, 156, 162
  and political dissatisfaction, 133, 135
  what the media do not do, 163, 168, 172
  positive media effects, 125, 130, 170, 172, *see also* digital pessimism, pluralism, media malaise, mean world effect.
media malaise, 7, 10, 123, 135, 137, 167, 168
  mobilisation and malaise effects of news, 125, 130, 135, 137
  and general and entertainment TV, 130–134
  Newspaper and TV effects, 127, 129
  A Virtuous Circle, 129, 130
  real world and media effects, 130, 135
  falling into the news and self-selection, 136, *see also* mean world effect, bad news, entertainment TV
medium is the message, 171, 172
Miller, W., 114
Moore M., 116
motivated reasoning, *see* belief preservation, hostile media effect, confirmation bias
Murdoch, R., 24, 25, 178, 182, 185

news: accepting media messages, *see* accepting media messages
news avoiders, *see* avoiding the news
news: believing what the papers do not say, *see* convictions and behaviour with little or no media support
news diets, 37, 54
  multisourcing, 42
  cross- media use, 46, 47

news diets (cont.)
  of the young, 47–48
  and entertainment media, 37, 38
  and apathy, 15, 38, 127, 175
  individual attributes of, 39–49
  as a sideshow of a sideshow, 22, 49, 50, 52, 183
news landscape
  importance of, 17.
  TV, 18
  radio, 19
  newspapers and magazines, 20, 21
  online, 21, 23
  and the news system, 23, 34
  market forces, 24–26
  public service and commercial media, 26–34
  hyper-pluralism of, 23, 34, 52, 157, 163
  concentration of ownership and control, 9, 19–23, 79, 160
  small news content of, 21, 22, 34
news literacy, 37, 51, 140
newspapers and print media
  in the news landscape, 20–21, 160
  online papers 79–80
  local papers, 24
  broadsheets and newspapers of record, 24, 82, 128, 129, 161
  economic interests of newspapers, 24–26, 181
  rejecting newspaper voting advice, 60, 62
  believing what the papers do not say, 47, 62–66
  the spreading of political information without papers, 67, 68
  trust in, 82, 164, 165, 173
  and voting behaviour, 97–122, 165–166
  reinforcement effects, 112, 113, 118, 119, 165
  and agenda-setting, 113, 117, 119, 120, 165
  and news diets, 1, 39–49, 52, 67, 137, 149
  tabloids, 35, 51, 79, 97, 100, 104, 123, 137, 158, 160, 164, 173
  Influence on political knowledge and attitudes, 126, 147, 153, 161, 164, 165, 171.
  prime ministers and tabloids, 178, 182.
  and partisanship, 161, *see also* magazines
newspapers and voting, 97, 112, 117, 118, 160, 165, 166
  and cross-pressures, 101, 103
  problems of cause and effects, 101, 102
  in the 1992 and 1997 elections, 102, 109
  in normal times, 109, 112
  and the standard model, 121–122
  swing votes and the ceiling effect, 109, 118, 119
news system, 12, 14, 23, 34.
Norris, P., 5, 6, 10, 129, 130

'old' and 'new' media, 52, 53, 79, *see also* legacy media, digital media
online news
  lack of information about 108–110, 174
  in news landscape and system, 10, 21–23, 34
  legacy media in, 34, 36
  pluralist nature of, 22, 36, 156, 161
  small amount of, 22, 53
  consumption of, 39, 48, 50, 53, 54, 79, 137, 159, 167
  and fragmentation of the political system, 53, 167
  and echo-chambers, 53, 79–84, 166
  and digital pessimism, 78, 95, 96
  and polarisation and populism, 84, 85, 167
  and fake news, 86, 93
  and Russian and American bots, 93, 94
  digital natives, 34, 42, 44, 46, 48, 53
  political talk online, 146, 151
  trust in, 164, *see also* social media, algorithms, Facebook, Twitter.

partisanship of media
  difficulties of classifying newspapers, 98, 100
  and internal pluralism, 14, 35, 52, 157, 160, 161
  newspapers and voting, 98–121
  and political reinforcement, 112, 113
  alignment with reader partisanship, 24–26, 98, *see also* newspapers of

Index

record, bias in the news media, propaganda, priming.
partisanship of people
  and self-selection of partisan news, 61, 62, 71, 78, 98, 101, 165, 172
  partisan cheerleading, 66
  and political polarisation and populism, 84, 86
  reinforcement of, 112, 113
  and political talk, 150, 151
  and political knowledge, 92, 93
  importance for explaining media effects, 71–72, 121, 172
  and cross-media traffic, 46, 47, 95, 166, *see also* hostile media effect, trust in media., belief preservation, beliefs of conviction and convenience, party identification
party identification, 31, 102, 115, 136, *see also* partisanship
personal experience, 11, 138, 155
  the standard model of explanation, 140–146
  everyday life effects, 140, 146
  personal experience as a reality check, 143, 145
  and agenda-setting, 115, *see also* political talk
pluralism of the British media, *see* hyper-pluralism, *see also* internal pluralism
pluralist theory
  classical theory of, 14, 157, 158
  problems of classical theory, 36, 157–162
  and the market for ideas and news, 158, 161
  measurement problems, 23, 34, *see also* internal pluralism, hyper-pluralism
podcasts, 9, 23, 48, 50, 51, 66
polarisation, 75, 79, 84, 86, 95, 152, 167
political bias, *see* hostile media effect, partisanship of media, partisanship of citizens; belief preservation
political blogs, 22, 50, 66, 159, 174
political fragmentation of the country, 53, 163, 167, 171

political fragmentation of the media market, 35, 53
political identity, 54, 106, 113, 130, 136, 139, *see also* party identification, standard model
political instability, 4, 53, 54, 100, 163
political interest, 30, 32, 54, 79, 125, 128, 136, 139, 146, 147, 162
political leaders and the media, 177, 182
political talk, 146, 153
  as part of everyday life, 146, 151
  historical examples, 67, 68
  and the public sphere, 147
  and the two-step flow of communication, 147, 148
  online discussion, 151
  effects and importance of, 151, 154
  political talk and belief preservation, 154, *see also* personal experience
populism and populists, 85, 95, 167, 175, 184
Postman, N., 4, 135, 171
practical lessons
  real causes, 176, 177, 183–184
  and Covid-19, 183, 184
  Finnish social engineering, 184, 185
  consequences of a realistic view of media power, 182–185
priming, 137, *see also* agenda-setting, framing
propaganda, 1, 3, 79, 91, 158
public service media, 26, 33
  and internal pluralism, 28, 29
  and political bias and neutrality, 27, 28
  in media landscape, 24, 85, 170
  trust in, 27, 164, 173
  and news diets, 24, 38, 44, 48, 50, 51, 53, 118, 136, 167
  political effects of, 29, 34, 171
  and media pluralism, 36, 127, 160
  and echo chambers, 53
  and populism, 53, *see also* BBC, ITV, Channel 4

radio, 170, 172
  trust in 54, 164
  in the news landscape, 8, 19, 22

radio (cont.)
  in news diets, 39, 45, 49, 50, 54, 95, 104, 118, 149, 168
  ownership and control, 19, 21
  public service regulation, 26
  news content and quality, 27, 29
  wholesale and retail outlets, 35
  and pluralism, 22, 23, 34, 36, 125, 159, 161
  lack of evidence about, 8, 34, 174
Ramsay, G., 116
reading and watching the news, 51, 54, 65
real causes, 96, 126, 143, 146, 168, 169, 170, 175, 176, 183
reinforcement, 112, 113
Romer, P., 159

Schudson, M., 6
self-reported responses, 39, 46, 149.
self-selection, 8, 32, 38, *see also* causes and effects, supply and demand of the news
Seymour-Ure, C., 181
social media
  lack of evidence about, 9
  as part of news landscape, 10, 46, 79
  political impact of, 91, 92, 93–95, 96, 116, 168
  distrust of, 51, 149
  in news diets, 27, 43–48, 54, 80, 125
  and digital pessimism, 78, 85
  and polarisation, 75
  and fake news, 54, 88–90
  and information about Covid-19, 92–93.
  convenient to blame, 153, 164
soft news, 29, 30, 54, 170
Sokal, A., 74
Sprague, J., 148
standard model of the social sciences, 107, 121–122, 131, 136, 139, 140, 146, 169, 171, *see also* real causes
The Sun, 23
  and voting behaviour, 60–62, 97–112, 118, 165
  commercial interests and editorial policy, 24, 25
  and news diets, 44, 47, 80
  and populism, 85
  trust in, 100, 118

influence on prime ministers., 178, 182. *See also* Murdoch R.
supply and demand of news, 12, 52, 78–79, 156, 159, 161, 174, *see also* causes and effects, self-selection
Sutherland, S., 70

tabloids
  concerns about, 1, 97
  compared with broadsheets, 35, 158, 160
  and news diets, 47, 51, 79, 123, 137
  and voting and agenda-setting, 99–100, 103–108, 114
  trust in, 100, 104, 134, 164
  impact of, 128, 129, 175
  in news landscape, 158, 160
  and political leaders, 178, 182, 185
Tarde, G., 146
Temple, M., 112
Tetlock, P., 74
Trivers, R., 71
trust and distrust in the media, 1, 12, 100, 170
  importance of, 33, 71, 72, 138, 162, 164
  in BBC, 27, 47, 48, 50
  in social media, 48, 51, 82
  in radio, 174
  in newspapers, 161
  in public service, 33, 120, 173
  in the news media generally, 38, 39, 45, 52, 75, 91, 94, 160
  in journalists, 110
  in psychological experiments and the outside world, 91
  and partisanship, 71–72
Twitter, 42, 44, 46, 53, 83, 87, 92, 93, *see also* social media

Virtuous Circle, 6, 31, 129
voting and elections, *see* elections and voting

wholesale and retail news, 35
word of mouth, 67, 68, 146, 154, 169, 174

Zaller, J, 6

Printed in the United States
by Baker & Taylor Publisher Services